A biography of one of a
ering his incredible three
the first multi-engined ai
Clippers of the 1930s, an
revealed as a humble geni
piety, and humor, whose ....telligence made his
"impossible" dreams come true.

THE BANTAM AIR & SPACE SERIES

To Fly Like the Eagles . . .

It took some 1800 years for mankind to win mastery of a challenging and life-threatening environment—the sea. In just under 70 years we have won mastery of an even more hostile environment—the air. In doing so, we have realized a dream as old as man—to be able to fly.

The Bantam Air & Space series consists of books that focus on the skills of piloting—from the days when the Wright brothers made history at Kitty Hawk to the era of barnstorming daredevils of the sky, through the explosion of technology, design, and flyers that occurred in World War II, and finally to the cool daring of men who first broke the sound barrier, walked the Moon and have lived and worked in space stations—always at high risk, always proving the continued need for their presence and skill.

The Air & Space series is published every other month as mass market books with special illustrations, and with varying lengths and prices. Aviation enthusiasts would be wise to buy each book as it comes out if they are to collect the complete Library.

IGOR
SIKORSKY

His Three Careers
in Aviation

With illustrations from the personal photographic collections of Igor I. Sikorsky, Dmitry D. Viner, and Galina Viner Godkin.

IGOR SIKORSKY

His Three Careers in Aviation

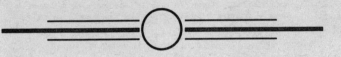

Frank J. Delear

REVISED EDITION

Foreword by
General James H. Doolittle USAF (Ret.)

BANTAM BOOKS

NEW YORK · TORONTO · LONDON · SYDNEY · AUCKLAND

This edition contains the complete text
of the original hardcover edition.
NOT ONE WORD HAS BEEN OMITTED.

IGOR SIKORSKY

A Bantam Falcon Book / published by arrangement with the author

PRINTING HISTORY
Dodd, Mead & Company edition published 1969
Bantam edition / December 1992

The photographs on pages 18 and 22 are used courtesy of the
National Air and Space Museum, Smithsonian Institution.

ISBN 0-553-29701-5

Published simultaneously in the United States and Canada

PRINTED IN THE UNITED STATES OF AMERICA

OPM   0 9 8 7 6 5 4 3 2 1

For my wife, Marion, who suggested that this book be written, and in memory of my mother, who first stirred my interest in books

Acknowledgments

Through their generous gifts of time, talent, and encouragement, several persons contributed significantly to this book. I am especially indebted to Charles and Anne Lindbergh, Lauren and Kay Lyman, Eugene Wilson, and C. B. Allen, all good friends of Igor Sikorsky; and to Mr. Sikorsky's son Sergei, his daughter Tania von York, and his cousin Igor A. (Prof) Sikorsky. Grateful acknowledgment is made also to Catherine Simokat, Dmitry Viner, Galina Viner Godkin, and Frank Gregory, each of whom helped in different ways and in varying degrees. The kind cooperation of Igor I. Sikorsky was, as always, a source of immense help and inspiration.

Contents

Foreword

All of us who know Mr. Sikorsky well enough to call him "Igor"—and a mere acquaintance would not encourage this familiarity because of his quiet, unassuming dignity—admire him very much and greatly value his friendship.

He is a truly unusual person. He is a genius. He has great natural ability. He has, throughout his entire life, increased his inherently high capabilities by study, observation, and analytical consideration. He is able, and willing, to concentrate and think through. He is not only intelligent but wise. These are both very important attributes in the decision-making process.

He is a good man. His life and character exemplify those essential basic virtues and values which, in the mad rush and scramble of today's living in our modern, very complex society, are sometimes forgotten.

He has spirituality. He believes implicitly in a Divine Creator. He is sure that a universe as vast and orderly as ours—from the microcosm to the macrocosm—could not have "just happened." It had to have a Divine Creator. It must be organized and ruled by a Divine Purpose beyond the mind of man.

He lives by the Golden Rule. "Do unto others as you would have them do unto you." Far too many people today, here and elsewhere, accept the Law of Expediency which in substance says: "The end justifies the means." With this philosophy any evil can be accepted and excused if one's purpose—whether good or bad—is achieved.

He has humanity. He believes that he is his brother's keeper. He is interested in and cares for his fellow man. He is thoughtful of others. He is courteous, polite, and unselfish. He is a gentle person who instinctively—without the necessity for conscious thought—does the kindly, the right thing. A true gentleman, of the old school.

He has integrity. He is honest with others and with himself. His word is as good as his bond. I cannot conceive of him, knowingly, misrepresenting anything—telling a lie—for any reason. With integrity one is a whole man. Those without it are not.

He practices and believes in well-organized hard work. So did our forefathers. This is certainly one of the cornerstones of our national greatness. A willingness to work, to strive mightily to attain our ends. The will to achieve and succeed. (But not at the expense of others.) His works attest to his dedication.

He rigorously disciplined himself. This is the best kind of discipline. A person who disciplines himself does not have to have discipline imposed on him by others.

He has courage. He has physical courage and moral courage. All his life he had the courage to take great risks for great achievements. He had the courage of his convictions and the tenacity and determination, despite almost insuperable problems, delays, and disappointments, to carry his ideas through to completion and fruition.

His three greatest aeronautical achievements were the multi-motored airplane, the big flying boat, and the practical helicopter. He spent a full lifetime in developing and producing each in its turn. Almost every possible problem and frustration was faced and overcome. A less courageous and determined man would not have succeeded, as he did, in any of the three areas.

He dared to dream dreams—to dream the near impossible—and he made those dreams come true.

GENERAL JAMES H. DOOLITTLE, USAF (RET.)

Los Angeles, California; 1969

Preface

The young reporter waited, pencils sharpened and notebook ready. It was one of his biggest assignments: an interview with the famous aviation pioneer, Igor I. Sikorsky. At the age of fifty, Igor Sikorsky had carved two brilliant careers in aviation. Now—it was 1940—he was well launched on a third, the helicopter. As a result he was news almost anywhere in the world. In the Bridgeport, Connecticut, area where the Sikorsky plant was situated, his name was a byword. Even so, the local newspaper had yet to publish a reasonably complete story of his life and achievements. It was the reporter's job to write the story, but first to get the facts. So he waited.

The three-minute wait seemed much longer. Finally, a secretary said, "Mr. Sikorsky will see you now." The reporter entered a modestly appointed office and was greeted with the warm smile and courtly bow that over the years endeared Mr. Sikorsky to thousands. He sat down, stated his business—the story of Mr. Sikorsky's life—and promptly forgot most of his carefully prepared questions.

Sensing the situation, the aeronautical pioneer took over. He began to tell his story, slowly, precisely, his excellent English spiced with a Russian accent. The reporter wrote down almost every word, for every one was worth writing. Mr. Sikorsky watched the moving pencil, pacing his words with the young man's frantic scribbling, slowing the narration or stopping it altogether when the pencil seemed to fall behind. His kindness saved the day. The resulting story covered almost two pages in the *Bridgeport Sunday Post*.

As the reader may have guessed, the young reporter was this author who has told this brief story to show why it was and is a privilege to write about Igor Sikorsky.

Igor Ivanovich Sikorsky, in the twilight of his life, looks back on a career that seems almost too rich in achievement for one man. His story is one of courage, of never giving up, no matter what the odds. It is a story of a man whose mind always leaped into the future, ignoring those who said this or that could not be done. It is a story, too, of a man who, despite his great strength of purpose, remains ever kind, courteous, modest, and humble. Of his work, which long ago brought him world renown, he once said: "If I had not done this someone else would have. So I do not overestimate the importance of anything I have done."

In 1952, Thomas K. Finletter, then Secretary of the Air Force, presented Mr. Sikorsky with the National Defense Transportation Award, one of almost one hundred honors that have come his way over the years. Mr. Finletter likened Mr. Sikorsky to the Wright Brothers, to the great French air pioneer Santos-Dumont, and to the German inventor Count Zeppelin. Then he added: "Mr. Sikorsky is a milestone in the history of aviation, an equal giant and pioneer. Look upon him well and remember him." Mr. Finletter's words summed up Igor Sikorsky's high place in the world of aviation.

Five years later, upon Mr. Sikorsky's retirement as engineering manager of the company which bears his name, his friends presented him with a gold-lettered scroll which said, in part:

"Igor Sikorsky's greatness, in the finest sense, is of the heart rather than the mind. His deeply religious and humble nature, his strength of purpose, and his humor—made the more engaging by its subtlety—have won him the respect and affection of all who know him.

"These qualities, and others reflecting nobility of soul, have brought to Igor Sikorsky the acclaim of men, the goods of the world and the satisfactions of the spirit. We wish him a continuation of these blessings which are so justly his."

Those words summed up Igor Sikorsky's equally high place in the hearts of all who know him.

FRANK J. DELEAR

1

Igor the Boy

"As long as we have men like Mr. Sikorsky, men of imagination and determination, free men—free to imagine, free to achieve, and free to apply their knowledge—there are no limits to what we can do in this great nation of ours, no problems in this poor, troubled world of ours that, if we try hard enough and work long enough, we won't be able to solve."

The speaker was a United States senator and the object of his spontaneous praise was Igor I. Sikorsky. It was the night of December 14, 1967, and Mr. Sikorsky had just received one of aviation's highest awards, the Wright Brothers Memorial Trophy. Although he had accepted seventy-seven previous official awards and honors during his long career, this one had a special meaning. The Wright brothers' early flights had started him on his career in aviation and he had been one of their strongest admirers all his life.

The trophy committee of seven experts in the aerospace world had chosen Mr. Sikorsky for the Wright Brothers award "for the design and production of the world's first practical helicopter; for the conception and construction of the world's first four-engined aircraft; and for the design and production of a series of flying boats which pioneered transocean air transportation."

The presentation took place at the annual Wright Brothers Memorial Dinner in Washington, D.C. The audience of more than 1,000 persons included many leaders in the fields of aviation and government. It also included members of Mr. Sikorsky's family and many of his old friends and associates.

The handsome trophy which he received had two parts. The base was a replica of a plaque commemorating the Wright brothers' epic flight at Kitty Hawk, North Carolina. The tiny plaque was set in a piece of granite. Mounted atop the granite was a shining silver model of the original Wright biplane.

The man who accepted this trophy was of medium height. His Slavic face was kind, with sombre blue eyes, deep and piercing, that somehow seemed always about to twinkle with good humor, and often did. The smooth brow and strong voice belied their owner's seventy-eight years. Mr. Sikorsky's brief speech of acceptance was well organized, eloquent, and deeply moving. As always, he quickly won and firmly held his listeners' attention. His delightful Russian accent captivated them further.

United States Senator George Murphy was the toastmaster who responded to Mr. Sikorsky's remarks. He added: "It is seldom that you find a man who has achieved so much as our honored guest who combines with great ability one of the nicest and warmest personalities it's ever been my good fortune to witness." Then the Senator concluded: "I can think of no evening that has given me more pleasure, or greater honor to share, than this."

Many people came forward to shake Mr. Sikorsky's hand, to wish him well, to tell him how much they enjoyed his talk and, in many cases, to ask for his autograph on the dinner program. Typically, he was gracious to all. But he left early for his hotel room. The evening had been long and demanding. The bright lights had bothered what he called "tired eyes," and his hearing was not what it used to be in those long ago days when he heard the "heavenly music" sung by the little engine of his first airplane. Indeed, on this night of praise and appreciation, his thoughts may well have flashed back over the long years of his almost incredible three careers in aviation, years that had their disappointments and failures as well as their successes and rewards.

In memory he may have lived again those thrilling seconds of the first lift-off in his VS-300 helicopter twenty-eight years before. He may have felt once more the gentle sway of the big amphibian which carried him high over the Carribean to blaze new air routes southward in the early 1930's. Or, reaching back more than half a century, he may have walked again the open deck atop the fuselage of the huge *Ilia Mourometz*, enchanted anew by the dazzling wonderland of blue and white he had found on his first flight above the clouds.

The long trail that led to that December night in Washington, a night of friendship, respect and love, began in the romantic city of Kiev, capital of ancient Russia. Kiev, lying on the Dnieper River in the Ukraine, was a city of timeworn shops and streets, dim, mysterious churches, white walls, and golden turrets and domes. Often called the "Mother of Russia," Kiev had been founded in the year 430.

Igor Ivanovich Sikorsky was born in Kiev on May 25, 1889, the youngest of five children. He had three sisters, Lydia, Olga, and Helen, and a brother, Sergei. Had he been able to choose his mother and father he could hardly have done better. From them he inherited talents and received the inspiration that remained with him all his life.

Igor's father, Dr. Ivan Alexis Sikorsky, was the sixth of twelve children of a priest of the Russian Orthodox Church. Born May 26, 1842, in the village of Antonovka in the province of Kiev, he was, from his earliest childhood, thoughtful and serious far beyond his years. He scarcely participated in the games of his brothers and sisters. Very early, almost by himself, he learned to read, and read constantly. He even read aloud to his brothers and sisters, pointing out the morals contained in his favorite book, *Krilov's Fables*.

Years after Dr. Ivan Sikorsky's death, Igor's sister Olga, wrote a brief and moving biography of her beloved father. In 1968, Igor's daughter, Tania, a professor of philosophy at Sacred Heart University in Bridgeport, Connecticut, translated that biography into English. The translation reveals the fortunate heritage that was Igor's in having Dr. Ivan Sikorsky as his father.

"At the age of nine," wrote Olga of her father, "his parents placed him in the minor seminary in Kiev. He studied much and well, outstripping his fellow students and often astonishing his instructors with the extent of his knowledge. Coming home for vacation, he continued to be interested in

In 1904, Igor Sikorsky (right), a Naval Academy student at the time, with his sisters, Olga, Lydia, and Helen, and his brother, Sergei.

his studies, going out into the garden with his books and, most frequently, going up into the church belfry there to spend whole days in reading, often forgetting to come home for dinner.''

Upon entering the major seminary, he similarly distinguished himself with his deep and extensive knowledge, ranging far beyond the seminary curriculum. He easily read and translated the classics, and showed an active interest in natural science, literature, and philosophy; he also learned the French and German languages. Both his instructors and his fellow students showed him especial respect. He was respected, also, at home by his parents who, notwithstanding his youth, consulted him on serious matters.

In his last year at the seminary, just before the final examinations, Ivan told his parents that he was going to leave the seminary and prepare for the entrance examination to the University of Kiev. His parents were upset by this decision but they did not oppose it, feeling that it had not been lightly arrived at by their son. In the spring of 1862, Ivan studied at home and brilliantly passed final examinations required for high school graduation. Then, by virtue of a special exception, he was accepted by the university as a scholarship student from high school.

Ivan Sikorsky was interested in man, especially the mind of man. But before approaching the study of man, he decided to study the science of plants and animals, for which purpose he entered the department of natural science.

Living far from the university, he attended class daily, even visiting the classes of other professors than those of his own department. After classes he tutored, since it was necessary for him to earn his living, and only at night would he return home to study. There formed around him a group of students similarly eager to acquire learning, and the professors noted the young man's abilities and thirst for knowledge.

Ivan began to collect books. Toward the end of his life the collection was to become one of the largest private libraries in the world, containing more than 12,000 volumes, mostly on medical subjects. When he died in 1919 this library, as he had instructed, was given to the University of Kiev.

Ivan Sikorsky transferred to the school of medicine, completing his studies there in 1869. Two years later he obtained his degree as a doctor of medicine. He moved to St. Petersburg to work in his chosen field, since there was no department of psychiatry and nervous disorders at the University of Kiev. On the strength of his published writings, especially one entitled "Concerning the Symptoms of Fatigue in Mental Labor" which had already been translated into French and English, he was put in charge of a clinic on mental and nervous disorders. He spent long hours at the clinic, observing the ill and their illnesses, studying them and at the same time helping them. He was constantly surrounded by students who listened to his precise and vivid descriptions of the illnesses and heard his calm and sympathetic talks with the patients.

Dr. Sikorsky's reputation grew. He was named instructor in the department of psychiatry and nervous disorders at the Military Medical Academy. In 1882 his report, "In Regard to Difficult Children," presented at the International Congress of Hygiene, in Geneva, Switzerland, won the attention of the

Dr. Ivan A. Sikorsky—doctor, author, teacher, and his father—aroused young Igor's interest in science and the universe.

entire Congress; it was the first time this subject had been touched in science. He wrote a whole series of books on the rearing of children. One, "The Mind of the Child," drew world-wide attention, was translated into all the languages of Europe, and became the standard textbook in Germany, with over fourteen printings. He turned down several offers to head psychiatric hospitals, preferring to continue his research and teaching. In 1885, when the University of Kiev established a chair in mental and nervous disorders, Professor Sikorsky returned to his home province and was named professor at Kiev's University where he taught for the next twenty-six years.

At Kiev, the scope of his work was almost beyond belief, and his neighbors used to say he "worked a thirty-six-hour day." He lectured to medical and law students, to doctors and teachers. He taught psychology and worked in clinics and hospitals. He treated patients who came to him from all over Russia. He wrote into the early morning hours and had more than a hundred works published, many of them raising new and original scientific questions. He was active in community service, either heading or holding membership in many medical associations and societies. He founded the Psychiatric Society and organized a "Union for Sobriety" to fight alcoholism. He organized a kindergarten and served as its president for many years. He directed the construction of two buildings for students at St. Vladimir's and organized reading and discussion groups. "Teaching others, he continued to learn himself," commented Olga.

His annual vacation trips to other countries were, in part, extensions of his studies. He spent some of his time visiting museums, galleries, libraries, and monuments, acquainting himself with the life and psychology of different peoples. Even in his declining years, during these trips, he continued to walk, look, think, and observe with youthful enthusiasm.

He loved his books and his library was always in perfect order. From the start, every book was carefully entered in a catalogue. The purchase of new books was an occasion for happiness in his family. Often, when a new book was expensive, this was reflected in the family budget, but everyone willingly endured sacrifice for the sake of the library. Professor Sikorsky loved to recall an incident from his student days when thieves entered his room and took his only suit, his coat, shoes, and hat, so that he had to stay in bed until a fellow student rescued him from his difficulties. He remembered this as one of the happy days of his life because the thieves did not touch his books.

"Professor Sikorsky," Olga wrote, "did not drink or smoke; he played no cards, neither did he sit on soft furniture. He ate the most simple foods. Summer and winter he arose at 6:30 in the morning and went out into the garden for a twenty-minute walk. He himself had landscaped the garden and planted many of the trees there. Returning, he would have coffee and read the papers. He began his work at 8:00 in the morning—lecturing, calling at the hospitals, doing charitable and community endeavors, working with disturbed children. At midday, a half-hour for a hurried dinner and again the various activities—reception of the ill, meetings, and only after 8:00 in the evening did the working day end. At evening tea the provincial and foreign papers were read, and finally books were read and his own writing done."

Olga's description of her father's personal attributes are all the more interesting because, as events turned out, many points apply equally as well to Igor Sikorsky, the son, as to the father.

"In spite of constant strenuous work, Professor Sikorsky maintained always the same *even, brave, and enthusiastic mood. His eyes were serious and gentle. On his face there always lay the imprint of serous thought and at the same time the witty, kindhearted joke and smile were customary. His speech was expressive, definite, lacking in exaggerations. He keenly felt and understood the meaning and connotation of words, so that his speech, expressive but distinguished by a simple grace and exactitude of thought, attracted attention.* He regarded exactness in the use of words as very important and said that people often used words carelessly.

"*His mind was always in a condition of deep attention, his spirit in full peace and tranquility.* Professor Sikorsky could be seen not infrequently in a fatigued state, but he then sought solitude; *no one ever saw him irritated, much less angry.* Even in situations where it would be natural to feel spite or anger, these were replaced by wonder or more frequently by sorrow.

"*Balanced, far removed from the trivialities of life, high-minded, always philosophical calm, he spread this peace of mind around himself,* and both the well and ill were able, after taking counsel with him, to arrive at suitable decisions and to find peace of mind. His finely developed feeling gave him strength and ability to penetrate the recesses of the human soul and made him in every sense a psychologist and psychiatrist.

"These special qualities were widely known and the number of people coming to him in search of mental peace was great. *In his dealings with others he was known for gentleness and tact, patience, sincerity, and respect for an opinion different from his own. An order was always put in the form of a request.* Toward the end of his life, when he was ill, motionless, a dying man, he retained these same ways of dealing with people. 'Won't you please read me something?' 'Won't you please give me a small drink of tea?' 'Won't you please turn me?' he would say, rather than 'Read to me,' 'Give me tea,' 'Turn me'."

Professor Ivan Sikorsky died February 1, 1919, at the age

of seventy-seven, his mind alert and clear almost to the end. All his life he had acted in the belief that life is short, science is long. All his life was a service to science and to man. This belief, this deep spiritualism and curiosity about man and the universe, he passed on to young Igor, both by word and example. He was a father to be loved and respected.

Igor's mother was also a source of much inspiration to the youngster. She was a medical school graduate, and worked tirelessly for her family and for others. She loved music and taught her children to share this love with her. Although Igor early favored scientific pursuits, he spent long hours at the piano. He developed an appreciation for music which stayed with him throughout his life, often inspiring him and bringing calm in time of trouble.

It was Igor's mother who first turned his mind toward flying machines. She used to tell him about Leonardo da Vinci, the great Italian artist and inventor of the fifteenth century. She told him that one of da Vinci's designs was for a machine that could rise straight up in the air, but that da Vinci was a dreamer, far ahead of his time. Although a man could envision a flying machine, there was not sufficient mechanical knowledge at the time to provide the craft and power needed for actual flight. Young Igor, his lively imagination stirred, daydreamed of flight at an early age. Although his mother's influence on him was great, it was destined to be of short duration; Zinaida Sikorsky died March 5, 1907. Igor was only eighteen years old at the time.

Igor's earliest memories were of a large, fairly well-to-do family living in a big roomy house with a large garden and grounds. Since he was not physically strong, he devoted much of his time to hobbies. He worked well with his hands, carving wooden toys and building electrical batteries and small electric motors. By the time he was twelve he had made a flying model of a helicopter, powered by rubber bands, which could rise into the air.

One night when he was about eleven years old, the youngster had a dream that he never forgot. He dreamed that he was walking along a narrow passageway. A bluish light from overhead cast a glow on walnut doors on either side of the corridor. The floor had a fine carpet and beneath his feet Igor

*In the living room of the Sikorsky home in Kiev (Left to right):
Igor's sisters, Helen and Olga, and his mother.*

could feel a slight vibration. It was not like that of a train
or steamboat and Igor knew at once he was aboard a large
flying ship and that it was in the air. He reached the end of
the corridor, opened a door to a decorated lounge—and then
woke up. (Some thirty years later he was to relive that dream,
only then it would be real.)

It was at about this time that Igor's father exerted his
strongest influence upon the imaginative boy. Dr. Sikorsky
said that hard work, either physical or mental and even over
long periods, was not harmful, providing there were reasonable periods of rest. However, he warned that hard mental
work, combined with worry, could destroy a man's health
and abilities. Dr. Sikorsky put these beliefs into practice in
his own life. Every summer he would leave the cares and
demands of his work to visit for five or six weeks some quiet
place, usually in Germany or Austria. He took Igor with him
in the summer of 1900, to the beautiful mountains of the
German Tyrol. There, each afternoon, father and son walked
the wooded trails, the father talking and the son listening, or

asking an occasional question. Igor never forgot that trip, for it shaped his life.

His father told him about electricity, physics, and astronomy. He aroused the boy's curiosity in the world around him and his wonder about the endless universe beyond. Igor's interest in astronomy began at that time and stayed with him all his life. Dr. Sikorsky told his son of his work with the mentally ill and of how he was often called in as an adviser for difficult court trials. He described a new instrument he had invented, which was much like the lie detector now used

Sikorsky family home in Kiev. Dr. Sikorsky had offices on the first floor; living quarters were on the second floor; the top floor was used by Olga Sikorsky as a school for retarded children.

in criminal cases. He showed Igor how it worked, and the boy learned the terrible effects that fear, worry, and hate could have on a person. The father's experience as a teacher enabled him to explain things in a way that the boy could easily understand.

When he was twelve years old, Igor became interested in chemistry. He bought chemicals, test tubes, and Bunsen burners and began experimenting. The family maid refused to clean his room, fearing that she would be "poisoned" by the evil-smelling concoctions it contained. Later, Igor found a pamphlet written by anarchists which described how to make a bomb. He made several, exploding them in the garden at some distance from the house. A contractor who was rebuilding a house next door complained to Igor's mother. "It's not the noise," he said, "nor the danger. It's my men. They keep leaving their jobs to watch these experiments and I can't get any work out of them."

Like his parents, young Igor loved books. He read with great interest the stories of Jules Verne and was especially interested in Verne's description of a helicopter. Igor believed that heavier-than-air vehicles, in contrast to the lighter-than-air dirigible, would become the airships of the future. So many people believed that the heavier-than-air flying machine was impossible that Igor began to think that his dreams would remain just dreams.

In 1903, still not certain just what his lifework would be, Igor entered the Naval Academy at St. Petersburg. Unknown to him at the time, something else also happened that year. On the wind-swept dunes at Kitty Hawk, North Carolina, some 5,000 miles away, Wilbur and Orville Wright flew for the first time in history a powered, man-carrying, heavier-than-air machine. This achievement eventually was to change the course of Igor's life, even as it changed the course of human history.

Igor remained a naval cadet for three years. He enjoyed his studies, especially the duties aboard a vessel at sea. However, as he read books other than the naval textbooks, he became more and more convinced that a military career was not for him. Reading the few brief reports in the Russian newspapers of the Wright brothers' flights, he found himself again dreaming of flying. His mind continued to reach into

Igor in uniform of the military academy.

the future, far beyond routine textbooks. He wanted to become a creative engineer, to play his part in writing the textbooks of tomorrow. But where could he go to learn about aviation since there were no schools and almost no books on the subject? He decided to become either an electrical or mechanical engineer as the best way to move toward his real goal of flying.

Igor resigned from the Naval Academy in 1906 to enter a technical school and study engineering. Unfortunately, many of the engineering schools were closed because of an attempted revolution in Russia. The years 1905 and 1906 were troublesome ones. The Russo-Japanese war had come to a bad end for Igor's homeland. Strikes and peasant uprisings took place. Study in most of the schools and universities was interrupted. In order not to lose time from his studies, Igor went to Paris where he spent six months in the engineering school of M. Duvigneau de Lanneau. He loved the city and became an alert observer of Parisian life. He never lost his affection for the culture, color, and gaiety of the French capital and he returned to it many times. In his retirement years, more than half a century later, he was delighted when various aviation events, such as the big Paris Air Show, required his presence.

In 1907, when the situation improved in Russia, Igor went home and entered the Polytechnic Institute of Kiev. He did well in his studies, but preferred his home workshop where he continued to experiment with many mechanical devices. He even built a motorcycle that was driven by steam. He was torn between the theoretical courses at school and the creative efforts in his workshop. Which would win? The decision came during his summer vacation in 1908 when he again went to Germany with his father.

This visit lasted six weeks. As soon as he arrived Igor began to read German newspaper accounts of Count Ferdinand von Zeppelin's flights in one of his early dirigibles. Far more important, he learned for the first time the details of the successful flights of the Wright brothers. Strange to say, the aeronautical successes of Orville and Wilbur, which began five years earlier, were still generally unknown throughout the world. This was true, even in America. Or, where they were known, they were believed to be of little importance. However, in 1908, Wilbur Wright went to Europe and made a series of flights. Reports and pictures printed in a German newspaper gave young Igor, for the first time, a trustworthy and accurate description of the Wright brothers' accomplishments. When he read it he was surprised that it was printed inside the paper and not blazoned in headlines across the front page.

Twenty-four hours later, Igor had made the firm decision that aviation would be his lifework. Those hours had brought all his dreams into focus. He decided that his entrance into aviation would be by way of the helicopter. He thought again of the flying ship of Jules Verne. He knew that his own dream was to build an aircraft that could hover over one spot, that could rise vertically and land vertically, and fly in any direction chosen by the pilot. He wanted to be able to hover

over a tree, a house, or a mountain, and then start flying in any direction he desired. He realized that the airplane as then known could never do that. At the age of nineteen, he decided that his career would be devoted to flying machines, especially the helicopter.

2

An Early Failure

Once he had made up his mind to enter aviation, Igor went quickly to work to make his dream come true. His hotel room in Germany became his "engineering department." While his father worked on a book, Igor drew sketches of various helicopter designs. The design he liked best at the time was a twin-rotor helicopter with one rotor mounted above the other, the rotors turning in opposite directions.

Since there was almost no information on the subject, Igor had to figure out how many pounds a rotor might lift, and how much power might be needed to turn the rotor blades. At this point his hotel room became a test laboratory. He fashioned some rough testing equipment, including a four-foot propeller made of thin, wood strips from a window shade and some wire (both purchased at a nearby hardware store), a wood stick as a rotor shaft, a weight, some string, and a small, spring scale.

Igor attached the weight to the string which he then wound a few times around the wood shaft. The weight, when released, descended and provided the power to turn the rotor. The young inventor used the second hand of his watch to determine the velocity of the descending load. The spring scale made it possible for him to measure the thrust of the rotor. This primitive test device gave primitive answers. The first results showed that a rotor could lift as much as 80 pounds per horsepower. Igor soon learned from further tests that such a figure was too high and could not be obtained in a full-size helicopter. (For comparison, today's modern helicopters lift between seven and eight pounds per horsepower.) When his early tests were finished, Igor was convinced that a full-size helicopter could be built even using the low-powered engines then available.

Back home in Kiev after vacation, Igor continued his research. He set up improved test equipment in his home workshop. He read everything he could find on aviation, learning as much as possible from the accomplishments of the few men who had built successful flying machines. He was ready to build his own machine except for one problem—money. He needed money to buy a motor and the many parts for his proposed helicopter.

Igor told his family of his plans for a helicopter. He said he wanted to leave school and go to Paris and buy a motor. His father gave him his blessings and in December of 1908, his sister, Olga, offered him the money needed to go to Paris for the motor and also to further his study of aviation. The rest of the family as well as the neighbors were stunned. "A helicopter? Simple nonsense," said Igor's brother. "It will never fly." He reminded Igor that there was some natural law that limited flight to creatures and machines weighing less than thirty pounds. The ostrich, a big bird that could never fly, was pointed out as an example of this.

Distant relatives joined in warnings at the "folly" of permitting a boy not yet twenty to interrupt his studies and go to Paris with a large sum of money. They predicted that the money would go for purposes other than a motor and that the young man would return home penniless. They were wrong. They underestimated Igor Sikorsky's devotion to what he now considered his lifework—aviation.

Igor's arrival in Paris was one of the many milestones of his career. He described it best in 1963 in a lecture before the Wings Club in New York. "At that time," he said, "Paris was the center of the aviation world. Aeronautics was neither an industry nor even a science; both were yet to come. It was an art and, I might say, a passion. Indeed, at that time it was a miracle. It meant the realization of legends and dreams that had existed for thousands of years and that had been pronounced again and again as impossible by scientific

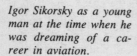

Igor Sikorsky as a young man at the time when he was dreaming of a career in aviation.

authorities. Therefore, even the brief and unsteady flights of that period were deeply impressive. Many times I observed expressions of joy and tears in the eyes of witnesses who, for the first time, watched a flying machine carrying a man in the air.''

Early in February, 1909, Igor met Captain Ferdinand Ferber, one of the great pioneers of French aviation. Captain Ferber was one of the earliest followers of the German glider pioneer, Otto Lilienthal, and the author of an aviation book with the prophetic title of *From Ridge to Ridge, from City to City, and from Continent to Continent*. Igor found his talks with Captain Ferber both interesting and inspiring. He remembered all his life Ferber's remark: "To invent a flying machine is nothing; to build it is little; to make it fly is everything." Captain Ferber also told Igor to forget about helicopters. "You will waste your time on a helicopter," he said. "My advice is to work on an airplane. That is much more promising."

Wherever he turned, Igor found arguments against building a helicopter. A noted Polish scientist and propeller designer, Drjevietzky, strongly advised the young man against spending his time on a helicopter. He even went so far as to write a magazine article entitled "The Wrong Way," explaining the hopelessness of the helicopter as a flying machine.

In 1909, Wilbur Wright penned the following lines which, although they sounded logical over half a century ago, look strange today: "Like all novices, we began with the helicopter (in childhood) but soon saw that it had no future and dropped it. The helicopter does with great labor only what the balloon does without labor, and is no more fitted than the balloon for rapid horizontal flight. If its engine stops it must fall with deathly violence, for it can neither float like the balloon nor glide like the aeroplane. The helicopter is much easier to design than the aeroplane but it is worthless when done."

As he studied aviation in Paris, visiting the airfields and talking with the pioneers, Igor found more discouragement. When he asked one flier for advice as to which engine was best for his helicopter, the flier replied, "There are no best engines; they are all bad." Igor then asked him which was the "least bad." It turned out that the French Anzani engine was probably the "least bad" because it had fewer parts than the others. Therefore, it would have fewer bad parts.

Those early days of aviation brought many failures and tragedies. Captain Ferber was to die in an airplane crash a short time after Igor had met him. In 1909, there was about one death for every 1,000 miles of flight, and probably several crashes every 100 miles. Aviation facts which later were taken for granted were learned through these failures and accidents. The need to build wings to withstand downward forces as well as upward forces was not generally known. This lack of knowledge brought death to George Chavez, a famous aviator of the time. As Chavez approached for a landing after completing the first airplane crossing of the Alps, the wings of his monoplane snapped downward as he flew through slightly turbulent air.

On many a night Igor sat in his hotel room, or wandered the twisting streets of Paris, thinking to himself: "Helicopters are impossible; all engines are bad; the failures in aviation far outnumber the successes. Who am I to think I can succeed?" Still, he was determined to go on. The final prize—the ability to climb high into the skies and see the earth from above—was simply too great to be abandoned.

As the weeks passed by in Paris, Igor continued to learn all he could about aviation. He enrolled at a new school started by Captain Ferber. Classes consisted mostly of standing around in a hangar at an airfield, talking and arguing aviation. The chief advantage was meeting the men who were active in aviation—pioneers like Henri Farman, the airplane builder, and Alexander Anzani, the engine manufacturer.

After visiting the few engine factories that existed, Igor made his choice—the Anzani, which was built in a small plant on the outskirts of the city. The plant boasted a total work force of thirty-five men; the engine had three cylinders, produced 25 horsepower and was a development of a motorcycle engine. At the Anzani factory, Igor met another French air pioneer, Louis Blériot, who also had ordered a 25-horsepower engine. Blériot planned to put the engine in his little Blériot monoplane in which he hoped to make the first flight across the English Channel. In July, 1909, Blériot accomplished the twenty-two mile flight, to become the most famous airman of his time.

After four months in Paris, Igor returned to Kiev, bringing with him the Anzani engine and various materials for building his helicopter. He also brought back books, papers, some experience, and a great many ideas. He realized that although he had learned a little about airplanes, he had learned practically nothing about helicopters. He knew he would have to rely almost entirely on intuition.

In the beautiful gardens of the Sikorsky family home stood a one-room summerhouse. This became Igor Sikorsky's first factory. There, with much enthusiasm and almost unlimited working hours, Igor built his first helicopter. The body of the machine was a square wooden frame. Attached to one side was the Anzani engine and to the other a seat for the pilot. In the center was a transmission box, which would deliver the engine's power to the rotor blades overhead.

Two hollow metal shafts, one inside the other, ran vertically up from the transmission. Each shaft was attached to a two-bladed lifting propeller or rotor. A pulley and belt system drove the rotors, which turned in opposite directions. The blades were held firm by piano wires above and below. The wires could be shortened or lengthened to change the pitch, or lift, of the blades. Control was to be provided by small wing surfaces placed in the downwash of air from the rotors.

In July, 1909, the helicopter was completed and first tests were undertaken. The motor was started and various troubles began. The drive belt was slipping. When that was fixed, the power to the rotor became greater. Then the two hollow shafts shook so badly that the engine had to be shut down without delay. Igor removed the rotor blades, took them apart, and carefully adjusted them for weight. But that didn't help. With great patience and ingenuity, he found the trouble: the inner shaft vibrated about 120 times a minute. He knew that the rotors turned at 160 revolutions per minute. So he hammered a four-foot length of hard wood down into the inner shaft until both vibrations and rotor revolutions per minute were about equal. That solved the problem. On the next test, the shaking was gone.

Igor stood near the frame opposite the engine, his hands on a throttle and switch. He gave the engine almost full power and the machine started to topple over toward the heavier side where the engine was attached. Igor quickly cut the power and the helicopter fell back to the normal upright position. It was a narrow escape, for had the whirling blades struck the ground, they would have destroyed themselves and quite likely have injured the young inventor who was standing under them.

Despite his close call, Igor was happy. For the first time he could feel the power of the machine and he knew that it was trying to lift itself into the air. As he stood on one side of the frame which was about a foot in the air (the other side still on the ground), he noticed that when he cut the power, the side in the air did not fall. Instead, it settled slowly to the ground, held in check by the unseen force called "lift."

Igor continued to test his first helicopter for over two months. The machine danced and slid along the ground, kicking up clouds of dust and leaves, and obviously supporting much of its own weight. When he attached the helicopter to a scale, Igor found that the machine could lift just over 350 pounds which was about 100 pounds less than the helicopter

The first helicopter in the summer of 1909.

weighed. When he ended the tests in October, 1909, he realized that his helicopter number one could never take off with a man aboard. It was, in short, a failure.

Young Sikorsky, who was twenty years old at the time, looked on failure as a steppingstone to success. He refused to become discouraged. He had learned much from his first attempt to fly and already was planning helicopter number two. Before starting to build it, though, he once more visited Paris and the flying fields. For the first time he saw airplanes in actual flight, including the historic first flight of an airplane over the city of Paris. This was accomplished on October 18, 1909, by Count Charles deLambert when he flew a Wright biplane from Juvisy Airport, circled the Eiffel Tower, and returned to the airport, having reached the amazing altitude of 1,300 feet.

Igor returned to Kiev from Paris with two new Anzani motors, one of 25 horsepower and the other 15. The engines were for two propeller-driven sleighs which he built and drove through the snowy streets of Kiev the winter of 1909–1910. He wanted to gain experience with propellers and engines under conditions very much like those of an airplane. He had not given up on the helicopter, but was thinking more and more of the airplane as a simpler and quicker way to make his first flight. He made his first propellers of white pine, but soon found that walnut and mahogany were far more sturdy.

During that winter Igor was busy designing his second helicopter as well as his first airplane, the S–1. In February, 1910, he removed the engines from the sleighs and began building both the helicopter and the airplane. He completed the helicopter early in the spring of 1910. It was similar to the first one, with two rotors, one above the other. Each rotor had three blades instead of two and the helicopter, with its 25-horsepower Anzani engine, lifted almost its entire weight of 400 pounds. It was clear, however, that much more work and money would be needed to bring the machine to the point where it could lift itself and the pilot.

On the grounds of the family home, young Igor poses with his helicopter number two.

Later that spring Igor decided to put the helicopter aside temporarily. He had already installed the 25-horsepower Anzani in his S-1 airplane. Now he disassembled both his helicopters. As he recalled many years later: "I learned in those first two years the immense difficulty of pioneering in the helicopter field as well as my own vast ignorance on the subject. I learned later that it was far more difficult than I had thought at the time. I am glad I had sense enough to decide that at least temporarily I must enter the fixed-wing airplane business."

Igor's wisdom in this decision had already been matched by his good luck. If either of his earlier helicopters, with their primitive controls and structures, *had* lifted him into the air, he might not have lived to tell the tale. His career, destined to be one of aviation's brightest, would probably have ended where it started—in aviation's early pioneering period.

So Igor, still enthusiastic and healthy, took temporary leave of the helicopter, suspecting not at all that "temporary" was to mean almost thirty years.

3

An Early Success

Having put aside his plans for a helicopter, Igor increased his efforts to build a successful airplane. Although he still attended classes at the Polytechnic Institute, he spent almost every spare moment at a grassy pasture outside Kiev where he had built a small wooden hangar. There, with a few loyal helpers, he speeded up his work on the S-1 airplane which he had started to build while still working on the helicopter. The helpers included two carpenters and a plumber. They were paid a few rubles a week, thanks to the continued faith and generosity of Igor's father and his sister, Olga. Other helpers included some of Igor's classmates who asked nothing more than a chance to be a part of aviation, with all its promise of excitement and glamor.

The S-1 was a light biplane, with the pilot's seat mounted on the lower wing, out in the open. The 15-horsepower Anzani engine, also mounted on the wing, drove a pusher propeller behind the wings. A tapering framework of wood extended to tail surfaces at the rear. Two bicycle wheels and a tail skid made up the landing gear. A pair of skids extended forward of the wheels to prevent the plane from nosing over in case of a sudden stop.

While still trying to learn how to design and build an airplane, Igor now had to start learning to fly. The first problem was keeping the S-1 moving in a straight line along the bumpy field. As soon as the plane began to roll it would swing quickly either to one side or the other. It proved especially hard to handle at low speeds. Igor blamed the rudder and installed a larger one. When that did not help, he decided that the trouble was his own slow reactions on the rudder pedals. He soon learned to kick the opposite rudder at the instant the plane started to turn. After that he was able to propel his plane from one end of the pasture to the other at 25 to 30 miles per hour.

At these speeds, with the little engine at full throttle and the tail in the air, the S-1 sounded and felt as though it would take off at any moment. But it never did. It simply lacked enough power. When Igor pulled back on the control stick, lowering the tail to point the airplane's nose up for the hoped-for take-off, nothing would happen. Each time he had to cut the throttle and bump to a stop at the end of the pasture. On one windy day the plane suddenly rose into the air for a few seconds. However, it quickly settled back to the ground. Igor had gotten into the air at last, but he knew that the plane had merely been lifted by a freak gust and had not actually flown. He hadn't even had time to move the controls, so short was the hop.

Although the S-1 did not really fly, Igor was able to learn much about controlling an airplane on the ground. He learned also about the design improvements which he would have to make if he expected to build a successful airplane. His new-found knowledge led to the S-2 which used basic parts of the S-1 with four major changes; he built a new wing center section, installed the 25-horsepower Anzani engine from his helicopter number 2, placed the propeller at the front of the plane only a few inches ahead of the wing to make it a tractor plane, and constructed twin fins and rudders on the tail section for better directional control. In early June of 1910, Igor was ready for another attempt at flight.

Of the changes made, the placing of the engine at the front of the plane was by far the most important, especially from the viewpoint of safety.

"Having the engine at the front of my planes saved my life," Igor recalled in later years. "In 1909 and 1910 there was a big dispute among fliers as to whether aviation was safe or dangerous. Blériot said it was safe, and lived to an old age, dying a natural death. Delagrange, another famous pilot of the day, said flying was dangerous, and later was killed in an air crash. Blériot said that the real danger in flying was from the engine being placed behind the pilot. The planes of the time, he pointed out, were flimsy and even a minor accident would tear the engine loose and kill the pilot. One of the most famous fliers of the time, Captain Ferber, died this way; his plane made a good landing, but rolled into a ditch and the engine broke loose and killed him. In the S-1, I had the engine in the rear, but it bothered me and, so, in the S-2 I placed it in front. Later, in several of my accidents, I would have been killed if the engine had been in the rear.''

After testing the engine the previous day, Igor and his helpers rolled the S-2 out on June 3. Several factors convinced Igor that this might be the day of his first flight. He could feel the engine's extra power and the stronger wind blast of the propeller. Encouraging, also, was a light wind that blew steadily across the field. As the S-2 started its run along the pasture the tail came up at once and the speed proved to be much faster than that of the S-1. Igor eased the stick back and suddenly the plane was in the air.

Igor's first flight lasted about twelve seconds and covered approximately 200 yards at a height that varied from two to four feet. The flight ended when the S-2, without apparent

Igor made his first airplane flight as pilot of his S-2 in 1910. The 200-yard flight lasted about twelve seconds.

reason, suddenly flopped back to the ground. Nobody at the field had ever seen an airplane off the ground before and there was much excitement. Igor decided not to try his luck any further that day; instead he talked about the flight with his helpers and other witnesses to learn as much as possible about how the plane had behaved while in the air.

During the next few days Igor flew the plane on slightly longer and higher flights. He permitted the S-2 to build up more speed on its take-off runs; then when he pulled back on the stick he would find himself climbing higher—finally as high as fifteen or twenty feet. However, on each flight, the S-2 would eventually settle to the ground, no matter what its builder did with the controls. (In later years Igor described the S-2 as a plane whose take-off, cruising, and landing speeds were all the same. "When I pulled back on the stick it would go up," he said, "and when I pulled back again it would go down. Of course, if I pushed the stick forward it would also go down.")

One day the S-2 settled to the ground from a height of about twenty feet, despite the fact that it was flying at full throttle. The landing gear collapsed and there was other damage, including a broken propeller. It was Igor's first crash and he escaped unhurt. Three weeks later, with the S-2 not only repaired but improved, he was back in the air again. This time the plane did not settle. Igor was able to fly the entire length of the field, throttle down the power, and land as he wished. The cross-field flight took about thirty seconds. He repeated it and, with growing confidence, decided that the time had come to fly beyond the field, make a turn, and land at his starting point. Although he still had less than eight minutes total flying time to his credit, he was determined to attempt this risky flight the next day.

To make the circular flight, he would have to cross a wide and swampy ravine, continue the turn over level fields, cross a small river, and complete his turn to land at the point where he had begun his take-off run. All went well at first. The plane was crossing the ravine at a height of about eighty feet. For the first time Igor experienced the real feeling of flying; the ground now moved slowly far below, instead of rushing by as in the previous flights.

Igor had only a few seconds to enjoy the new and wonderful sensation of flight. In the turn, the plane suddenly began to lose altitude. In spite of a frantic pull on the control stick, the plane piled into the far slope of the ravine. The S-2 was completely wrecked, but Igor walked away with only a few scratches and bruises. The S-2's career was finished, after a total flight life of eight minutes. The longest flight, the final one, lasted forty-nine seconds.

What had caused the crash, since the engine was at full power and the airplane flying normally? A pilot of today will quickly give the answer—a stall. The S-2 flew only a few miles faster than its minimum, or stalling, speed. In straight flight it had just enough power to stay in the air. But in a turn it slowed down, lost its lift (stalled), and plunged to the ground. Igor, with neither instruments nor experience to warn him, became the innocent victim of one of aviation's worst traps, the stall at low altitude. A downdraft over the cool swamp contributed to the crash. It was not until much later that Sikorsky, safely crossing the ravine in faster, more powerful planes, fully understood the causes of the accident.

The S-2 was washed out. Igor salvaged what he could, mainly cables, bolts, and turnbuckles. In July he designed his next airplane, the S-3, which was to be larger and more powerful than the previous one. Visiting Paris again, he bought a 40-horsepower Anzani motor. By late November the S-3 was at the field and ready for its first flight. The lessons that Igor had learned from his earlier attempts had been put to good use; the S-3 not only had more power, but also larger ailerons, tighter control cables (for quicker response), and wings that were built and covered with greater care.

Although the S-3 was clearly a better airplane than the S-2, its career turned out to be much the same. Igor made a dozen flights across the field and then decided to try, once again, the circular flight which had ended in a crash a few months before. Not superstitious, he took off on this thirteenth flight on December 13. Igor cleared the boundary of the field at a height of almost 100 feet and turned to the right. Continuing the climb, he looked down on snowy fields and ice-covered ponds. He was off to a good start. Suddenly the engine sounded as though its spark were retarded. It lost power and the plane started down. Igor kept his head in the emergency. He pushed the stick forward to maintain flying speed, leveled out, and landed—on one of the frozen ponds. The ice broke and the S-3 sank nose first into about four feet of water, its tail and wing trailing edges protruding above the surface. Igor, soaked, climbed out and waited on a solid section of ice for his helpers.

Before going home for tea and a hot bath, Igor—since he could not get any wetter than he was—returned to the icy water to examine the submerged engine. He found the distributor in the retarded position and so knew the cause of the engine's failure. The spark had slipped to the retarded position, probably from vibration. No wonder the engine had sounded as it did!

In the days that followed, Sikorsky realized that he had reached a fork in the road. One way, school, led to a diploma and the security of a steady job. The other, aviation, could promise only hard work, risk, and insecurity. Igor now understood that he could not follow both roads, that he would have to make a choice. Aviation was taking too much of his time. His marks at the Institute were down and he was falling farther and farther behind his classmates. Two years of trying to fly had shown him that aviation needed 100 per cent of a person's time. To design, build, and fly a plane required all of one's energy and enthusiasm. Igor realized now that flying, despite its romance and fun, was really a deadly serious business. He had found that the slightest error or piece of bad luck could mean big losses in time and money, and even disaster. He knew that it was his own time that was being lost, but someone else's money. His father's income was only modest. His sister ran a school for retarded children, and her income was even less. Igor knew that their hard-earned money could not be expected to support his experiments indefinitely.

In later years, Igor confided to his eldest son, Sergei, how hard it was for him to continue. "To go back again and again and ask for more money caused my most crucial moments," he said. "I knew I could build a successful plane, but they didn't. Yet they mortgaged the family jewelry and other possessions to raise the money for me. I had to fight with myself because the whole family was exposed to criticism. It was bitter to lie awake at night and to force myself to go back and ask for more money. And after the money was offered, I'd lie in bed again worried sick because now if I failed again I'd betray their trust. And then, after another crash, it would be the same bitter thing all over again. In those days, of every ten airplanes built, nine never even got off the ground. Men were killed and families went bankrupt. This was one of the most bitter periods I ever lived through.''

After much thought, Igor made his choice: aviation. He decided that giving up aviation would be to admit failure. It would mean that all the support and confidence given him by his family would be wasted. Finally, it would mean choosing a comfortable living in place of the work which had won his whole heart and soul. He decided to push on with his attempts to fly, diploma or no diploma. He knew he had chosen the more difficult of the two roads open to him. He also knew it was the only one that would make him happy. With the decision made, Igor put all his doubts firmly aside. Time and money were running out. He made up his mind that he had to succeed and maybe even rise to a place of real leadership in aviation. He began to work harder than ever before.

For the first time Igor laid out a detailed program. His plans for the winter and spring called for building two more airplanes. The first one, the S-4, used as many parts as possible from the crash-damaged S-3, and several improvements. The second, the S-5, was a new design, with a larger engine, more wing area, and different control arrangements. Under the program, both planes were to be ready for flight tests in early spring. By working long hours Igor and his men met the schedule.

Building the S-5 had been practically a neighborhood project. Igor built the propeller at home. A plumber and bicycle repairman contributed their talents to many other parts of the plane. A collection of springs used to close doors served as shock absorbers on the landing gear. Only the engine was built elsewhere.

The S-5 was the favorite and received almost all the group's attention. Its water-cooled Argus engine developed 50 horsepower. Instead of two control sticks (one for the elevators, one for the ailerons) used in Igor's previous planes, the S-5 combined the controls in a single wheel. This was similar to the control system widely used today. Igor crossed

In 1911, Igor posed with the S-5 in which he first experienced the real thrill of flying, climbing to an altitude of 1,500 feet.

the rudder control cables so that steering was the same as for a sled: pushing the right pedal turned the plane to the left. This seemed more natural to him, but not many aircraft builders agreed. The opposite method became the rule as the years went by—push left to go left, right to go right.

When flight tests of the S-5 began in late April, 1911, Igor followed a careful plan. He remembered his two crashes and the delays and expense they had caused. He was determined, this time, to complete the test program with his plane still in one piece. For three weeks he flew from one end of the field to the other. He stayed low, usually flying a straight line, but occasionally making shallow turns. Onlookers who came to see a real flight, or some excitement, maybe even a crash, became bored and began to heckle Igor. But the young designer ignored their taunts and stuck to his schedule. After all, it was his neck and he had spent only fifteen minutes in the air prior to these training hops in the S-5.

On May 17 Igor believed that both he and the plane were ready. It was early in the morning and only his assistants were on hand as he took off on his third attempt to leave the field and return to his point of departure. Climbing higher than ever before, he made a turn and headed back with the field on his right. The S-5 responded well to the controls and, with growing confidence in his ability as pilot, Igor was able to look about and enjoy the thrill of flying as never before. He went by the field at a height of about 300 feet, flew on for a while and then made another turn, banking the plane slightly. With the field ahead, he pushed forward on the control wheel, reduced engine power, and started down. Leveling out over the pasture, he made a fairly good landing only a short distance from the spot where he had started his take-off about four minutes earlier. Igor knew that after two and a half years, he had made a real flight and achieved a real success.

The flight of the S-5 came almost exactly one year—and three crashes—after Igor's first flight, the twelve-second hop in the S-2. After that, progress came faster and a little easier. The flights got longer and higher. By the middle of the summer Igor was staying aloft a half-hour at altitudes up to 1,000 feet. By the end of the summer he could fly for an hour at 1,500 feet. That summer of 1911 was one of the happiest in his flying career. Sitting in the open just above and behind the S-5's lower wing, he had a clear view in all directions. Cruising along in the slow biplane, he viewed the hills and woods around Kiev from a new and marvelous perspective. And those below looked on Igor with different eyes. Maybe, they thought, he had not been wasting his time when he went off to Paris to buy an airplane engine back in 1909!

More success came that fall. The Imperial Aero Club of Russia issued Igor Sikorsky F.A.I. (Federation Aeronautique Internationale) pilot license number 64. In September the Army invited him to take part in its maneuvers near Kiev. This led to his first cross-country flight—a thirty-five-mile hop from Kiev to the village of Fasova. During the maneuvers he met Emperor Nicholas II. Later that fall he earned his first money in aviation by making an exhibition flight at a nearby town.

During the exhibition Igor experienced his fourth crash, and again showed his coolness in an emergency. He had taken off from a race track surrounded by houses and trees when the motor quit at a height of 150 feet. With the trees coming up fast, Igor quickly selected a narrow railroad yard as the only place to make a landing. The area was only 200 feet long and was bordered by a stone wall on three sides and a freight train on the fourth. He sideslipped into the yard, deliberately smashing the landing gear and overturning the plane only fifty feet short of the stone wall. A normal landing would have sent him crashing into the wall.

Only shaken up, he had time to inspect the engine before anyone reached the scene. What he found proved to be a turning point in his career: he had been brought down by a mosquito! The insect lodged in the tiny jet of the carburetor, choking off the engine's fuel supply. If an engine could be stopped by something as insignificant as a mosquito, Igor decided, then airplanes ought to have more than one engine. Forced landings because of engine failure were far too common, he thought. As he considered his narrow escape, he reached the firm belief that aviation would have to find some way to reduce the number of forced landings. Less than a year later he took positive steps to make that belief a working reality. The ultimate result was the multi-engined airplane which, with the helicopter, was destined to be most closely associated with the name of Igor Sikorsky.

Igor's next airplane, the S-6, was similar to the S-5, but larger. Its 100-horsepower Argus engine gave it twice the power of the S-5 and there were seats for the pilot and two passengers. When the S-6 was rolled out of the hangar for its first flight in November, 1911, everyone who had worked on it expected the new plane to be the fastest and best in Russia. They were quickly disappointed.

Despite its power, the S-6 was only slightly better than the S-5 in lifting capacity and climb. Its take-off and landing runs were too long and it was hard to handle during landings. What had gone wrong? Why didn't the new craft's perfor-

Igor Sikorsky's first pilot's license. The picture shows him at the controls of his S-5 airplane.

mance reflect the greatly increased power of its engine? Igor halted the flight tests and went to work on the problem.

He remembered that the S-5 had proved faster than the Russian Army planes in the maneuvers of the previous September. He thought he knew why. The Army planes, chiefly French-built craft, were powered with air-cooled rotary engines of the same horsepower as the S-5's Argus. However, the rotary engines, with their cylinders exposed to the airstream, had more air resistance, or drag. Even the lighter weight of the air-cooled engine did not offset the added drag.

Convinced of the importance of keeping air resistance as low as possible, especially as speeds increased, Igor decided to streamline the S-6. He built a machine for measuring the drag of different parts of the airplane. A crude device, its main function was to whirl the various parts around so that their resistance at different speeds could be determined, at least approximately. The test device served much the same purpose as today's wind tunnels. Using the information gained from these tests, Igor rebuilt the S-6, calling it the

S-6-A. He replaced the plane's open frame body with a long and tapering fuselage built of plywood sheets. Inside he installed seats for the pilot and two passengers in the familiar cockpit style that was to remain standard for many years. This and other streamlining greatly reduced the plane's drag.

Although less drag contributed toward greater speed, it did not help to produce a slower and better landing. At that time the theory of drag was not generally known. Nevertheless, by pure intuition, Igor came to the conclusion that it was not so much the added wing area as a greater span which would improve the quality of the aircraft. As a result, he added about five feet on each side to the span of the plane. It was mainly this feature which greatly improved the take-off, landing, climb, and lifting power of the aircraft, making it an outstandingly high-performing airplane for that time.

With these improvements the S-6-A now flew even better than its builders had expected. Its take-off and landing runs were shorter, it climbed faster, and could carry more weight. Earlier, Igor had carried one of his helpers on the short straight hops across the pasture, only a few feet in the air. Now he was able to reward a helper with a real flight. The lucky passenger was his mechanic, Vladimir Panasiuk. His

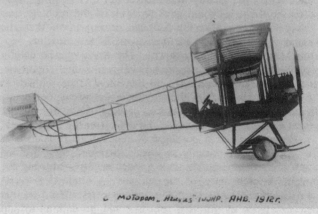

The S-6 in January, 1912.

carpenter, Ilya Foursoff, also went up for a flight. Later, Igor flew two passengers at a time until, finally, all his loyal band of workers had been aloft. On one flight the S-6-A flew at about 70 miles an hour, which topped the world speed record for an aircraft with three persons aboard.

Success followed success for the S-6-A, by far Igor's best airplane to date. In February, 1912, it won the highest prize in the Moscow aircraft exhibition. This achievement attracted the attention of one of Russia's largest industrial companies, the Society of Russia Baltic Railroad Car Factories. The company had an aircraft division at St. Petersburg and, in the spring, Igor became the division's designer and chief engineer. Under the contract the company bought all of Sikorsky's designs, including the S-6-A, as well as rights to all the designs and inventions which he would make for the following five years. Igor also received the right to build at least one new experimental aircraft each year at the company's expense.

In three years Igor's efforts in aviation had grown from a home workshop and a helicopter that could not fly to one of the country's leading aviation jobs. In those brief but busy years he had designed, built, and tested two helicopters, two propeller-driven sleighs, and six airplanes. He had received much support, both moral and financial, from his family. He enjoyed the loyalty of the little band of men who worked with him. But it was his own imagination, vision, courage, and hard work that earned this support and loyalty.

Many years later, in the twilight of his life, he was asked by a reporter if teamwork had not reduced the importance of an individual's work. "I am convinced," he replied, "that the work of the individual still remains the spark which moves mankind ahead even more than teamwork. Teamwork comes into existence after the spark, the intuitive spark, of a living man has started something."

In the first three years of his career, Igor had surely "started something." Now he was ready for bigger things. Now he had a bigger team—an entire airplane company backed by the resources of a large and powerful parent company. Even so, the real progress would continue to depend largely upon the creativity, courage, and dreams of a single, dedicated man.

4

Bigger and Better

In the late spring of 1912 Igor Sikorsky, then twenty-three years of age, traveled 800 miles north to begin his new job in St. Petersburg. He found hard work and marvelous opportunities awaiting him. The aircraft subsidiary of the Russian Baltic Company was only a few months old. It consisted of a small factory, recently rented, and a few employees. By the middle of the summer the number of workers had reached thirty, including six of Igor's men who had come north with him.

Igor's workday seemed to have no end. He spent his days at the factory, his evenings at the airport, then devoted the late night and early morning hours to planning, sketching, and designing in the quiet of his home, an ancient house near the factory.

His mind was still occupied seriously with thoughts of a four-engined airplane. He envisioned a huge craft able to carry eight to twelve persons 300 or 500 miles in the comfort of an enclosed cabin. The project was to include real pioneering work, for several of the ideas Igor had in mind had never been tried before. He did much preliminary design work for a big airplane. However, before he could advance the project beyond the drawing board, he first had to complete some activities with the smaller single-engined planes.

By far the most urgent of these activities was a military aircraft competition scheduled to be held in St. Petersburg during August and September. The competition represented a most important opportunity for the new company. Winning first prize, or just making a good showing, would probably mean orders for a number of planes. There were cash prizes, also: 30,000 rubles ($15,000) for first place, 15,000 rubles for second, and 10,000 for third.

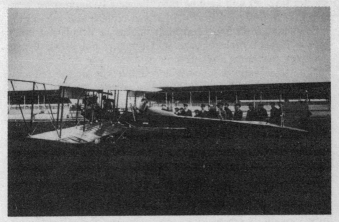

The S-6-A in the spring of 1912.

As the competition neared, the company concentrated its work almost entirely on the two airplanes it had entered. Igor was to fly the S-6-B, an improved version of the S-6-A. A company test pilot, George Jankovsky, was to fly the S-7, a new two-place monoplane. The S-8, a training plane fitted with a rotary engine of 50 horsepower, had been completed in the early summer, but was not entered in the competition.

Eleven airplanes were expected to compete. Under the rules they all had to be built in Russia, although foreign designs were eligible. Points were to be given for high speed, low speed, rate of climb, take-off run, and useful load in excess of the normal load. The normal load was determined by the power of the engine and the plane's size. In addition, each plane had to take off and land within a given short distance, climb to 4,900 feet in less than fifteen minutes, make an endurance flight of one hour, thirty minutes, and take off and land on a newly ploughed field. Failure to perform any of these requirements would disqualify a plane for the competition, no matter how many points it had won.

The contest for points proved to be close. The S-6-B showed better speed and climb, but several of the other aircraft, with their lightweight rotary engines, were making shorter take-off and landing runs. Especially impressive were two French-designed craft—a Farman biplane and a Nieuport monoplane. Both had been built in Russia. Unofficial entry was a Fokker biplane built in Germany and flown by its designer, Anthony Fokker.

Igor was well on his way to completing all the required flights when trouble struck. During a practice landing a group of men ran onto the field and Igor had to groundloop and crash his plane to avoid striking them.

The landing gear and propeller were smashed and other parts of the plane damaged. Igor and his mechanic climbed out bruised and shaken. The mechanic was sent to a hospital. Igor, tired both from the competition and his long hours in the factory, asked that the plane be repaired with all possible speed, and then went off to Finland for a rest. Returning four days later, he found that the workers, by toiling day and night, had performed a minor miracle. The plane was ready for flight.

As he prepared to finish the required flights, Igor received bad news. The officials had decided that he must repeat his earlier flights. They reasoned that the repairs to the S-6-B had been so extensive that the plane's flight qualities might have been changed. Despite delays caused by bad weather, Igor completed almost all of the required flights by mid-September. Among those remaining was the flight from the ploughed field.

The S-6-B was leading in speed, climb, and useful load, and first prize seemed almost certain. However, the almost daily rains had made a quagmire of the ploughed field, and a take-off was impossible. To make matters worse, Igor's competitors had completed their ploughed field flights in August when the field was dry. Unless the muddy area improved by the end of the month, the S-6-B would be unable to make the flight and would be eliminated from the competition.

The seventeenth of September dawned with threatening

clouds and rough air. The ploughed field was as muddy and hopeless as ever. To add to his troubles, Igor received word late in the afternoon that impossible flying weather was forecast for the next few days. In the general gloom and dampness there was no hint at all that this day was to be one of the most memorable of his life.

The weather prediction spurred Igor to complete two official requirements in a single flight. He climbed to 4,900 feet in less than fifteen minutes and continued in the air to finish the endurance flight of an hour and a half. It was dark when he landed near a fire set by his co-workers to guide him. He walked to the hangar, weary and chilled from his long flight in the open plane. There he found a message from Michael Vladimirovich Shidlowsky, chairman of the board of the Russian Baltic Company. Igor was invited to dinner that night at the chairman's home!

A former naval officer and government official, Mr. Shidlowsky had invested in the Russian Baltic Company a few years before. Through reorganization, new methods and new equipment, he had vastly improved the company's position. In addition to railroad cars and farm machinery, the company, under his direction, began to produce automobiles and airplanes. Young Igor Sikorsky had appeared on the scene at just the right time to obtain the leading job in the airplane division.

After dinner Igor's host invited him to his study for coffee. Igor described the situation at the military competition, but the chairman did not seem interested. After a few minutes of silence Igor introduced a subject which he hoped would prove of real interest to Mr. Shidlowsky—his dreams of building a big, four-engined airplane. With youthful enthusiasm, he explained the many advantages of a multi-engined plane. He said that the future belonged to the large, multi-engined aircraft, a plane that could stay in the air if one engine went out of commission. He described a plane which would have not a single pilot, but a crew of at least four—two pilots, a navigator, and a mechanic.

Igor stopped several times, afraid he was boring or tiring his host. But Mr. Shidlowsky urged him to continue. The young designer gave more details. The plane should have an enclosed cabin because of the cold Russian winters. The crew should be able to reach the engines while in flight to inspect and repair them. As he talked, Igor drew sketches of the proposed aircraft.

Finally, toward midnight, Igor ended his remarks with a suggestion: "If we win the military competition," he said, "let's use the prize money to build a four-engined airplane." The chairman's reply was short and to the point: "No," he said. "Start building the plane immediately."

Almost unable to believe his ears, Igor thanked the chairman and hurried to the factory. He asked the night watchman to telephone his engineers and foremen and tell them to come to his house. Despite the hour—it was now after one o'clock in the morning—he felt the news was too good to wait. When the men gathered at Igor's home, sleepy and mystified, he served each a glass of wine. Then he told them what had happened.

Years later, Igor Sikorsky recalled in these words: "The great news was received enthusiastically, of course, and for the next three hours I had one of the most effective business engineering conferences I ever had in my life." The meeting was so efficient and the little group's enthusiasm so great that the work of preparing drawings and buying parts was started the very next day. Within a couple of weeks actual construction was under way.

Meanwhile, returning to the competition, Igor faced again the problem of the ploughed field. His temporary home at the time was an aircraft shipping box at the military airport where the tests were being held. A stove and two windows had been installed to make it livable. He stayed there to be close to his plane and to take advantage of any break in the weather. With only four days left, the rain pelted his box-house and the ploughed field remained a sea of mud.

On September 28, with only two days remaining, the field looked about the same—impossible for a take-off. But the weather had taken a turn for the better. It was sunny, almost windless and the temperature was falling. After visiting the city for dinner and a change of scenery, Igor went back to the field at about nine o'clock in the evening. He was glad to notice that the cold was now nipping his fingers and ears. If the muddy field froze he might be able to take off from it on the next day—the last day of the competition. He went to his box-house for a few hours of sleep. At 4:00 A.M. he was up, dressed, and heading for the ploughed field a half-mile away. He found the ground partly frozen and apparently offering at least a fair chance of a successful take-off.

Shortly after sunrise the S-6-B was ready for its hazardous attempt. The fuel and useful load had been checked and two military duty officers were on hand as official witnesses. There was still no wind, so Igor decided to take off diagonally across the field, from corner to corner, to obtain the longest possible run. The decision proved a wise one, for the plane needed almost the entire run to get off the rough surface. The landing wheels broke through the furrows at times, as they bumped along the uneven surface of the field. But somehow the plane staggered into the air, its tail skid dragging the last few feet, and slowly gained speed and altitude. Igor found the landing easier. He brought the plane in as slowly as possible, pulled the nose up high, and plumped down to a full stall landing. For the first time in days he relaxed. He had finished all the requirements. Now everything was in the hands of the judges.

On the next day, September 30, the judges announced their decision: the S-6-B was the winner, with the Farman taking second prize and the Nieuport, third. The Russian Baltic Company accepted half the 30,000-ruble first prize and gave Igor the other half. Now the young designer-pilot had enough money to repay a large part of the debt he owed his family. And, as a result of the victory, the new airplane company received an order for several S-6-Bs.

With the competition over, Igor turned all his attention to his four-engined airplane. Construction was progressing favorably. So huge were the wings and fuselage that the workers quickly gave the plane its name: the *Grand,* after the French word for "large."

As it took shape in the factory, the *Grand* looked bulky and unwieldy. Visitors shook their heads and predicted failure. Skeptics and pessimists appeared uninvited to offer their gloomy theories: nature's flying creatures were far lighter than those that lived on the ground; the *Grand,* the skeptics said, would be unstable and impossible to control. They of-

Close-up of the Grand, *world's first four-engined airplane, showing balcony, pilots' cabin, and inboard engines.*

fered "scientific" reasons why the lift of a wing would not increase beyond a certain limit, no matter how much larger the wing were built.

They reminded Igor of his experience with helicopters: the little, rubber-powered models actually flew, but when he built a full-scale helicopter it remained firmly on the ground. They pointed out, also, that a pilot in an enclosed cabin would have no wind stream to tell him his air speed and whether or not his plane was skidding. Therefore, he would be unable to maintain control of his craft.

Sikorsky and his men were too busy trying to build their big airplane to pay much attention to the critics. It was a difficult job. There were no wheels available for an airplane of the *Grand*'s size. So they had to design a special landing gear using sixteen airplane wheels and a framework of skids to save the plane in case the wheels collapsed. There were no steel wires in the infant airplane industry light and strong enough to support the huge wings of the *Grand*. They finally obtained suitable wires from a piano factory.

The builders had to consider seriously the problems of control of the ungainly craft. Suppose an engine failed.

Wouldn't the sudden imbalance in thrust throw the plane out of control, as the critics predicted? Not necessarily, Igor decided. Let's meet that problem by making the fuselage extra long to provide plenty of leverage for steering. And let's add more steering strength by using four big rudders on the tail section. And finally, let's mount the engines in tandem, two on either side of the fuselage, close to the center line, one behind the other, with both pusher and tractor propellers. These design arrangements, they believed, should solve the problem of directional control in case of an engine failure.

The *Grand*'s long, narrow wings were designed for the best stability and lift. Here, Igor was using a mysterious faculty which many years later he recognized as intuition. In 1912, airplanes were built with relatively short, wide wings, or "low aspect ratio." There was no reason to try long, narrow wings, or "high aspect ratio." Yet something, luckily, told Igor to do it. Later, when he and other pioneers had learned much more about the facts of flight, Igor realized that the *Grand,* heavy and underpowered, would never have gotten off the ground if he had used the low aspect ratio wings common at the time.

Busy as he was during the time the *Grand* was taking shape, Igor could not completely ignore the views of those who predicted failure. He did not argue with them nor did he lose faith in himself or his dreams of success. However, his critics caused him to spend many a long night reviewing his calculations to make sure he had the correct answers. Sometimes his conclusions were based only on guesswork or intuition. But more often they came from his growing experience and knowledge. None of the work of the previous four years had gone to waste. He gained confidence, for example, when he recalled his experience in converting the S-6 into the S-6-A. The latter, though heavier than the S-6, showed greatly improved performance because of its streamlining and additional wing span. Igor still believed the same principles would apply to the *Grand* and that the plane would surprise the critics and doubters.

In April, 1913, the major parts of the *Grand* were finished at the factory and trucked to the military airport for final assembly. In May the big plane stood fully assembled and was starting to attract crowds to the field. With its wingspan of ninety-two feet, its ten rows of struts and its overall height of more than twelve feet, the *Grand* made an impressive sight by its sheer size. Nobody had ever seen an airplane with more than one engine, and here was a giant with four! The power plants were four-cylinder, water-cooled Argus motors developing 100 horsepower each.

Equally as impressive as the *Grand*'s size, the crowds noticed, were innovations and luxuries for both crew and passengers. The nose of the plane was an open balcony with room for two or three men to stand. Back of that was the enclosed pilots' cabin. A door connected the pilots' area with the balcony. A second door led back from the pilots' cabin to the passenger cabin where there were four seats, a sofa, a table, a washroom, and a small closet for clothes. This was luxury almost beyond belief when one realizes that open cockpits, helmets, and goggles were still standard more than twenty years after the *Grand* was built. Igor's brainchild had surely arrived far ahead of its time. It seemed like a Jules Verne dream come true.

Though the *Grand* was big, impressive, and luxurious, the questions in everyone's mind were "will it fly and, if it does, can it be landed without a crackup?" As the zero hour drew near, the crowds began to bet as to what would happen. Once again Igor had to defy the pessimists and also the superstition of 13. The day that the *Grand* stood ready for its first flight happened to be May 13, 1913.

Although the *Grand* was ready to go that afternoon, the military authorities told Sikorsky he would have to wait until a group of Army planes had finished their flights at the field. It was not until after nine o'clock that evening that the last plane landed. Spring days in northern Russia are long, and there is light enough for flying even as late as 10:30 or 11:00 in the evening. At Mr. Shidlowsky's suggestion, Igor decided to try the first flight despite the lateness of the hour. Since the light was ample, there seemed to be no reason to wait until the next day—except the "unlucky 13th."

As Igor taxied the big plane out to the end of the field, his confidence increased. He reviewed the flight plan which he had been mentally rehearsing for weeks: take off, test the plane's general control qualities, climb to 600 feet, simulate a landing at that height to see how the *Grand* behaved at slow speeds, fly a few miles downwind, and turn back for the landing, depending largely on decreasing and increasing the power of the engines to control the final descent and landing.

Seated high above the ground in the enclosed cabin, Igor turned the *Grand* into the wind and revved up the motors. On the platform before him stood his flight mechanic, ready to signal the men who were restraining the plane by holding its wings. Aft in the passenger cabin, the co-pilot, Captain Gleb Alenchovich, had a more important job. After the take-off, he was to move forward if the plane proved to be tail heavy, or back if it was nose heavy, a function performed by the elevator "trim tabs" of modern planes.

Igor ran the engines to full throttle, the mechanic signalled the wing-holders, and the *Grand* began to roll along the grassy ground. It seemed to gain speed slowly, but soon the control surfaces took effect and the plane raced across the field with its tail high in the air. Igor eased the control wheel back and

During an inspection of the Grand *in 1913, Czar Nicholas II talks with Igor Sikorsky on the balcony of the big airplane.*

suddenly the vibrations of the wheels on the ground disappeared. The world's first four-engine airplane was in the air and climbing steadily. The take-off had been perfect.

The lack of an air stream felt strange, but Igor was glad to notice that the *Grand*'s homemade air speed indicator showed 60 miles an hour. Two other homemade instruments—a bank indicator, and a metal tube mounted in front of the cabin windshield to show the plane's angle of incidence (the angle at which the wing entered the airstream)—also helped him control the big plane from within the unfamiliar closed cabin.

As Igor held the *Grand* in a slow but steady climb he noticed the engines and propellers seemed to be functioning flawlessly and that the plane flew smoothly. He concentrated on the controls, trying to learn as quickly as possible the flying qualities of this long-winged aircraft. He soon discovered that the big plane answered the controls much more slowly than the small ships he had been flying.

When the altimeter showed 400 feet Igor turned the plane 90 degrees to the left. He made a similar turn at 600 feet which brought the *Grand* back over the airport and hangars. The mechanic, enjoying an unobstructed view from his balcony, joyfully waved to the huge crowd below. Back in the passenger cabin, Captain Alechnovich had nothing to do but look from the windows. There had been no need to run back and forth to "trim ship" as the airplane rode steadily, showing no signs of being either nose or tail heavy. Already a good number of pessimists had been proved wrong. The *Grand* was flying well and under good control.

With his strong, square hands on the wooden control wheels, Igor was growing more confident with each passing moment. Now it was time to think about the next challenge—landing the *Grand*.

Igor approached the problem of the landing with the same methodical care that had marked his flying since he had first hopped his little planes across the pasture in Kiev. Pulling back on a throttle, he reduced the power of one of the left engines, at the same time pushing the opposite rudder. The *Grand* held its course. This removed somewhat his anxiety about veering out of control if an engine failed.

Next he reduced the power on all four engines and pulled

back on the wheel to see how the ungainly craft would act in a landing position. At the slower speed and with the nose high, the plane still showed sufficient response to the controls. As a result, Igor changed his landing plans: instead of landing in a "power stall," he would bring the plane down in a normal glide for a power-off landing.

Igor turned the plane again and headed back for the field which was about a mile away. With power reduced, the *Grand* descended in a gentle glide and crossed the boundary of the field at a height of about fifty feet. Things were going so well that he decided to hold the plane in the air a little longer in order to land closer to the hangars. He increased the power and flew low over the runway, then pulled the throttles back and brought the huge ship to a smooth landing near the center of the field. The first flight of the world's first four-engine airplane was all over but the cheering.

The cheers turned out to be loud and long, but Igor and his crew did not hear them at first. As the *Grand* rolled to a stop they saw the crowd of many thousands moving in a solid wall toward the plane. Igor quickly cut the throttles and the roar of the motors and propellers was replaced by the even louder roar of the thrilled and happy crowd. As the propellers spun to a stop, the throng surrounded the plane. All three crewmen were on the balcony, smiling and waving. They started climbing down but never reached the ground. The onlookers seized them and carried them to the hangars where they received the greetings of a beaming Mr. Shidlowsky. For Igor, just twelve days short of his twenty-fourth birthday, it was a scene that would remain one of the most vivid and wonderful memories of his life. If those who said the *Grand* would never fly were still on hand, they were lost to sight in the surging throng.

For the next year and a half Igor Sikorsky enjoyed a unique distinction: he was the only pilot in the world who had taken off and landed a four-engined airplane!

During the months that followed the *Grand*'s maiden flight the people of St. Petersburg grew accustomed to the long-spanned craft droning slowly overhead. As the number of flights increased, much information was gathered. The plane's chief drawback was poor take-off performance and a slow climb. Apparently the tandem mounting of the motors, while

The Grand *forms a backdrop for Igor Sikorsky (center), with Czar Nicholas II at his left, and a group of government and military officials in 1913.*

safer from a control viewpoint, had a bad effect on performance. The efficiency of the rear propellers was reduced by the air blasts of those driven by the forward-mounted motors.

Since the flights had shown that the *Grand*'s big rudders provided more than enough control when an engine was shut down, Igor decided to make a major change in the engine arrangement. In June he ordered the engines installed four abreast along the leading edge of the lower wing. The resulting gain in propeller efficiency gave the big plane a shorter take-off run and better climb. And even with two engines stopped on one side of the fuselage, Igor was still able to keep the plane flying in a straight line, thanks to the big rudders.

Igor continued his test flights of the "new" *Grand* during the summer of 1913. In July he proudly accepted an invitation from Emperor Nicholas II to fly the plane to an Army airport near Krasnoe Selo, about twenty-five miles from St. Petersburg. There the plane underwent the royal inspection of the Emperor and the Grand Duke Nicholas. The Emperor walked around the plane and, his curiosity aroused, climbed a rickety wooden ladder to the front balcony. Igor, properly respectful, spoke only when the Emperor asked a question. Soon the questions came more rapidly and before long the youthful aviator and the middle-aged monarch were chatting freely and informally. Igor later described the Emperor's questions as "correct, intelligent, and sound from an engineering point of view."

In a few days Sikorsky learned how impressed the Emperor had been with him and his airplane. Nicholas sent him a gold watch on which was mounted the imperial Russian eagle. He kept this prized gift all his life, even though his work was to take him far from his motherland.

The life span of the *Grand* turned out to be just over four months. During its total of fifty-eight flights the historic plane

Czar Nicholas and Igor on balcony of the Grand.

gave no trouble. The end came in late August, 1913, when it was parked on the military field, protected all around by an eight-foot fence and seemingly free of all danger. But, as warplanes were soon to prove, there is little protection from the sky. A biplane, one of the entrants in the military competition that year, was passing over the field at a height of about 1,000 feet. Suddenly, parts flew off, the engine tore loose from the wing just behind the pilot and, almost beyond belief, plunged straight down through the right wing of the grounded *Grand*.

Ironically, the biplane's pilot was Gaber-Vlinksy, one of Igor's closest competitors in the military contests a year before. The pilot guided the plane to a crash landing despite loss of the engine and badly damaged elevators. He climbed from the wreck uninjured.

The *Grand* fared worse. Igor, who had witnessed the accident from start to finish, found the plane too badly damaged to repair. Besides he was, as usual, already dreaming of the future and other large airplanes. He ordered the *Grand* taken apart and its usable parts salvaged.

Watch and medal given to Igor Sikorsky by Czar Nicholas II. Inscription reads: "To Igor Ivanovich Sikorsky from the Municipality of the City of Kiev."

An engine, tearing loose from a biplane overhead, plunged through the wings of the parked Grand *in a freak accident which ended the* Grand's *life after only four months of flying.*

Though its life was short, the heroic *Grand* had earned a lasting place in aviation history. Truly it can be considered the forerunner of the multi-engined airliners that, many years later, were to link cities, nations, and continents in a vast network of commerce and communications.

5

On the Edge of Eternity

The year 1914 brought the outbreak of World War I. Its shattering aftermath in Russia was to affect drastically the life and career of the young air pioneer, Igor Sikorsky. But it would have been a memorable year for him, even without the threat of war disrupting his country, for in 1914 he faced the greatest dangers of his life. It seems almost miraculous that he survived.

Aviators have long agreed with the often repeated comment of the unknown pilot who said: "I don't want to be the bravest pilot, only the oldest." By the time 1914 had passed into history Igor Sikorsky not only proved himself one of the bravest pilots but, merely by surviving the year's hazards, seemed a good bet to become one of the oldest.

The new year began with no hint of the exciting days that lay ahead. The little aircraft plant of the Russian Baltic Company had been enlarged to handle a few small production orders and to make room for a second four-engined airplane. The orders, from the Army, were for the S-10, a biplane with an 80-horsepower French Gnome-Rhone rotary engine. During the previous fall the S-10 and the S-11, the latter a monoplane also powered by the Gnome-Rhone engine, had taken first and second prizes in the annual military competition. The planes were flown by two company pilots, Gleb Alechnovich and George Jankovsky.

Igor's second four-engined airplane was named the *Ilia*

Ilia Mourometz, *equipped with skis, lands at a snow-covered airfield near St. Petersburg in 1914. Note two crewmen standing atop the fuselage catwalk.*

Mourometz after a tenth-century hero of Kiev. Mourometz, according to the folklore of the centuries, fought gloriously against the enemies of Mother Russia. His story was an inspiring one, and the several airplanes which bore the *Ilia Mourometz* name lived lives as hazardous and thrilling as that of the legendary warrior.

The new plane was larger and had better performance than the *Grand*, even though its total (of 400) horsepower remained the same. Its wingspan of 102 feet exceeded the *Grand*'s by ten feet. The wings were of improved design and were spaced wider apart to reduce the air interference of one with the other. The gap between the top of the fuselage and the upper wing also was widened. The fuselage, though larger and roomier, caused no additional drag; its improved form made up for the increased size. The new plane had an open balcony in the front and a platform along the top of its fuselage about fifteen feet back of the wings. A stairway led from the cabin to the platform for those who wanted to enjoy the breeze. Handrails around the platform made it safe, providing the air was smooth.

Comfort and safety again received Igor's attention: part of the engine exhaust gases passed through two steel pipes in the cabin to provide heat against the Russian winter. A wind-driven generator gave electric current to illuminate the cabin, which was roomy and had four big windows on either side. The new craft even boasted a private cabin with a berth, table, and cabinet. Mechanics could reach the engines in flight by climbing through openings in the cabin and walking along the lower wing.

Since the *Ilia Mourometz* was completed in midwinter and was to be flown in January, it was mounted on skis. But it was an unusually warm winter with little snow. Some remained in ditches near the airport and was carted to the grassy runway and spread in two lanes for a distance of about 150 feet. The *Ilia Mourometz*, with Igor at the controls, got off to a fast start on the snow, but slowed down when it hit the grass. However, there were many pools of water along the grassy strip and the plane gained speed when its skis hit these. Finally, it lifted into the air.

The first flight was held to only a few minutes, as the plane proved very tail heavy. Later, with that defect corrected, the *Ilia Mourometz* made many flights in the area of St. Petersburg. On one flight the plane carried sixteen persons, a world record at the time. Sometimes the engines were shut down so that the mechanics could practice climbing out on the wings. On occasions they crawled all the way to the outboard engines to change spark plugs. The many struts and wires provided plenty of hand holds against the 60-mile-an-hour slip stream. The plane also was flown with landing wheels and later from the water with pontoons.

The *Ilia Mourometz* attracted thousands of visitors to the field. Interest in the huge plane even caused members of the Czar's government and left-wing members of the Douma, or Council, to forget their differences and speak to each other. In those days of growing enmity between the rulers and their opposition, this was highly unusual. Several opponents of the monarchy became frequent visitors. One of them, I. F. Polovzev, became a friend of Igor and provided much needed help in arousing the government's interest in the big plane.

Many in the government thought it foolish to spend money on anything as risky as an airplane. Even when the company built a second and more powerful *Ilia Mourometz II,* in April of 1914, the scoffers continued to scoff. One ''expert'' told members of the Douma that the big Sikorsky planes never climbed much over 1,000 meters (3,300 feet) and therefore were almost worthless for military or even for civilian use.

Igor's new friend, Mr. Polovzev, told him of the damaging remark. Sikorsky replied by inviting him and other members of the Douma to fly with him in the *Ilia Mourometz*. They accepted, and that evening found themselves aboard the plane as it climbed for altitude. The two outboard engines of 140 horsepower each and the inboard engines of 125 horsepower each brought the airplane to a height of just under 7,000 feet, which was considered sufficient for bombers of that time. The flight ended further criticism of the *Ilia Mourometz'* ability to attain a good altitude. The Army became more interested and began to consider four-engined airplanes for use as heavy bombers.

Although Igor's big airplanes had been performing well, they had never left the St. Petersburg area. Even during a long flight of six hours, thirty-three minutes on June 18 to test fuel consumption, the *Ilia Mourometz II* did not fly more than forty miles from the airport. However, the flight established a world duration record for a plane carrying six passengers. Encouraged by this performance, Igor decided that the time had come to take the big plane on a long, cross-country flight. He selected as his destination his home city of Kiev, 800 miles to the south. If all went well, it would certainly be a triumphant return for the young inventor. If he could fly the *Ilia Mourometz* across the rugged Russian countryside, through the always uncertain weather, and land safely at Kiev, it would be a proud day for his family and friends. It would also provide another surprise for the cynics who said that an airplane weighing a ton or more would never fly.

Careful plans were made for the long flight. It was to start before daybreak and continue in the light of the long summer day in the hope of reaching Kiev before darkness fell late the same day. One stop was planned for refueling, at the city of Orsha, well over halfway to Kiev. The *Ilia Mourometz* would be loaded as never before. In addition to a capacity load in the craft's regular fuel tanks, there would be extra gasoline in cans in the cabin. Extra containers of oil would also be carried in the cabin. Pumps and hoses would transfer the spare fuel and oil to the tanks when they ran low. Tools and spare parts, including an extra propeller, added further to the weight. Getting the overloaded plane into the air, Igor realized, would be only the first of the dangers to be faced and overcome. What other hazards might lie ahead along the route he could only guess. The engines must not fail, navigation and piloting would have to be good, and reasonably clear weather would be required, since Igor and his crew had neither the experience nor proper instruments for blind flying.

At the airport, late in June, Igor and his crew of three awaited the first light of dawn. On hand were the navigator— co-pilot Navy Lieutenant George Lavrov; the second pilot, Army Captain Christopher Prussis; and Igor's mechanic from the early days in Kiev, Vladimir Panasiuk. Lavrov and Igor had been close friends ever since their days as classmates at the Naval Academy. The eldest son of an admiral, Lavrov had long been interested in flying. He had told Igor about gliders and had shown him pictures of Otto Lilienthal's gliders before either of them had ever heard of the Wright brothers. Now in his mid-twenties, intelligent and physically strong and wiry, Lavrov commanded the respect of his associates. As Igor's friend, he had remained close to the development of the *Ilia Mourometz* planes. Later, though a Naval officer, he requested and was given a transfer to the Army squadrons which flew the *Ilia Mourometz* bombers during World War I. Prussis and Igor first met at the military airfield in St. Petersburg where Prussis served as a pilot and instructor. He was an excellent pilot, especially well qualified on Farman biplanes.

About 1:00 A.M. the four men boarded the *Ilia Mourometz*. It was light enough so that they could see the line of the horizon, but little else. The big plane stood at the start of the runway, wood blocks holding it in place while its engines were run to full throttle. With the engines still at full power, about twenty men pushed the plane over the blocks and the overloaded craft lumbered slowly down the runway. The take-off run was longer than ever before, but the *Ilia Mouro-*

metz finally staggered into the air and droned low over the still dark countryside.

Fifteen minutes later, and with the engines still at full throttle, the plane had barely reached a height of 500 feet. As fuel was consumed, the ship climbed slowly and after about an hour and a half in the air, had reached a safe cruising altitude of 2,000 feet.

The air was so smooth and the flight was proceeding so well that Igor twice climbed out on the wing to one of the outboard engines. He wanted to make sure that the engines could be reached if an emergency should occur in flight. Years later he described the sensation: "Behind the motor there was a space reasonably well protected from the air stream," he said. "It was beautiful and interesting to watch from this point the huge body of the ship and the wide, yellow wings. It was a strange feeling to see these wings apparently motionless in the smooth, clear, and cool air of the early morning."

Igor Sikorsky peers from the cabin of the Ilia Mourometz *in early 1914, prior to the historic cross-country flight from St. Petersburg to Kiev.*

The *Ilia Mourometz* flew steadily for the next few hours, cruising at about 65 miles an hour and gradually climbing to 5,000 feet in the clear, still air. The flight seemed to be proceeding too well, almost beyond Igor's best hopes. Seated at the cabin table, the men took turns enjoying a breakfast of sandwiches, fruit, and coffee. Probably the first meal ever served aloft, it was a forerunner of the hot meals now enjoyed daily by thousands of passengers in today's jetliners cruising at 600 miles an hour, 30,000 to 40,000 feet above the earth.

About eight o'clock in the morning the *Ilia Mourometz* passed over the city of Vitebsk where two telegrams were dispatched—one to Igor's home and one to the factory. The flyers placed the messages in slender aluminum tubes, along with the money needed for delivery, and tossed them from the plane. Strips of colored cloth attached to the tubes were easily seen from the ground. Igor learned later that the two telegrams reached their destinations as did several others tossed out later in the flight.

Orsha, end of the flight's first leg, came into view shortly after 9:00 A.M. and Igor brought the plane to a smooth landing on a field that had been selected and marked earlier. He taxied up to a row of fuel drums containing 400 gallons of gasoline. When the men left the plane they were surrounded by the usual large and excited crowd, most of whom had questions to ask about the strange machine. Igor and his navigator, after much effort, shook off the throng and walked across the field to study the problems of their next take-off in the fuel-heavy aircraft.

The field lay just across the river from Orsha. Only some 1,200 feet long, it sloped from a row of trees downward toward the river where it ended abruptly over a 100-foot-bluff. Even though it meant a downwind take-off, Igor decided to make the attempt toward the river rather than try to clear the trees. He reasoned that even if he did not get off the ground in the 1,200-foot run, he would have 100 feet of altitude as soon as the ship went over the cliff.

Refueling took at least two hours longer than had been planned and it was 2:00 P.M. before the last tank was filled. The crew became anxious, knowing that darkness came earlier in the south and that the pilots had no experience in night flying. If they reached Kiev after nightfall they would face serious problems, not only in finding the airport but in making a safe landing anywhere in the dark. They estimated that the flight to Kiev would take about six hours. It would be close, but they decided to take the chance.

As the plane gathered speed in its downslope take-off run, Igor decided not to attempt a normal lift-off. He simply drove the ship right over the cliff. The crew held their breaths as the craft dipped down toward the river, recovered, crossed the stream and skimmed low over the rooftops of Orsha. The city lay well behind them before the plane started to climb. The *Ilia Mourometz* had survived another overloaded take-off, one downwind from a short field.

Despite this success, the airplane was in trouble. In the hot and bumpy afternoon air the ship barely held its own at 250 feet, refusing to climb higher even with all four engines at full power. A downdraft dropped it toward the treetops below and Igor ordered cans of water and oil thrown out to lighten the load. He found it was taking all his modest flying skill to keep the heavy craft in the air.

After fifteen minutes of ups and downs in the turbulent air, the flight suddenly turned into a pilot's nightmare. Panasiuk and Igor, almost at the same time, stared in horror at the right inboard engine—gasoline was streaming from a broken fuel line. The engine continued to run for a few seconds, using up the gas in the carburetor. Then it backfired, igniting the fuel streaming out of the broken pipe. A twelve-foot tongue of flame shot out, searing the wing fabric and enveloping one of the wooden struts.

With the instinct of desperation, the crew sprang into action. It was a life or death situation and the next few seconds might decide which. Igor became busier than ever as he tried to keep the now badly underpowered plane in the air long enough to make an emergency landing, hoping that in the short time allowed him there would be no explosion or that the strut would not burn away.

Meanwhile, Panasiuk and Lavrov had scrambled through the fuselage opening and were crawling along the wing to the flaming engine. They beat at the fire with their overcoats, but the fuel-fed flames showed no lessening. Lavrov then leaned across the flames and turned the shutoff valve, choking off the fuel. The men attacked the flames again with their coats and this time were successful. The fire subsided and the two crewmen, almost exhausted from their efforts, returned to the cabin.

As the overloaded plane continued to settle toward the trees, Igor recalled a small field they had passed a few minutes before. He completed a careful turn back toward the field and reached it just as the plane ran out of altitude. The landing was good under the circumstances.

It was only then that the men realized how lucky they had been. First, the fire had flared just below the huge fuel tank. Second, the presence of the little field, with swamps, woods, and hills all around, had enabled the plane to land without further damage. And third, the undercarriage had proved sturdy enough to withstand the impact of landing with a full load of fuel.

With the flight to Kiev off for that day at least, Panasiuk repaired the fuel line while the others walked over the field to see if it provided enough space for a safe take-off. It was narrow and sloped toward a swamp. Once again Igor decided to take off downhill, no matter what the wind direction. By this time crowds from a nearby village reached the scene and helped push the plane to the high end of the field. There it remained for the night, Igor, as commander, sleeping in the cabin berth while the others curled up under blankets on the floor.

When the men awoke at about four o'clock in the morning they found a new danger—bad weather. Rain splattered off the cabin roof and the clouds overhead pressed low and threatening. Despite the outlook and the fact that they had no way of knowing how much worse the weather might be farther south, Igor and his men decided to resume their flight. There would be times during the next few hours when they would regret having left the safe little pasture on which they now stood.

The take-off proved a pleasant surprise. Racing down the slope, the *Ilia Mourometz* picked up good speed and lifted from the field well before reaching the swamp. In the cool morning air the ship climbed better than the day before. It cruised in and out of the clouds at about 1,500 feet and, for the first time, Igor found himself using his primitive instruments to fly blind. The instruments, hardly adequate by today's standards, included four tachometers to show the revolutions per minute of the engines (which would also indicate if the plane were gaining or losing speed), and a ball in a curved glass tube to serve as a bank indicator. Also aiding the pilot was a crude air speed indicator consisting of a U-shaped glass tube filled with colored alcohol. While flying in good weather, Igor had been able to mark the instrument with figures from 40 to 100 kilometers an hour. By watching it he could detect any changes from normal cruising speed. The final instrument was a horizontal tube mounted on a vertical rod, which was in turn attached to the end of a rod extending a few feet from the nose of the plane. In conjunction with this, Igor had painted a horizontal line on the windshield. By noting the positions of the windshield line and the horizontal tube in relation to the horizon, the pilot could tell if the plane were flying level, climbing, or descending.

As the ship flew in and out of the clouds, Igor was able to give himself a "cram course" in instrument flying. The plane would enter a cloud and then, in a few seconds, emerge on the other side. It seemed a safe and effective way to practice blind flying and, as things turned out, was time and effort well spent.

As long as the air remained smooth, Igor, with the help of his navigator, found it fairly easy to keep the *Ilia Mourometz* level and on course. Trouble came, though, when the plane plunged into a rainstorm. The ship staggered in the turbulent air. Lavrov watched the compass readings, shouting to Igor to "turn left" or "turn right," while Igor kept his eyes glued to the tachometers and bank indicator to hold the ship in level flight. In the driving rain and gusty air the plane could barely hold 3,000 feet of altitude and was constantly driven lower by strong downdrafts. Suddenly the left wing dropped in the heavy turbulence. The compass spun wildly and the altimeter showed a rapid loss of altitude. The controls became sloppy and ineffective. In a matter of seconds the *Ilia Mourometz'* brave flight to Kiev had become a terrifying fight for survival. Igor had lost control of the plane and he knew that the earth, hidden somewhere in the mists below, was coming up rapidly. It was a time for action. The lives of all rode on his next move. There would be no second chance.

Again, instinct or some higher power saved the day. Instead of pulling back blindly on the control wheel in an attempt to halt the plane's plunge, Igor neutralized the controls. He pushed both feet firmly forward on the rudder bar, held the throttles at full power, and waited. The plane stopped lunging, regained its air speed, responded again to the controls and appeared to have gotten back once more to level flight. Later, when Igor had gained more air knowledge, he realized what had happened. The big plane had fallen into a spin which would have continued right into the ground had he not made the correct move of neutralizing all the controls.

Although they were out of the near-fatal spin, the *Ilia Mourometz* and her crew remained in grave danger. Some 1,200 feet of precious altitude had been lost, they were still flying blind, and the rain and rough air continued as bad as ever. They could not climb up out of the clouds, and remaining in them would invite another spin and now there was probably not enough height left for a recovery. Besides, Igor had had enough of this blind flying. "All I wanted," he recalled later, "was to get down out of the soup so that we could see something."

The narrow escape had thrown the *Ilia Mourometz* off course, so that the crew could not be sure of what lay below or ahead of them. With no radio or weather information they could not know if there were a safe ceiling beneath the clouds or whether the clouds reached right down to the hills hidden below. As Igor reduced the engine power and nosed the plane down, groping blindly for the ground, the dangers of the situation could hardly be overstated.

With the engines throttled back, the crew heard the wind whistling through the struts and wires. Their anxiety grew as the altimeter showed less and less distance to the ground. They peered hopefully ahead and down, but were rewarded with nothing but the milky whiteness of the mist which even blotted out the wingtips. Less than 800 feet of height remained when the whiteness seemed to darken a bit. The darkening turned into a hazy green and then, the most welcome sight of their lives, the green became woods and pastures visible through a screen of rain. They were out of the soup at last, with the nerve-wracking ordeal of their first blind flight over, for the moment, at least. Now they had to determine their position and get back on course.

Lavrov guessed they had been off course to the east for at least twenty minutes. He advised Igor to head the plane southwest for a while, which proved good advice. The new heading soon brought them to the Dnieper River, about halfway between Orsha and Kiev. They followed the winding river southward, flying as high as possible—only about 800 feet—always keeping the ground in sight. With the fuel load lighter and the air not as rough, the ship was able to cruise and hold its altitude under reduced power. Except for the rain, which continued heavy, the situation seemed much improved. Maybe they would reach Kiev after all!

After about an hour the strain of flying through the downpour at low altitude became increasingly severe. With the plane in a much lighter and better flying condition, Igor decided to try to climb up through the clouds and get "on top." Pushing the engines to full throttle, he pulled back on the wheel. Almost immediately the ground disappeared and they were once more flying blind. This time things were not so difficult. The air was less turbulent than before and Igor had learned something about instrument flying. Lavrov's navigation again proved a big help and the *Ilia Mourometz* held its course, steadily climbing up through the dark, damp recesses of the clouds.

At 4,000 feet the rain slackened, but the darkness persisted. A few minutes later a brightness appeared overhead and the *Ilia Mourometz*, its yellow wings glistening with moisture, arose from the clouds into a world such as its crew had never seen before. It was a scene of breath-taking beauty—dazzling white clouds below, and the clear blue sky above. They shielded their eyes from the glare and it took several minutes for them to get accustomed to the brightness. The beauty of the scene, together with the smoothness of the air, were too pleasant to leave. They decided to stay above the clouds until the dependable Lavrov had guided them to a position over Kiev.

Captain Prussis took over the controls and Igor went to the cabin for a cup of tea. Lavrov, free of darkness and bumpy air for the first time in hours, relaxed in a wicker chair over his charts and maps. Igor, adventurous and curious as usual, donned his overcoat and climbed the stairway to the platform atop the fuselage. There, literally standing in the sky, he leaned into the cold blast of the slip stream, gripping the handrails and looking out on a scene he would never forget.

"Only a few times in my life have I seen such a majestic and beautiful spectacle as I did then," he recalled a quarter of a century later. "With the power of the engines reduced to slow cruising, our ship was gliding along a few hundred feet above a sparkling white surface. The air was calm and the plane seemed motionless with its huge yellow wings stretched out some twenty feet ahead of where I was standing on the upper platform. All around me there was a fairyland, formed by clouds. The surface was not at all even. From time to time we would pass close to a strange looking mountain. Next there would be a gigantic mushroom several hundred feet high. When we passed close to it, the cloud motion below its huge head would become apparent and a few bumps would be noticeable. For a long time I stayed alone on the platform admiring the wonderful fairy panorama—the strange beauty of which I will never forget."

Igor hated to leave the magnificent and thrilling scene, but his freezing hands forced him to return to the cabin. There the view from a window, while still beautiful, seemed like a framed picture in contrast to what he had seen while standing in the open on the narrow fuselage. Igor Sikorsky flew many times above the clouds in later years, and in most parts of the world, but nothing ever matched the enchantment of the morning he walked the sky atop the *Ilia Mourometz*.

Captain Prussis flew the plane for the remainder of the flight to Kiev. Igor had done his share and was glad to lean back in his wicker chair and gaze on the cloud carpet below. Three overloaded take-offs, fire in the air, a forced landing, rain, turbulence, hours of blind flying, and a nearly fatal spin—all combined to make him feel he had lived a lifetime of flying in little more than one day.

After two and a half hours without seeing the ground, Lavrov said he thought they were only about five miles short of Kiev. Igor took over the controls. He faced the final challenge to be overcome if they were to complete the flight to

Kiev successfully—a blind descent through the deep cloud layer. Again the crew prayed that there was a clear space beneath the clouds. And again the men had no way of knowing for sure if the clouds reached right to the ground. Igor throttled the engines and nosed the *Ilia Mourometz* down, leaving the sunlight and dropping once more into the murky darkness of the clouds to grope again for the earth almost a mile below. As before, the crew's worry increased as the altimeter showed them descending under 1,000 feet with still no sign of the ground. Suddenly, they were out of it. Directly ahead and about 900 feet below appeared the golden domes of Kiev's Lavra Cathedral. Lavrov's navigation had been uncanny in its accuracy. They had hit their target on the nose.

After that it was easy, for this was Igor's home territory. He guided the plane low over the Dnieper River with its bridges, over the familiar suburbs, finally over the woods and fields and down onto Kourenev Airport where he had made his first flight three years before.

For Igor it was a triumphant homecoming. Only a few persons were at the field to greet the big plane, for nobody expected it to arrive that rainy morning. But the great news soon spread and the city gave its heroic pioneer and his crew a warm welcome. For days crowds visited the airport to watch the *Ilia Mourometz* make demonstration flights. Igor's father, though ill, was brought to the field in a closed car and looked on with pride as several members of the family went up for a flight in the huge plane. Igor and his men were guests at a gala all-night dinner and celebration arranged by military aviation officers. The party was held at the exquisite garden house of the Chamber of Commerce on a hilltop with an unsurpassed view of the Dnieper River.

The return trip to St. Petersburg, while mild compared to the hectic flight southward, was not without its moments of tension. The Army had ordered Captain Prussis to return earlier, so the crew numbered only three, with almost all the piloting chore falling to Igor. The *Ilia Mourometz* took off from Kiev early on July 11 and seven and a half hours later landed at Novo Sokolniki, more than halfway to St. Petersburg. A compressed air device enabled the refueling job to be done in forty-five minutes, compared to over four hours on the earlier flight. The ship took off at noon on the final leg of the trip. Rough air and smoke from forest fires made the first part of the flight difficult for the low-flying plane. As fuel was consumed, the ship climbed until, at 5,000 feet, flying conditions were much improved.

The *Ilia Mourometz* was cruising smoothly along, with only an hour to go, when the crew saw gasoline streaming from the left outboard engine. Lavrov took over the controls while Igor climbed out to the engine. There he found that four screws on top of the carburetor had been loosened by vibration and that two were missing altogether. He tightened the two that remained and the leak stopped. Again his theories regarding the safety of multi-engined planes had proved sound.

The *Ilia Mourometz* touched down at five o'clock in the afternoon at the military field in St. Petersburg. For Igor and his men the 1,600-mile round trip represented not only adventure and danger, but a strong sense of accomplishment. No airplane had ever before made such a trip and the obstacles and troubles overcome only added to the scope of the achievement. The epic flight proved beyond doubt the worth of multi-engined airplanes and provided only a hint of what could be expected in the future. Military leaders were much impressed and it was not long before the Army placed an order for ten planes of the *Ilia Mourometz* type. Planes able to fly such distances and with heavy loads should make good bombers.

The remainder of the year brought hard work, tragedy, and one more narrow escape to Igor Sikorsky. The first bit of news he had heard after his triumphant landing in Kiev was that Archduke Franz Ferdinand of Austria had been assassinated in Sarajevo, Serbia. It was the spark that was to set off World War I. With the outbreak of hostilities between Russia and the armies of Germany's Kaiser Wilhelm, the days brought sadness. Captain Prussis was killed in the crash of a small plane while serving as an instructor. Many of the young officers who had attended the gay party in Kiev died in the first months of the conflict.

From the Baltic Sea came even more crushing news. Igor's older brother, Sergei, a graduate of the Military Academy of Law, was a naval officer. He was serving safely ashore in the Court of Kronstadt when he wrote to the commander of the Russian Fleet, requesting active sea duty. He was accepted. Two weeks later the light cruiser, *Pallada,* tied up at a dock in the Baltic, was blown up by a German torpedo with the loss of her entire crew of 800. Among them was the young naval officer, Sergei Sikorsky.

(Many years after, in Berlin, Igor Sikorsky chanced to meet the commander of the German U-boat that sank the *Pallada.* "We shook hands as friends," he recalled later. "After all, he had merely done his duty in the service of his country.")

For Igor, aviation—and life—became a stern and somber business, with the fun and elation of the earlier days wiped

Ilia Mourometz *bomber at a Russian military airfield.*

out by the grim demands of war. His responsibilities increased each week.

He performed not only his regular duties of directing the aircraft factory, but also had to teach the young Army pilots to fly the new planes. For more than a year he had been the only pilot in the world who could fly a four-engined plane. Others, like Lavrov and Prussis, had handled the controls of the *Ilia Mourometz* in the air, but only Igor had taken off and landed the huge planes. His schedule ran almost around the clock: fly all day with the Army pilots; direct production activities at the plant all evening; and work late into the night designing a new four-engined plane specifically for military missions.

The new ship was a lighter, smaller version of the *Ilia Mourometz*, with the emphasis on speed rather than comfort. The narrow fuselage had a single cabin fitted out for carrying bombs. The new craft, known as the Military *Ilia Mourometz*, Type V, was designed to climb faster and higher than the cumbersome earlier ships. Its destination was the fighting front where its job was not only to drop bombs, but to evade anti-aircraft fire and return safely to base.

In October the Army asked Igor for use of the *Ilia Mourometz* to test some new bombs at its proving grounds outside St. Petersburg. The Army had no racks for the new bombs, so the plan was to place them in the cabin and drop them by hand one by one through an opening in the floor. A colonel explained the situation to Igor who, for the first time in his life, found himself within arm's length of a powerful explosive.

The bombs, the colonel said, were six 40-pounders and one of 80 pounds. They were of the detonation type and would be armed during their drop to explode on impact. Before he dropped each bomb through the floor hatch, the colonel would screw in the fuses. A little propeller on each bomb would unscrew in the air stream as the bomb fell earthward and this would arm the missile. Once the propeller fell free, even a minor shock would cause the bomb to explode. "As long as the propeller remains in place, the bomb is harmless," the colonel assured Igor and his co-pilot, Lieutenant Lavrov.

During the drops, Igor stayed in the cabin watching the procedure both with interest and anxiety. Lavrov handled the flight controls, keeping the big plane steady and on course over the proving grounds, some 4,000 feet below. One by one the 40-pounders were dropped through the hatch. Each time the little propellers spun and fell free. About sixteen seconds after being dropped the bombs would strike the ground with flashes of fire and clouds of smoke and dust. A few seconds later the *Ilia Mourometz* would shake under the shock waves.

The colonel handled the 40-pounders alone, but asked for

Igor's help with the larger bomb. The air was bumpy and the men struggled and stumbled as they brought the missile into position at the opening in the floor. Suddenly, to their dismay, they noticed that the little propeller was spinning, started by a blast of air through the cabin. The propeller continue to spin and, to Igor's further displeasure, dropped out on the cabin floor. Now the big bomb was ready for action. The slightest bump would set it off and the plane and its occupants would be blown to bits.

Scarcely daring to breathe, Igor and the colonel raised the armed bomb over the hatch, lowered it slowly, making sure it did not touch the edge of the opening, and released it. Not until the bomb was well below the level of the plane did the two men look at each other and shake hands. A flash of orange flame and a black cloud of dirt erupted on the ground below.

Igor had survived another brush with death. Luckily, the remainder of the year found him too busy building the new bombers to get himself into any more personal danger. His tightrope walk on the edge of eternity had ended, for the time being, at least.

6

A Career—and a Way of Life—Ended

In the aerospace world of today it takes not months but years to bring a new aircraft from drawing board to first flight. Team after team of experts in almost endless array all contribute their special skills and knowledge to the complex task to be done. Their fields are many—aerodynamics, structures, materials, hydraulics, avionics, weights, metallurgy, power plants, tool engineering, manufacturing, quality control, to name but a few. It seems almost beyond belief that the new bomber, the *Ilia Mourometz* V, made its first flight *only seven weeks* after Board Chairman Shidlowsky had said to Igor Sikorsky: "We must have a better heavy bomber. Design and build three of them."

Spurred by a desire to do his part to help halt the invading armies of the Kaiser, Igor worked into the late night hours, a cup of coffee always at hand to keep him awake. Previously he had often stayed in the plant at night to solve design problems after the din of the day's production work had ended. But now the factory was buzzing twenty-four hours a day as parts of the new plane were built while others were still being designed. It was no place to seek the solitude needed for creative thinking.

Earlier, in the silence of the factory at night, but now in the quiet of his room, Igor applied the mysterious faculty, intuition. In the field of engineering, he said many years later, intuition probably makes it possible for some persons to solve problems almost at once rather than through hours or even weeks of calculations. Time and again in Igor's life it has enabled him to say that a particular design was good and would succeed or was bad and would end in failure.

Once, during World War I, this kind of intuition saved his life. Late one night he studied the tail assembly of the *Ilia Mourometz* D, one of the many models built during the war. The plane stood in the factory, finished and ready for test flights. Igor returned repeatedly to the tail, shaking it and bending it by hand. It looked good and the design knowledge at the time indicated that there would be no great flight loads or stresses on the tail. But something kept telling Igor that the spars and supporting wires of the horizontal stabilizer were just not strong enough, even though they looked good.

"It was an unpleasant thing to do," he recalled later, "but in the morning I ordered the entire tail removed and thrown away. We built a new and stronger one." A few years later, with greater understanding of the stresses on an airplane's tail section, Igor found definite evidence that the first tail would have broken off in flight. Igor was the test pilot at the time and such a failure would have meant certain death for him and anyone else aboard.

Once in a while Igor found time for recreation in the form of an evening walk about the city. With the coming of war the city's name had been changed from St. Petersburg to Petrograd. (Later, after the Revolution, it was to be called Leningrad.) Men in uniform were everywhere. Hotels, cafes, and places of amusement were crowded as people went on spending sprees, trying to forget the war which was drawing ever closer. Igor avoided the gaiety, knowing that not many miles away the wounded filled the hospitals and that the white crosses were spreading across vast cemeteries near the front.

The design changes in the *Ilia Mourometz* V paid off. When the new plane made its maiden flight it flew twenty miles an hour faster than the previous model, even though it had the same four engines. It could climb to an altitude of 10,000 feet with full military load, about 4,000 feet better than the previous bomber. The improved plane was badly needed. The first two *Ilia Mourometz* types had been sent to the front while the new ship was being built. They had not done well, the Army reported. One had been cracked up in a bad landing before even reaching its destination, the Austrian front. The other was judged unsafe for flying over enemy territory because it could not climb high enough. The Army announced it wanted no more big bombers, only the smaller, single-engined planes.

Even though the first two bombers had proved inadequate, Igor and his associates knew that the principle of the big, multi-engined plane was a good one. But how to change the mind of the Army's general staff? After several days and nights of conferences, Igor and Mr. Shidlowsky sent their answer to the Army: true, the two planes had not proved completely successful, but the failure was due largely to the crews who were not fully trained in handling the big ships. More important, a much better plane would be in the air soon, and they asked for another chance to prove the value of the big, four-engined bomber. Finally, Mr. Shidlowsky, a retired Army officer, requested that he be returned to active duty and put in charge of the new planes.

The company's reply went to the Secretary of War, who showed it to Czar Nicholas. The Czar favored another trial of the big bombers, returned the sixty-year-old Shidlowsky to duty as a major general, and appointed him chief of a new "Squadron of Flying Ships."

Before the end of December, 1914, the squadron had arrived at a new air base at Yablonna, about twenty-five miles behind the lines. Igor went along as technical adviser. The new bombers were flown to the base where military equipment and armament were added. Again Igor worked almost around the clock—as designer, test pilot, and flight instructor. In only five weeks the planes and crews were ready. On February 15, 1915, Captain G. G. Gorshkoff flew an *Ilia Mourometz* V on the first bombing raid on the enemy, dropping 600 pounds of bombs on German forces near Plotsk. The plane carried a crew of five, including Lieutenant Joseph Bachko, second in command, who later became a squadron commander. A German plane retaliated the same day, dropping a few bombs on the new base. After that it was give-and-take as the pace of the air war increased.

The plane flown by Captain Gorshkoff was the second *Ilia Mourometz* V to be built, but was the first operational bomber of this class. It was named the "Kievsky." Nine days later it bombed the railroad station at Willenberg, Germany, returning the next day to destroy two ammunition trains detained by the previous day's attack.

In late February, 1915, Igor was busy in a hangar when an air raid sounded. He looked up to see five German planes approaching at high altitude. Reasoning that the bombs would be aimed at the hangar, he ran toward the center of the field. One plane seemed almost directly above him. Just back of it he saw a small dot in the sky—a bomb. The dot looked motionless, but grew in size. Still running, Igor passed General Shidlowsky in mid-field. They looked up; the bomb was going to strike dangerously close. No matter which way they turned it seemed the bomb would hit right where they were. There was no time to run any more; the bomb was so close they could hear it whistle.

"Throw yourself on the ground," Igor shouted to General Shidlowsky.

"Do you think that is best?" the general replied calmly.

"Yes, get down, quickly," yelled Igor, who was already flat on the ground.

The bomb struck between the two men, the earth shook, and they were showered with soil. Igor ran to the bomb crater about fifteen feet away and scooped up a few of the still

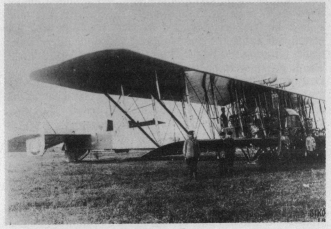

Ilia Mourometz *C*.

warm fragments which he kept as souvenirs. Most of the fragments had gone upward at various angles. If the men had remained standing they would have been killed by the bomb splinters.

The successful operation of the new *Ilia Mourometz* at the front had an impact on both Russian and German thinking as to the use of large bombers. The staff of the Russian First Army issued a report praising the performance of the big planes in destroying enemy railway terminals and in conducting aerial photography and observation flights. The report asked for all encouragement of further development of the big bombers and for the training of more squadrons. From that time on—March, 1915—the problem was no longer how to convince the military of the worth of the bombers, but how to build enough of them to meet the demand.

The appearance of the *Ilia Mourometz* bombers at the front showed the Germans what could be done in the way of long-range bombing. The ruggedness of the Russian bombers impressed the German pilots who met them in combat and found them difficult to shoot down. One bomber made it back to its base with 374 shrapnel and bullet holes and a wing strut shot away. Others returned with one and two engines out of commission. The gun crews of the *Ilia Mourometz* bombers could also hit back; they claimed thirty-seven enemy aircraft shot down.

The *Ilia Mourometz* spurred the German big bomber program. This led to the German giants called the "R-planes," which turned out to be the largest airplanes of World War I. The R-planes were built in only small numbers, probably a total of fifty-five to sixty-five. Of these, about thirty reached the front. The remainder either crashed, were used as trainers, or were ready for service when the war ended. They were huge planes, most of them with wingspans of almost 140 feet. One had a span of 157 feet, while another—on the drawing boards at the time of the Armistice—was to have had a massive double-decked fuselage and a wing span of 175 feet. These giants, and others in England, traced their ancestry to the *Grand*, the world's first four-engined airplane, and to the *Ilia Mourometz* V, the first four-engined bomber.

While the factory was turning out as many bombers as it could build, Igor spent most of his time at the front. There his duties included test flying the new planes as they arrived and helping in the design and structural changes that became necessary to make the planes safer and more effective in combat.

During 1915 the squadron of *Ilia Mourometz* bombers moved from one sector of the front to another, as required by military activities. German pursuit planes attacked them again and again, but the bombers always managed to get back to their bases. Sometimes they were badly shot up and landed with dead and wounded men aboard. Igor worked closely with the returning crews to devise ways of making the planes less vulnerable to attack. This work brought improved methods of fire prevention aboard the big bombers and better protection from the enemy's machine guns.

Braving the assault of the pursuits, the bombers inflicted much damage on the enemy's ground installations. On June 5, 1915, an *Ilia Mourometz* blew up a munitions train at a station in Prjevorsk, Austria, destroying the train and 30,000 shells and badly damaging the station. The bombers also did a good job of observation and photography, penetrating far deeper into enemy territory than was possible with the smaller planes.

Because of these attacks, the Germans increased their efforts to bring down an *Ilia Mourometz,* both by strengthening their antiaircraft defenses and sending more and more fighters after the bombers. One bomber, torn by shrapnel and with three engines damaged, limped back to a Russian field with its commander unconscious and its co-pilot at the controls. Upon landing, the plane's right wings fell to the ground. The load wires had been shot away and only the supporting air pressure of flight had kept the wings in place!

The *Ilia Mourometz* bombers had side guns, but could not defend themselves against attacks from the rear. The German pilots would fly directly behind the tail and open fire from short range. The squadron finally came up with the answer to these attacks—a tail gunner who would have a clear shot at the approaching pursuits, keeping them at a distance or shooting them down if they approached too close.

To make a place for the tail gunner Igor removed the central rudder and enlarged the rudders at either end of the horizontal stabilizer. He also increased the size of the stabilizer to carry the added weight of the gunner and his machine gun. An ingenious way was devised to enable the gunner to get to his position in the tail: a low sled mounted on rollers ran on lightweight tracks from the main cabin back to the tail. The gunner would lie prone on this "trolley" and slide smoothly under the many cross wires and braces inside the cramped confines of the aft fuselage.

The *Ilia Mourometz* tail gun was the first ever installed in an airplane. However, on September 25, 1915, before the improvement in defense had been completed, an *Ilia Mourometz* was shot down by German fighters, with the loss of its entire crew. A short time later the bombers with tail guns began to appear and from that time on not a single *Ilia Mourometz* was downed by pursuit planes.

Two new models, the *Ilia Mourometz* G and the *Ilia Mourometz* E entered service with tail guns. The new ships showed the advances that had been made in the bombers' wing area, weight, and power in only about two years. The first *Ilia Mourometz* had a total of only 400 horsepower, a wing area of 1,700 square feet, and a gross weight of just over 10,000 pounds. The G model had a total of 740 horsepower, while

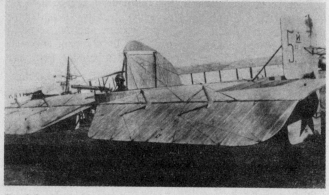

To defend against enemy pursuit planes, Ilia Mourometz *bombers were fitted with tail gun positions in the fall of 1915. This was the first time tail guns were used on bombers.*

This Mourometz *was flown by the Red Air Force following the 1917 Revolution.*

the E, the largest *Ilia Mourometz* built, had 880 horsepower, a wing area of 2,050 square feet and a gross weight of 17,600 pounds. The E obtained its power from four French-built Renault engines of 220 horsepower each. All of the *Ilia Mourometz* planes were powered by various combinations of engines produced outside of Russia, chiefly in France and England. This situation limited production, since it was impossible to obtain enough engines to keep pace with the factory's output of planes.

In late 1916 four engines designed and built by the Russian Baltic Car Company were installed in an *Ilia Mourometz* and quantity production of the new engines was planned for the next year. For the *Ilia Mourometz*, however, there was no "next year." The Russian Revolution in the spring of 1917 brought an end to all plans.

Of the seventy-three *Ilia Mourometz* bombers that were built, about half were used at the front, while the remainder served as trainers. Only one was shot down over enemy territory. Another was brought down, but over Russian territory. A third spun into the ground in a training accident, while a fourth crashed, probably as a result of Bolshevik sabotage, killing the crew of five. Among those who died in the crash was Igor's personal friend and co-pilot-navigator on the epic flight to Kiev, Lieutenant George Lavrov. The plane broke up in mid-air and there was evidence that an outer wing strut had been deliberately weakened.

The overthrow of the three-hundred-year-old Romanov dynasty, which forced Czar Nicholas II to abdicate his throne, shocked the country but did not come as a complete surprise. During the third winter of the war, widespread discontent swept through Petrograd, the capital. The presence of 400,000 war workers brought overcrowding. Living costs climbed, food supplies dwindled, and people stood in long lines waiting for bread. As the Czar's armies suffered defeat after defeat, more disloyalty and unrest spread.

Onto this scene of growing confusion came radicals with promises of peace, prosperity, and freedom. Hundreds of thousands of war-weary and despairing people seized on this hope and on a cold and windy March day in 1917, the Russian Revolution flared. Workers held meetings in the factories and then swarmed out into the streets shouting for bread and peace. They carried banners which read, "Down with Autocracy." Fifty factories closed.

Within a few days 200,000 workers were on strike. They tried to cross the bridges over the Neva River to reach the government offices, but were blocked by the police. Undaunted, they stormed across the frozen stream. University students joined them in the demonstrations. They attacked the police, which brought the only bloodshed during the early days of the Revolution.

The troops of the Czar offered only token resistance to the revolt. Soon they too were joining the rebels, bringing rifles and machine guns. The mutiny spread from regiment to regiment. To add to the confusion, newspapers ceased to appear. The city became a place of disorder and chaos.

Work at the aircraft plant came to a halt. Igor walked the streets of the city watching the turmoil with growing anxiety. He stood one icy night on the banks of the Neva and heard the crowds cheer as the District Court Building went up in flames. He wrapped his long parka coat about him and trudged home in sadness. It was not difficult to see that the world he knew was coming to an end, that his career and way of life were almost finished.

Alexander Kerensky, a socialist, headed the provisional government which took over after the Czar abdicted. Kerensky urged that Russia keep its pledges to its Allies by continuing the war against Germany. But the new government was weak, and disipline continued to decline in the Army. In November, 1917, the Bolshevik revolutionary leader, Lenin, appeared, calling for a separate peace with Germany. His Military Revolutionary Committee overthrew Kerensky's government.

There had been some reason for hope, Igor believed, while Kerensky's government existed. Now he could see that there was no longer a future for him in his native land. He believed deeply in moral and spiritual truths, but these were being wiped out by Bolshevik disbelief and violence. Men of great ability were being shot by the new regime. Colonel Gorshkoff and other officers of the "Squadron of Flying Ships" were executed, and Igor feared that the killings would continue. As the Germans overran the Russian forces, many of the *Ilia Mourometz* bombers were destroyed to prevent their capture by the enemy. Thirty bombers were burned by their own crews at one airfield.

Despondent, with his services in aviation no longer needed, Igor pondered his future. He discussed the problem with his friends. He did not want to leave his homeland, but he could see that the Russia he knew was tumbling down in hatred, violence, and destruction. He was a builder, not a destroyer. He decided to leave Russia and offer his services to the Allies.

Igor and his brother-in-law, Dmitry N. Viner (husband of his sister, Helen), obtained passports in Petrograd in February, 1918. Their destination was Paris where Igor hoped to serve French aviation and where Viner, a painter, planned to pursue his career in art. The civil war in Russia had not fully erupted at the time they obtained their passports. They boarded a night train for Murmansk in the north where, in March, they caught a small steamer, the *Oporto,* a Portuguese-built vessel then under British ownership.

As the shores of his homeland faded into the distance, Igor was bidding farewell—for the moment, at least—to his family and friends. The decision to leave had been difficult, but in the turmoil of the day, no other course seemed sensible. Before leaving, he had arranged for his sisters to care for Tania, his infant daughter born of a short-lived marriage. He hoped to arrange for Tania and the others to follow him later to whatever country should become his new home. Besides the separation from his loved ones, Igor was giving up a fortune in money, real estate, and government bonds earned by nine years of hard work. Although not yet thirty, he was worth about half a million dollars. As he stood on the deck of the rusty little steamer he had only one suitcase and a few hundred English pounds.

Having watched individual freedom decline in his homeland, Igor felt that in leaving he would gain something far more important than material wealth. He hoped that somewhere ahead he would find again the freedom to create and, with luck, ingenuity, and hard work, carve another career in aviation. He also believed that his own losses did not amount to much when compared with the overwhelming tragedy being suffered by the Russian people. In this first great trial of his life, Igor was reacting with faith, serenity, and inde-

pendent thought, as he was destined to do throughout his life
when trouble came.

A week later, *Oporto* berthed at Newcastle and Igor went
by train to London. There he found order and cleanliness in
contrast to the dirt and disorder he had left in Petrograd. The
people of the British capital, despite four years of war, including bombings by Zeppelins and the giant German R-planes,
looked fit and confident in the critical closing months of the
conflict.

In a few days Igor and Dimitry left for Paris and found
the French capital also strong and orderly during this crucial
period. Only in the blacked-out night could they sense the
threat of the enemy. They saw and heard the city bombed.
However, the steel cables of barrage balloons, as well as
antiaircraft guns, kept most of the bombers clear of the city.

Igor had carried from Russia a letter of introduction written
for him by General Niessel, chief of the French Military
Mission to Russia. With the letter in hand, he went to the
chief of the French Air Service's technical section to offer
his assistance to the nation's air power. He found that the
French had a 2,200-pound bomb but no airplane large enough
to carry it against the enemy. Could Igor design such a
bomber? The visitor's answer was an immediate "yes."

As he worked on the design of a new bomber, Igor occasionally studied German airplanes that had been shot down.
The enemy planes, in various stages of damage, were scat-
tered about in a "graveyard" outside the city. Igor poked
through the hundreds of wrecks, probing them for design
advances that might be useful for his new plane.

Igor favored two 400-horsepower, American-built Liberty
engines for his proposed bomber, but the French technical
section ordered the use of four French Hispano-Suiza engines
of 180 horsepower each. Working in a hotel room through
the spring and summer, Igor completed the design and the
French government ordered five of the new aircraft. The Armistice ended this work in November, 1918. The order was
canceled and Igor's reason for being in Paris ended.

Sikorsky stayed in France for several more months in the
hope that peacetime aviation would provide new opportunities. For years he had dreamed of airplanes that could fly as
far as 3,000 miles non-stop, planes that could carry passen-

gers across the Atlantic Ocean. In France he sketched plans for such an airplane. But aviation was suffering a postwar slump and there was no place in Europe where he could bring his dreams to reality. Where else could he go? He could not return to Russia. His fears that the Revolution would bring more executions were coming true. He learned that, in the fall of 1918, the Bolsheviks had shot General Shidlowsky and the latter's son in Petrograd.

What of America? Igor thought of the United States as a pioneering land, a good place to make a new start. He admired trail blazers like Thomas Edison, Henry Ford, and the Wright brothers. Like thousands before him he obtained an immigrant visa, spent more of his dwindling supply of money on a second-class ticket, and on March 24, 1919, sailed aboard the French liner, *Lorraine,* from Le Havre for New York. His good friend, Dmitry N. Viner, elected to remain in Paris. He loved the great city and found his art career progressing satisfactorily there.

At the age of thirty, Igor Sikorsky was venturing into a new world and closing the door on the old. Soon all would be memories—the comfortable home in Kiev, the early attempts at flying from the pasture, the incredible *Grand,* the perilous flight of the *Ilia Mourometz.*

With mixed emotions he watched the French shores slip away. Then he went to his little stateroom to consider again the problem ahead: to start life all over again, in a strange land, with scarcely any knowledge of the language, with no friends, no job, and only $600 between him and destitution.

It seemed hardly an encouraging prospect. Yet Igor faced it with quiet confidence and his usual optimism, looking forward with curiosity and enthusiasm to what the New World might bring to him, and he to it.

7

A New Life

On September 6, 1967, Igor Sikorsky, then seventy-eight years of age, said in reply to a question from a reporter, "I came to the United States because I thought this is the place which I want to make my second mother country, where I want to come and stay and work out my destiny. I came because in America I hoped to find a chance for free, creative work. . . . I found this freedom of initiative and to my mind it still exists. Today it has shifted from going west and starting a farm or a ranch to maybe starting a new industry. But it is still there."

Before he could make full use of the freedom he found in America and apply his aeronautical experience and talents, Igor faced two serious problems. The first was the extremely poor state of aviation. Military aviation in the United States, which had lagged far behind that of Europe during the war, fell even lower after the Armistice. War-surplus engines and training planes, chiefly the 90-horsepower Curtiss OX-5 and the 400-horsepower Liberty engines and the Curtiss JN-4D Jenny, a training plane, were offered at prices just short of giveaways. A Jenny in flyable condition could be had for about $200. Contracts and appropriations were cancelled and activities at the few airplane factories came to a standstill.

If military aviation was dead, commercial aviation was practically unborn. There were no airlines and virtually no airplanes deserving to be called "transports." Even the famed barnstormers, who almost alone were to keep aviation alive in the early 1920s, had yet to appear at the county fairs to carry passengers in sputtering Jennies and Standards or to show off their daring young wing walkers and parachute jumpers.

Igor's second problem was his limited knowledge of English and his almost total ignorance of local customs and conditions. While problem one made it unlikely that he could earn a living in aviation, problem two raised the question of whether he could earn a living at all. Not that Igor ever thought in such pessimistic terms, for his natural optimism and enthusiasm left no room for doubts or misgivings. When he debarked from the *Lorraine* in New York on March 30, 1919, he first noticed what he described years later as "the majesty of the skyscrapers." Within a week he felt at home in the humming city, taking in stride its subways, hurrying throngs, busy streets, and bright lights. "I found what I had hoped for," he said, "a dynamic, forceful, progressive country."

Standing at last on American soil, Igor hailed a taxi and in his halting English was able to tell the driver to take him to an inexpensive hotel. The cabby's choice was a small hotel in downtown Manhattan on West Eighth Street, not far from Fifth Avenue. This was Igor's home for several months until his decreasing reserves of money forced him to make several moves into ever more modest places, the last of which was a furnished room at three dollars a week.

In the spring Igor learned in a letter from his family in Kiev that his father had died on February 2, 1919. With his ties to his native land weakened further by this loss, he redoubled his efforts to get started on a career in the New World. One of his best hopes was to be recognized and appreciated for his early achievements as a designer of large airplanes. This proved difficult because of the language barrier. People to whom Igor tried to explain his plans for large airplanes dismissed him as "another strange immigrant."

Working with other Russian immigrants, including Boris Sergievsky, an aviator, Igor set up a small company in the summer of 1919. But its activities consisted chiefly of making many sketches of multi-engined airplanes and, with no business and only meager capital, the company soon failed.

With his money melting away, Igor decided the time had come to use a letter of introduction that he had obtained in Paris. The letter, dated February 17, 1919, was from Major General Mason M. Patrick, U.S. Army, Chief of the Air Service, American Expeditionary Forces, Paris, and was addressed to the Director of Air Service, Washington, D.C. It said:

1—Mr. Sikorsky, Russian inventor of airplanes, is proceeding to the United States for the purpose of laying before the authorities there information concerning the success of his designs.

2—The general public at large knows but little of the result of the use of airplanes on the Russian Front. We have been able to collect the following brief information:

The Sikorsky multi-motored airplanes rendered excellent service to the Russian Army as battle planes, as confirmed by official documents, and made about 400 raids over the enemy territory, representing a total distance of over 120,000 kilometers. Only one airplane, brought down by enemy fire, failed to return to its base; long distances were covered in spite of being badly damaged by shots of the enemy, several times with one and even two motors stopped at the same time.

3—Mr. Sikorsky can furnish further information and photographs concerning the results of his work. It is felt that these are interesting enough to call the matter to the attention of the Air Service in America.

In Washington, Igor received help and suggestions from the Russian ambassador. (The Imperial Government still maintained its embassy in Washington despite the Revolution.) He was directed to the Air Service Headquarters where General William Mitchell and his deputy, Colonel Charles Deeds, were especially helpful with telephone calls and letters of introduction. One letter was from the Director of Air Service to Colonel Thurman H. Bane, Chief of the Engineering Division, McCook Field (now Wright-Patterson Air Base), Dayton, Ohio. The letter said:

"The bearer of this letter, Mr. I. I. Sikorsky, will need no introduction to you once his name is mentioned. Mr. Sikorsky has visited the Office of the Director of Air Service and all here expressed keen interest in designs he may be able to propose. Inasmuch as the Air Service is at present particularly interested in the design of a super-bomber, there is no doubt that the arrival of the most experienced designer of super machines in the world will be of very great interest to the Engineering Division.

"The undersigned has explained to Mr. Sikorsky the limitations of our project due to lack of funds so that you need not fear that his hopes have been raised or that he has any material idea of entering into any arrangements with your office. All such matters, of course, are entirely in your hands and any arrangements that are made or might be made in behalf of the Air Service will of course depend entirely upon your judgment and the policy laid down for the Engineering Division by your office."

This letter, dated October 28, 1919, and signed by Lieutenant Colonel B. Q. Jones, Assistant Chief, Supply Group, office of the Director of Air Service, led Igor to Dayton and his first job in the United States. Within three weeks he had signed a contract with McCook Field's Engineering Division to furnish "preliminary study and general views of two types of multi-seater airplane for three 700-H.P. engines."

The agreement, dated November 20, and signed for the Government by Major R. H. Fleet, Contracting Officer, added: "It is understood that this work will be done at McCook Field and will be completed and delivered not later than January 1, 1920, for the sum of $1,500. The Government will furnish you, for the performance of this agreement, a suitable place to work, and the necessary drafting, blueprint, and stationery supplies."

Igor knew that the job was only a temporary one. Colonel Bane told him frankly of the many aircraft contracts that had been closed out since the Armistice and described aviation as "a dying industry." Within six weeks Igor had submitted his designs and his brief return to aviation was over. It had been a pleasant experience and he had established friendly relationships with everyone he had met at McCook. The engi-

Igor Sikorsky in the spring of 1919, one of the thousands of White Russian refugees seeking work in New York.

neers had been proud to meet and work, if only briefly, with the famous Russian designer. Colonel Bane expressed these feelings in a letter on January 12, 1920, addressed to Mr. Sikorsky at the latter's little two-room apartment at 506 West 135th Street, New York.

"My Dear Mr. Sikorsky," he wrote, "I desire to take this opportunity of expressing to you my pleasure in the good fortune that McCook Field had in having you with us for the month of December. We had all watched with interest the development made in Russia by yourself during previous years and it was a real pleasure for both myself and our engineers here to become acquainted with you and learn your methods of designing.

"The two layouts for multi-motored airplanes, which you were able to complete in such a satisfactory manner during your short stay here, have been studied with interest. We regret exceedingly that we were not able to go any further with these designs, as they both bid fair to be very interesting. The engineers at McCook Field assure me that they were able to determine from your work while here that your methods of design indicate that you have had good practical experience in designing large bombing planes.

"I hope that your business in New York will not cause you to forget us entirely and that you will find it convenient to come out to McCook Field occasionally. With best personal regards and wishing you a successful and Happy New Year, I am, sincerely yours, Thurman H. Bane."

Despite the colonel's good wishes, 1920 was hardly happy or successful for Igor Sikorsksy. He tried several times to find employment in the aircraft industry but, caught between almost total curtailment of military contracts and an almost nonexistent commercial aircraft industry, he found no opportunities at all, especially for a foreigner competing with citizens of the United States.

For the first time, Igor was beset by doubts. Even the big city's glamor began to fade as he discovered how alone one can feel among millions of strangers. He walked the streets to escape his depressing living quarters. But soon his worn shoes prevented even that retreat. He took refuge in the library, fighting homesickness by reading his favorite Russian author, Dostoevsky, in his native language.

The spectre of hunger drew closer and he began to limit himself to two meals a day. Most of the time his meal would be a plate of Boston baked beans and a cup of coffee in a cheap restaurant where bread and butter were served free with the beans. Such a meal cost twenty cents. He enjoyed the rare treat of meat or eggs only when invited to the home of a fellow immigrant. His two suits, rapidly becoming threadbare, hung loose on his thin frame. His one overcoat, shabby from winters in Petrograd, Paris, and now New York, contributed little to his warmth and nothing to his appearance. No longer did he think only of aviation. He needed a job, any job.

With another winter rapidly approaching, Igor finally found employment. A fellow immigrant and former Russian naval officer, Leo Trofimov, suggested to him that he try teaching. There was an opening, Trofimov said, for a mathematics instructor at the Russian Collegiate Institute, a night school organized by a few Russian intellectuals. Classes were made up of Russian immigrants, chiefly workers from Manhattan's lower East Side, who wished to improve their station in life. Igor had never taught anything except flying, but he quickly reviewed his arithmetic, algebra, and geometry and became an effective and popular teacher. As he won new friends, he was invited to lecture to various small organizations on aviation and on his hobby, astronomy.

His lectures led him into the suburbs. Often he rode the subway to the end of the line, carrying lantern slides borrowed from the American Museum of Natural History and lugging a heavy projector. Much of the time he had to walk a mile or two beyond the subway to reach his destination. It was hard work, almost all of it at night. Although he was earning a living and no longer worrying about the future, he still stuck to his low-budget diet of beans and bread.

Eventually, the lectures paved the way for Igor's return to aviation. First of all, he improved his English, simply by reading and speaking the language. Increasingly, he was better able to express himself about his former work in aviation. He impressed his listeners, too, with his hopes and plans for the future. He told them of his dreams of a four-engined airplane carrying forty or fifty passengers from coast to coast. He drew sketches of such airplanes and talked about them with anyone who would listen.

During this period of teaching and lecturing, which ran through 1921 and 1922, the Russian society, Nauka (Science), became the center of Igor's social and working life. There, where he conducted adult night classes, he met a young Russian girl, Elizabeth Semion, who had been born in Manchuria and spent the first sixteen years of her life in that country.

Igor Sikorsky and his wife, Elizabeth, in 1930. They were married in 1924 in New York City.

Elizabeth's father was a professional soldier who was last stationed near the Mongolian-Chinese border. At the time of the Russian Revolution she was working at an American Red Cross field hospital set up in Siberia to help refugees from the Revolution. Her parents had already disappeared, probably victims of the terrible violence of the times. Danger and chaos were everywhere. Bands of bandits roamed the countryside, looting, pillaging, and fighting.

Elizabeth had studied English earlier while with the Red Cross and was serving as an interpreter when the revolutionaries abruptly ordered the Red Cross to get out of the country within twenty-four hours. Red Cross officials, who had been impressed with her ability and charm, managed to smuggle the young girl out of Siberia and into Japan. For the next three years she worked as a nursemaid for a wealthy Japanese family, learning the Japanese language and customs. She saved her money and traveled to the United States in 1920. At Nauka, she was a teacher in the children's school when

View of first Sikorsky "plant" at Utgoff farm, 1923. Chicken coop at right, garage at left.

she met Igor at a social gathering. They were married January 27, 1924, at the Russian Cathedral in New York.

The Nauka society also provided a turning point in Igor's professional life. Previously, despite many attempts, he had failed to obtain a job with the established aircraft companies. Similarly he had failed to win any American financial support for his aircraft designs. In contrast, he now found his ideas greeted with growing enthusiasm among his fellow immigrants. They urged him to renew his work in airplane building and even offered part of their own small earnings to help him get started.

Most of Igor's lecturing had been confined to evenings and weekends and for many months he had found time to keep up-to-date on developments in aviation. He had continued his sketching of new designs and once in a while visited airports to watch the latest airplanes in operation. More than ever he wanted to return to the only profession in which he felt at home. He realized that time was running out; his last real achievements in aviation dated back to his big bombers of 1916 and 1917, airplanes that had since become obsolete. Encouraged by the faith and confidence of his friends, Igor decided to try once again to organize an aircraft company.

Years later Igor Sikorsky recalled his return to aviation in these words: "It was a perfectly wrong way of entering aviation. Most of my listeners and students, who offered financial support to help me get started in aviation again, were men of very little means. When I decided to accept I was heavily criticized. It was almost said that it was dishonest to take people's money at a time when big, well-financed companies were going out of business. 'And here you are,' some people said, 'with no money, no connections, no nothing, so to say.' But, as I had become familiar with the geography of the United States I was sure that sooner or later this country would see a great expansion of air transportation. So I decided to take this risky way of returning to aviation. It seemed the only way."

Igor's formal return came on March 5, 1923, with the formation of the Sikorsky Aero Engineering Corporation

Fuselage of the S-29-A, first Sikorsky plane in the United States, takes form at the Utgoff farm at Roosevelt, Long Island, in the spring of 1923.

Stock certificate for Sikorsky Aero Engineering Corporation, the original Sikorsky company in the United States, formed in 1923.

under a charter from the State of New York. The corporation set up temporary offices at 114 East Twenty-fifth Street with Igor Sikorsky as president, W. A. Bary, treasurer, and L. A. Shoumatoff, secretary.

It was a modest beginning, to say the least. The company started with about $800 in cash and possibly a few thousand dollars in subscriptions or pledges for stock. What the new company lacked in money was more than offset by the faith and loyalty of the little group of men who were willing to risk their savings in the venture. Many of them were Russian immigrants who had been employed in factories in the United States but who had quit their jobs to invest not only their money but their labor in the Sikorsky company. Others were former Russian military officers for whom the new company meant their first jobs since leaving Russia.

All of the investors and workers knew well the gamble they were taking. The risks had been fully explained to them at meetings and in printed material. They were prompted by motives other than earning money, chiefly by a pride in their heritage. They wanted to show that, although they had fallen on troubled days, they were Russians who could help advance human progress through engineering and industry.

Early in the spring of 1923 the little company, which then

numbered only a half dozen employees, set up its operations on a farm in Roosevelt, Long Island, owned by one of Igor's friends, Victor Utgoff, a former lieutenant in the Russian Navy. Since payment of wages in shares was illegal, there was a gentleman's agreement with every worker that he would be paid only fifteen dollars in cash each week and would receive the balance of his salary in company stock. As president, Igor was to receive thirty-five dollars a week, his married assistants twenty-five, and his unmarried helpers fifteen. (A few years later the workers and other stockholders each received $2.60 for every dollar they had invested in the original corporation.)

The Sikorsky ''factory'' on the Utgoff farm consisted of a wooden shed worth about $250, a chicken house—and plenty

Igor Sikorsky at the Utgoff farm with the partially completed S-29-A.

of space outdoors. The plan was to use the chicken house as a drafting room, office, and workshop, and the shed for construction of some of the airplane parts. Assembly of the aircraft would be done in the open, a good plan if the plane could be completed before cold weather arrived—and if the summer did not bring much rain.

In these primitive facilities, with little money, only a bare hope of additional contributions, and not even a promise of any customers, Igor and his faithful followers began preparations to build an all-metal, twin-engined transport airplane of the most modern design then possible. This airplane, Igor hoped, would pave the way for new recognition of the name Sikorsky in the world of aviation, recognition which he hoped might surpass that which had been earned in Russia. Such was his dream. And such was the dream of his men as they started to look for materials and parts with which to construct the new airplane.

8

A New Career

With establishment of the Sikorsky Aero Engineering Corporation, Igor Sikorsky's four-years' residence in New York City's borough of Manhattan came to an end. In late February of 1923 he moved with his meager belongings to a rambling white frame house on the Utgoff farm in Roosevelt, Long Island, about twenty-five miles east of Manhattan.

In Roosevelt he occupied second-floor rooms that had been arranged for him and several relatives who had fled Russia a few weeks before. The group included two of Igor's sisters, Olga and Helen, together with Helen's two children, Dmitry Viner, Jr. and Galina Viner, and Igor's daughter, Tania.

Forced by circumstances to leave these loved ones behind when he himself had fled his homeland in 1919, Igor was happy to greet them when they arrived in New York on February 22, 1923. The newcomers were equally glad to see their renowned relative and countryman. They had gone to Riga, Latvia, and then boarded a small steamer, the *Latvia*, at the nearby port of Libau, some fifteen days before. Crossing the stormy north Atlantic in winter had been a frightening experience. Many passengers remained below decks, seasick, and often it seemed the vessel would sink under the pounding of mountainous waves. "I did not think we would ever make it," Tania recalled many years later.

Igor provided the money for the voyage of his relatives to America. It was still possible, despite the upheavals in Russia, to send a telegram to his sisters telling them that steamer tickets had been bought for them and could be claimed by going to Latvia. So he was able to bring about a reunion, and was especially happy to greet little Tania, then five years old, whom he had not seen since she was an infant.

Clearing through customs at Ellis Island, the new arrivals were relieved to see a familiar face and to learn that Sikorsky had arranged lodgings for them at the farm. The reunion was a morale builder for Igor, too, as it provided an emotional link with a past that was for the most part filled with pleasant memories. Dmitry Viner (whose name soon became the Americanized "Jimmy"), now fourteen years old, had vivid memories of being hoisted up into the *Grand* as a lad of six and romping on the plane's front balcony. Olga and Helen recalled their younger brother's futile attempts to fly his awkward, underpowered helicopters near their home in Kiev, and the fame he had won later with his big airplanes. They were happy to learn that after four years of effort he was returning to aviation.

Early in the spring work began on the S-29-A—"29" for the twenty-ninth type of Sikorsky aircraft and "A" for America. From the beginning the big problem was money—how to best use the few hundred dollars the company had on hand, and how to raise more money to continue construction of the airplane. Everyone helped. Igor and his men roamed from five-and-ten-cent stores to junkyards in their search for parts for the plane. Airplane builders during the week, the little group of workers became salesmen on weekends when stockholders and prospective subscribers visited the farm to find out what progress, if any, was being made.

"Every Sunday my aunt and mother prepared tea and sandwiches in the house for the prospects," Jimmy Viner recalled later. "Many people contributed money and this helped pay for more parts and materials during the coming week. Mr. Sikorsky worked hard and had practically no time off. Once in a while he would take us for a ride in the sidecar of his motorcycle. Later, he gave me the motorcycle."

Many persons who visited the makeshift "factory" considered the obstacles faced by the company to be almost insurmountable. Most of the work had to be done by hand as the shop boasted no machinery except a little quarter-horsepower

Left: Igor Sikorsky in S-29-A fuselage framework at Utgoff farm in 1923. Right: Jimmy Viner poses in the fuselage of the S-29-A.

drill press and a few hand tools. The airplane's design had to be changed from time to time to conform to the changing construction equipment and cheap materials.

The main structure of the fuselage was formed out of angle irons removed from discarded bedsprings found in a nearby junkyard. Turnbuckles, made for World War I airplanes and selling originally for fifty cents each, were found in a Woolworth's five-and-ten-cent store. There they were priced at ten cents each for use on radio antennae. At that price, Igor and his men bought all they could carry.

Bob Labensky, one of several resourceful members of the group, bought a bumper from a wrecked car in a junkyard and fashioned a pair of shears for cutting sheet metal for the aircraft. Two Hispano-Suiza (Nisso) engines of about 300 horsepower each were purchased from war surplus, even

Jimmy Viner as a young Sikorsky worker.

though both their power and condition would probably be inadequate. But the price was right—only $250 per engine.

Throughout the summer work progresssed on the S-29-A with the lush green foliage of trees forming strong walls for an aircraft plant and the sun, sky, and clouds providing an ever-changing ceiling overhead. In the outdoor assembly area the skeletal forms of fuselage and wings began to take shape, supported on wooden horses. Only rain and the dark of night halted production.

The work force now numbered about fifteen. Some of the men held other jobs and came to the farm after their regular hours to help as best they could. The youngest, Jimmy Viner, attended school in the village of Roosevelt and often skipped his homework to work on the plane. Most of the time he shopped, ran errands, dug ditches or just swept up the place. The youngster's ditch-digging ability was called for before the plane's landing gear could be installed. Since there was no jack to raise the fuselage, Jimmy dug under it to make space for the wheels and landing struts. With the gear installed, the ship was then pulled out of the ditch.

The group's enthusiasm and hard work won the respect and good will of investors and a good credit rating with suppliers. In many instances subscriptions for stock represented gestures of friendly help rather than investments. Such was the case with the famous composer and pianist, Sergei Rachmaninoff, who gave the company its brightest financial day of the year when he visited the farm one autumn Sunday and pledged a total investment of $5,000. The composer also accepted the position of first vice-president, adding much to the company's prestige as well as its financial well-being.

Rachmaninoff's support came at a time when it was badly needed. The cold weather of late fall had brought the work in the open to a standstill. Worse, it had greatly reduced the number of weekend visitors with their money and new subscriptions. The work force dropped to a mere handful, most of them going for weeks without pay. Despite these difficulties the S-29-A was more than half-completed by late autumn.

Thanks to Rachmaninoff's generous contribution, the company was able to rent a leaky, old wooden hangar at a corner of Roosevelt Field (now Roosevelt Raceway) near Westbury, Long Island, about ten miles north of the Utgoff farm. An ancient Reo car owned by Bob Labensky was used to tow the fuselage of the S-29-A to the airfield. The wings followed by trailer on a second trip, mounted on a triangular rack in the way that plate glass is now transported. The local police, who had come to like and respect the hard-working airplane builders, provided a motorcycle escort, halting traffic along the narrow roads between Roosevelt Village and the airport. A few days later Igor and his relatives moved into a rented house in Westbury, conveniently only a short distance by motorcycle from Roosevelt Field.

With the junkyards still a major source of supply, the S-29-A slowly took shape. Duralumin to cover the fuselage and wings was bought in small quantities from time to time to keep pace with immediate requirements. Money again became scarce and the men worked from twelve to fourteen hours a day without pay throughout the winter and into the spring. The few dollars that could be raised by stock subscriptions went mostly for food.

In April, 1924, the S-29-A appeared ready for flight. It

was an attractive aircraft for its day, with straight lines and a trim, sturdy look. The pilot sat far back in the fuselage in an open cockpit, closer to the plane's tail than to its nose. The passenger cabin extended from a point about midway between the cockpit and the wings all the way to the front end of the fuselage. Large, horizontal windows were spaced along either side of the cabin.

The S-29-A was a sesquiplane; that is, more than half of the lift was provided by the upper wing which had a span of sixty-two feet and a total area over twice that of the lower. The engines jutted forward from the lower wing to a point almost opposite the nose of the plane. The landing gear, standard for the 1920s, consisted of two wheels and a tail skid.

Despite its neat appearance, the S-29-A, Igor knew, suffered from hidden ailments. The weary Hisso engines, even at their best, provided barely enough power for an airplane of this size. Too many of the ship's makeshift and second-hand parts were of doubtful quality. The worn tires had blowouts even while the plane was safely parked in the hangar. Yet, for better or worse, the aircraft had reached the point of first flight. In addition, the shareholders, especially those who had invested their money when the company was first formed, were becoming impatient and demanding that the plane be flown without further delay.

Fueled with a few cans of gasoline from a nearby service station, the S-29-A was rolled from its hangar the morning of May 4. After the sputtering engines had been warmed up, eight workers scrambled into the cabin. Igor wanted to take only three, but found it impossible to say "no" to men who had worked so long and loyally for this chance.

After a long run down the field the plane lifted slowly into the air. From his lonely vantage point far back of the wings and engines Igor could see that the propellers were turning too slowly to provide sufficient thrust for a good climb. Apparently the Hissos were even more underpowered than he had thought. He wanted to land immediately, but the plane "ran out of airport," crossed the boundary of the field, and flew low across Mitchel Field, an adjacent Army airdrome. At an altitude of about 100 feet, Igor started a left turn and the ship dropped lower as the engines started to lose power.

Engines installed, the S-29-A takes shape at Roosevelt, Long Island. The entire work force at the time (left to right): a workman (not identified), D. D. (Jimmy) Viner, Walter Skory (Skorohodoff), Mr. Samilkin, Baron Nicholas Solovioff, Mr. Kotilevseff, Igor Popoff, Jacob Islameff (later killed in Fonck accident), Igor Sikorsky, Boris (Bob) Labensky, Colonel Victor Ivanov, Nicholas Glad, a workman (not identified), Al Krapish, and Ilya Foursoff.

He hardly had time to line up with the fairway of a golf course that luckily loomed ahead. He pulled up, barely clearing a row of telephone lines, and the plane settled to a hard landing on the uneven ground. After rolling about thirty yards the ship struck a low spot on the fairway and turned up on its nose, coming to rest bent and broken, with its tail pointing at the sky.

Jimmy Viner recalled the short flight. "I was crouched in the nose section with Al Krapish, another worker," he said. "The windows had not yet been cut in the metal at the front of the ship, so we couldn't see anything outside unless we looked back through one of the side windows. I didn't know anything was wrong, didn't even notice the loss of power. But I did know we were flying mighty, darned low."

When the plane came to rest on the fairway, Jimmy and

the others jumped from the cabin, bruised and shaken. It didn't take them long to see that the damage to the airplane was more serious than their own minor scratches. The wooden propellers were broken, water gushed from the cracked radiators, and the landing gear was smashed. Igor ordered the ship taken apart and trucked back to the hangar. He wanted to get away from the scene, to be alone to do some thinking.

As he started his motorcycle he heard Nicholas Solovioff, one of his most active workers, say, "This is the end." The words pounded in his brain as he headed his cycle eastward on the island, following the winding roads to wherever they might lead. Dusty, tired, and discouraged, he stopped at Port Jefferson, on the north shore of Long Island, some fifty miles from Roosevelt Field. There he slumped down on a park bench, gazing sadly out over the harbor. The end? he wondered. After building almost one hundred good airplanes in Russia, couldn't he build even one in his adopted country?

The sun had set before he climbed back on his motorcycle and headed for home. The long hours of solitary thinking had brought him to a decision: he would not give up. Too much time and work had gone into the S-29-A to admit defeat now. He owed a debt, also, to his faithful workers and investors and he would not let them down. He decided to call the men together the next morning and see what could be done to repair the plane, even though they had no money.

The next day everyone agreed on two main points: first, the S-29-A was a basically good design and simply needed more power; and second, they would begin immediately to repair the plane and would worry about the engine problems later.

Again the men worked without pay, often not sure of their next meal. These were days that Igor referred to years later when he said, "The greatest danger in aviation was starvation."

When Captain Charles Nungesser, the French ace of World War I, came to Roosevelt Field to give flight demonstrations, reporters covering the week's events helped pay for the Sikorsky workers' food—although they never knew it. Luckily, a telephone in the Sikorsky hangar had been paid for two months in advance. Luckily, also, it was the only phone in

Jimmy Viner, right, and Baron Nicholas Solovioff at the Roosevelt, Long Island, farm.

the area and the newsmen had to use it often. Each time they paid in cash. Igor and his men collected the change at noon and evening to buy bread and milk at a nearby store. Their pride prevented them from telling the reporters that their nickels were actually preventing hunger in the Sikorsky work force.

By midsummer the S-29-A was almost completely repaired, except that it had no engines. Igor had located two overhauled Liberty engines of 400 horsepower each—just the extra power needed. But the price tag for the engines and associated parts was $2,500, and at a time when the company was practically living on loose change and charity. Igor knew they had reached a crucial milestone and that some drastic action was necessary if the whole enterprise were not to fail. He called a special meeting of the stockholders, which included all the workers.

Throughout his life Igor Sikorsky showed strength and even a flair for the dramatic in time of crisis, or when arguing for a cause in which he believed deeply. In Petrograd his statements to Board Chairman Shidlowsky had paved the way for the world's first four-engined airplane. His coolness during the perilous flight to Kiev had saved his life and the lives of his crew. Years later his inspring arguments would lead to the helicopter and open up a whole new industry. Now, in the summer of 1924, on the verge of failure, he called once more on his own words and strength of will to win the day.

The special meeting was held in a small Manhattan office rented for the occasion. There was barely room for the fifty or so persons who attended. "It was a dramatic time," Sikorsky said in describing the gathering. "Many of our stockholders had lost confidence in us and some of them even wanted to call in the district attorney. This was not an official stockholders meeting and it had no legal power; I invited only the loyal shareholders, the ones who might be willing to invest more money even in time of trouble."

Igor opened the meeting by locking the door, putting the key in his pocket, and announcing firmly that nobody was going to leave the room until $2,500 had been pledged. He

Subscribers show up on a Sunday afternoon at the Utgoff farm to inspect progress on the S-29-A.

assured his listeners that the S-29-A was a good airplane and needed only the proper power to prove itself. He reminded them that it had taken off and climbed, even though far underpowered. He explained that $2,000 was needed to buy the two Liberty engines, plus $500 for stronger parts to handle the extra weight and power that would result.

Igor did not disclose at the time that his source for the engines was an enterprising businessman who had been buying war-surplus Liberties which he overhauled and sold to rumrunners who needed the extra power to outspeed Federal boats. "He was a very kind and friendly man," Igor said later. "He told me he was selling the engines cheaper to us than to the bootleggers, which seemed quite fair under the circumstances. Other aircraft companies were obtaining Liberty engines on loan from the government, but we were considered too poor and unreliable to qualify."

Igor's arguments brought initial pledges totalling $2,000. As he continued to plead, the extra $500 was subscribed. Igor unlocked the door and the men filed out, happy that the company was to receive another chance, but still far from convinced that they would ever see their money again.

The new engines were installed in August and the first time they were revved up Igor and his men could feel the extra power. On September 25 the improved S-29-A took to the air after a short run, climbed easily to about 1,000 feet, and landed after a successful test flight of ten minutes. Igor took only three workers on the flight, but it was obvious that the plane could have carried a much greater load.

Demonstration and charter flights followed, with Igor piloting the S-29-A on more than 200 flights. Carrying fourteen passengers at a cruising speed of 100 miles an hour—top speed was 115 mph—the S-29-A was the forerunner of the twin-engined, all-metal airliners which in the 1930's introduced air travel throughout the United States. In an era of barnstorming with single-engined, open cockpit planes, the big Sikorsky craft brought the comfort of a closed cabin and the safety of the extra engine. It proved to be one of the first twin-engined planes in the country capable of flying, and even climbing slightly, on one engine.

The publicity led to other opportunities, one of which had to be turned down for legal reasons. A flashily dressed visitor

S-29-A, first Sikorsky airplane built in the New World, was flown throughout the United States, arousing enthusiasm for aviation in the mid-1920s.

stopped at the hangar one day and offered the company several hundred dollars to fly a cargo of whisky from Roosevelt Field (where it would be delivered by trucks) to a field near Montauk Point, about 100 miles east on Long Island. This flight, presumably, would be to avoid Federal roadblocks. Igor's refusal to become an aerial rumrunner brought shocked disbelief and even outrage to the visitor. He left after threatening to report Igor's unbusinesslike behavior to the Sikorsky stockholders.

Many of the several thousand persons who took their first airplane ride in the S-29-A became friends of aviation at a time when flying's dangers were exaggerated and its promise for the future largely unknown. Besides showing people that a plane ride could be reasonably pleasant and comfortable, the S-29-A demonstrated in a dramatic way that a large aircraft could earn money as a cargo carrier. The company derived its first real profit with the plane by using it as an air freighter to fly two grand pianos from New York to Washington, D.C. One was delivered to the wife of President Herbert Hoover, the other to a department store for display. Sikorsky welcomed the $500 received for this job, but when additional subscribers appeared with their investment dollars he realized that the national publicity brought by the flight might prove even more beneficial in the long run.

For years a gnarled and broken tree limb on display in Igor Sikorsky's office reminded him of a flight one night in the S-29-A. He was flying the plane from Staten Island to Roosevelt Field late one winter day when darkness closed in. Through a misunderstanding, ground men had failed to provide landing lights at the field. Igor overflew the dark field and continued eastward over the Island. He lost his way, but knew he would have to land soon or find himself over the open ocean. He dropped the plane lower, barely able to distinguish woods from fields. Groping through the darkness for a landing spot, he felt a loud thump. He continued his descent and made a fair landing in a field. The broken tree limb imbedded in the left wing gave proof enough that the plane had clipped through treetops just before landing.

Captain Roscoe Turner, swashbuckling racing pilot of the 1920s and '30s, bought the S-29-A in 1926. He crisscrossed the country with the big plane, arousing enthusiasm for aviation and conditioning thousands to become the air travelers of a later day. He used the plane to make advertising flights for various companies, the long, flat sides of the fuselage providing ample space for company names in huge letters. At one point the ship was set up as a flying cigar store.

Turner's S-29-A once suffered the shame of having a tire blow out while the plane was in flight. "The tire was so rotten," Igor related with a chuckle, "that it could not stand the change in air pressure at altitude. The blowout was so loud and caused such a shock to the wing that Roscoe thought the end had come—that some vital part of the plane had failed. But he made a good, one-wheel landing with no further damage."

Through his many charter, advertising, and demonstration flights, Turner earned enough to pay the Sikorsky company the $11,000 price that had been agreed upon. When he sold the plane to Howard Hughes in 1928 for use in the movie, *Hell's Angels,* the S-29-A had fully proven itself a rugged and reliable aircraft. A telegram sent by Turner to Sikorsky from Hollywood, California, on February 26, 1928, provides a fitting epitaph for the S-29-A:

"The S-29-A successfully took off at 5,000 feet altitude,

Broken tree limb imbedded in the left lower wing of the S-29-A attested to the narrow escape in a night landing.

cleared mountains at 8,000, got into one tail spin going through mountain pass, came out OK. Never had any mechanical trouble. Plane a big show everywhere we landed. Tell Mr. Shoumatoff am writing. Regards. Roscoe Turner.''

In Hollywood, Hughes converted the S-29-A into a German bomber of World War I vintage, complete with machine guns and Maltese crosses. One gun sprouted from the mid-fuselage cockpit and a new cockpit was installed in the nose. The pilot put the ship into a spin and parachuted to safety. The old plane spun down for thousands of feet before smashing into the ground. The scene was probably the most spectacular of an epic film in which, as one movie historian said, ''The airplanes were the real stars.'' It was an ironic end for an airplane so safe it had never suffered a crash in its long and varied career. Tragically, one crewman who was releasing smoke flares far back in the fuselage failed to bail out and died in the crash.

Igor had become personally acquainted with several businessmen from New England, chiefly Arnold Dickinson of

Sikorsky Aero Engineering Corporation rented its S-29-A to many companies for advertising and promotional efforts. It was eventually sold to famed racing pilot Roscoe Turner (second from right), who continued to fly for a number of clients.

The S-29 disguised as a German Gotha Bomber, ended its days in the spectacular motion picture "Hells Angels," financed and directed by Howard Hughes. Here, the S-29 shows a splintered prop (left), dents and torn fabric after a close encounter with another aircraft.

Fitchburg, Massachusetts. The friendship, plus the reliable record of the S-29-A, so inspired the confidence of these men that they provided financial support for the still struggling young company. Dickinson proved especially helpful, both with money and his ability as a manager. He invested heavily in the enterprise and when the company was reorganized and refinanced in 1925 under the name of the Sikorsky Manufacturing Company he was named its president. Igor became vice-president, a change which enabled him to devote a greater portion of his time to the engineering and technical end of the business.

The pilots at Roosevelt Field did not pay much attention to their neighbors in the old wooden hangar until they suddenly realized that the Russians were making some remarkable aeronautical advances. "They were very genteel people and when we walked by their hangar they would often invite us in for tea," Jack Charleson, one of the pilots, said. "But we thought they were a bunch of dumb foreigners as far as airplanes were concerned. Then they built special wings for Roger Kahn's Jenny and from that time on we knew they had something. That Jenny showed tremendously improved performance."

Kahn, son of banker-philanthropist Otto Kahn, was one of several sportsmen fliers of the time who had bought war-surplus Jenny (JN-4D) trainers. The Jennies, remembered with much nostalgia by the early pilots who learned to fly in them, were slow, underpowered craft with bad wing stall characteristics. Pilots had to be especially careful while climbing after a take-off not to turn before they had obtained good altitude and ample flying speed.

With the new wings the Jenny became a new airplane. Its top speed rose from 70 miles an hour to about 90, and it performed as well with the pilot and a passenger aboard as it had previously done with the pilot alone. More important, with its wing stall tendencies reduced, it was a far safer airplane. The new wing was designed by Michael E. Gluhareff and was called the G-S-1, for Gluhareff-Sikorsky. (Gluhareff, who had joined the company in 1924, was to serve as one of its leading designers for many years. His wing airfoil sections were to contribute much to the success of the recordbreaking Sikorsky amphibians and flying boats a few

years later.) Eventually some twenty sets of the G-S-1 wings were built to improve the performance and safety of Jennies and other aircraft of the day.

In 1925 and 1926 the company built four small airplanes which provided valuable experience, but led to no production and only minor recognition. The planes were the S-31, a two-seat observation sesquiplane for the Colombian government; the S-32, a five-seat sesquiplane which, equipped with floats, was used by an oil company in South America; the S-33, a single-seat sesquiplane used as a racer by Al Krapish; and the twin-engined S-34, a six-seat amphibian built to test an entirely new design. The S-34 was the most significant of these aircraft, as it paved the way for the company's later achievements with big multi-engined amphibians and flying boats.

The next Sikorsky design of this period, the S-35, focused worldwide attention for the first time on the name Sikorsky. Although well ahead of its time both in performance and appearance, the S-35 was destined for a short and tragic life, possibly the most disappointing episode of Igor's life.

Michael Gluhareff and a Jenny with the improved G-S wings he designed.

The fate of the plane was especially disheartening because the S-35 might well have been his greatest triumph. Worse still, it brought death to two men, one a skilled and loyal co-worker.

In late 1925, during construction of the S-32, many parts were built for a large transport to succeed the S-29-A. The new aircraft was coming along nicely in the spring of 1926 when Captain René Fonck, the famous French ace of World War I, appeared in New York and disclosed that he was seeking an airplane capable of making a nonstop flight from New York to Paris. Fonck hoped to win the $25,000 prize that had been offered in 1919 by Raymond Orteig, hotel owner and philanthropist, for the first nonstop fight between New York and Paris, a distance of 3,600 miles.

After considering the various aircraft available, Fonck selected the new Sikorsky ship, but with changes. The new craft was designed as a twin-engined transport of medium range (about 1,000 miles). For a safe crossing of the ocean, Igor decided that a third engine was necessary and that the plane should be substantially larger.

Construction was halted as new designs were rushed through. The forward part of the fuselage was changed to take the third engine. Wingspan and area were increased by adding new sections, including a strengthened center section for the upper wing. An orginal fuel system was devised to move the huge quantities of gasoline to the three engines from the main tanks in the engine nacelles and from extra tanks in the plane's cabin. It was estimated that about 2,500 gallons of fuel would be needed for the long flight.

The completed S-35 was rolled from the leaky, old hangar in September of 1926. It was a glistening, all-metal craft built of Duralumin and steel, with all its parts either riveted or bolted together. Visitors to the field found it hard to believe that such a beautiful ship had been produced with primitive tools in a dilapidated "factory." Craftsmanship and determination, however, had overcome the handicaps and the S-35 appeared to be fully the equal of any plane produced in the larger and more established aircraft plants. Igor Sikorsky, its proud designer, later referred to the S-35 as a "huge, elegant, efficient, and modern-looking airplane."

Like previous Sikorsky designs, the S-35 was a long-

The S-34, built in 1926 at College Point, Long Island, helped pave the way toward Sikorsky's later successes with big amphibians and flying boats.

winged craft, its top wing spanning 101 feet, the lower wing 76 feet, compared to a fuselage length of only 44 feet. It, too, was a sesquiplane, with an upper wing area of 794 square feet, compared to only 301 for the lower lifting surface. The S-35's three engines were French-built Gnome-Rhone Jupiter 9A's, air-cooled radial power plants, providing a total of about 1,200 horsepower.

Captain Fonck and Igor were at the controls in the closed cockpit just aft of the nose engine when the S-35 took off on its first flight August 23, only two days after being rolled from the hangar. The big plane left the runway and climbed easily, although only two outboard engines were used, the center engine being held to idling speed. The flight lasted thirty-five minutes and the craft performed well. However, nobody knew better than Igor that many tests and preparations remained to be completed before it would be safe to attempt the long and hazardous flight across the ocean.

Other test fights followed. On September 7 several New York area Army and Navy representatives flew in the S-35 at Igor's invitation. One pilot, Frank W. LaVista, of the Department of Commerce, noted in his report that the plane "handled very well." He reported that the plane was loaded to a total weight of 20,031 pounds, and that with the three

Captain René Fonck
Ace
Army of The Republic
of France

Captain René Fonck, French ace of World War I. The crash of his plane on a transatlantic flight attempt was a tragic setback for the struggling Sikorsky company.

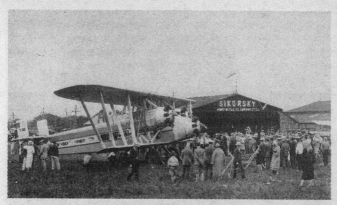

The S-35 in front of the Sikorsky hangar on Roosevelt Field, Long Island, sometime in early September, 1926.

Igor Sikorsky (directly below man on wing) joined others of the Sikorsky company in front of newly completed S-35 in the fall of 1926.

Another view of the S-35.

engines running at 1,550 revolutions per minute, it took off in 21 seconds, climbed to 1,000 feet in 1 minute, 15 seconds, and reached 2,000 feet in 2 minutes, 35 seconds. LaVista also recorded that with only two engines running the S-35 climbed from an altitude of 1,900 feet to 2,500 feet in 2 minutes, 35 seconds. He noted that he "flew the plane on one engine at 3,500 feet for 35 seconds and lost fifty feet of altitude flying at 82 mph airspeed." He concluded by stating, "The plane is very light on the controls and very sensitive on the ailerons. The plane showed a speed of 110 mph with engines running at 1550 rpm."

On September 9 Igor flew the S-35 to Bolling Field, near Washington, D.C., where demonstration flights were made for government officials. The big plane's ability to climb at full normal weight (20,000 pounds) on any two engines proved especially impressive to the officials. When flight tests were resumed later at Roosevelt Field the S-35's official performance figures showed a high speed of 145 miles per hour, cruising speed of 120 mph, landing speed of 65 mph, and an initial climb of 1,100 feet per minute. For several years no airplane of similar size and power surpassed these performances of the S-35.

During construction and flight tests of the S-35 two disturbing new elements appeared. First, pressure was exerted on the company to accept various advertising arrangements which would provide badly needed money. Second, those involved with the proposed flight insisted that the flight test program be speeded up and abbreviated since the days were getting shorter and the chances of bad weather over the North Atlantic were increasing. To Igor, these were dangerous and unwelcome intrusions on his work. They interfered with the steps necessary for the orderly and complete testing of a new aircraft, steps which were even more vital than usual in view of the hazardous and unprecedented flight to be attempted.

"The circumstances were unfortunate," Igor recalled many years later. "We were broke, we had no money, and I had to accept advertising and publicity tie-ins with oil companies. I hated it and I fought it, but in the end I had to give in."

When announcement was made that Fonck was seeking the $25,000 Orteig prize, public interest and curiosity were aroused. Advance publicity, inevitable in an undertaking that promised to be so perilous and dramatic, increased day by day. Visitors came to the field to stare at the huge plane which would soon be winging over the ocean on what many believed to be a foolhardy and impossible venture. As the news spread that the S-35 might take off at any time, the curiosity seekers grew in numbers.

Igor watched the publicity build-up with growing concern. He saw that persons who knew little about flying now were having much to say about the flight. They wanted it to be made as early as possible in September, realizing that otherwise the attempt would have to be delayed until the following spring. Igor preferred to wait, so that the ship could be adequately tested, but he and the little group that had produced the S-35 found themselves powerless against the excitement and the forces demanding an immediate take-off.

Igor believed the S-35 to be fully capable of a New York to Paris flight, but he wanted, particularly, to make gradual trials of its performance with heavier and heavier loads up to the heaviest which would be required for the transatlantic flight. This would have meant filling some of the fuel tanks with water as ballast and later steam-cleaning them and disassembling parts of the fuel system, and that would have brought further delays. He also wanted to test the plane's auxiliary landing gear in a series of take-off runs. The gear was intended to help support the fuel-heavy ship during its take-off run and was to be dropped when the ship became airborne. There was no time for these vital tests.

A false start was made on September 15. The weather looked good and the fuel tanks were filled. But a minor leak showed up in one tank and the take-off had to be postponed. Then the weather worsened and it was not until September 20 that another favorable forecast was received. Late that night Fonck decided to take off at dawn the next morning. At about midnight, Igor taxied the S-35 to the end of the runway, turned it to face into a barely perceptible breeze, and shut off the engines. There, for the remainder of the moonless night, in the glare of floodlights, some fifty barrels of gasoline were pumped aboard—about 2,500 gallons.

The crew arrived at the ship shortly after 5:00 A.M. Included were Captain Fonck, pilot; Lieutenant Lawrence Curtin, a U. S. Navy flier whom Fonck had chosen as his co-pilot; Charles Clavier, radio operator, who had accompanied Fonck from France; and Jacob Islamoff, mechanic, a member of the Sikorsky company from its beginning.

Upon their arrival the fliers found conditions which threatened to make the hazardous take-off even more hazardous. Thousands of persons, hearing of the impending flight, had driven to the field during the night and were milling about the runway. Igor's men drove a car along the runway, forcing the crowd back and opening up a strip not much wider than the wingspan of the plane. Adding further to the danger, the wind had dropped to zero. Igor, standing atop a knoll at the edge of the field, had hoped for even a slight head wind to help shorten the take-off run and get the heavy ship into the air. Now he noticed with misgivings that even a slight tail wind seemed to be stirring along the runway, and that would lengthen the take-off run.

At the plane, as the engines were started, someone jokingly yelled to Clavier, "Have you got enough money to take care of you when you reach Paris?" The radio operator, worried now, as were the other crewmen, shouted back, "A dollar is enough to take to Paradise."

A few minutes later the three engines were run to full power, the wheel chocks were pulled, and the S-35 started slowly down the runway, threading its way between the two rows of onlookers. On the knoll Igor was dismayed to feel a slight breeze blowing in the same direction that the plane was moving.

Perhaps the clearest view of what became a tragic take-off run was provided by a newsreel film made from a plane flying low and just to the right of the runway: As the S-35 reaches the halfway point along the runway a cloud of dust is seen to erupt suddenly behind it. The dust is raised by one of the auxiliary landing gears which has broken and is dragging along beneath the plane. Faltering in its run, the plane is seen unable either to take off or to stop. It passes the end of the runway and seems to become momentarily airborne as it plunges down a steep slope. It lands heavily at the bottom, veers to the right, and comes to rest. For a few agonizing seconds it lies motionless and silent. Then, in a flash of flame topped by billowing black smoke, the beautiful S-35 is no more.

When the first spectators reached the scene they found Fonck and Curtin standing near the blazing ship, pale and shaken. In the few seconds given them they had fought their way from the cockpit. They had tried to return to their two fellow crewmen, but had been driven back by the heat. Islamoff and Clavier, trapped far back in the fuselage, had no chance to escape before gasoline from the ruptured tanks burst into flame.

What caused this tragic end to an attempt which might well have been successful? No single cause was ever established and nobody was ever held responsible. Igor Sikorsky refused to blame Fonck, and years later would say only that "some poor judgment was used." Besides the factors already described, there was probably some unnecessary weight aboard.

Most aviation people, Igor included, agree that the pilot and a co-pilot-navigator would have been sufficient for the flight. "The other two were not needed," Igor believed. "They were extra weight. Six months later, Lindbergh proved it by flying alone. He took intelligent chances. Of course, such flights at that time involved hazards. But the S-35 was a good ship and might have made it. We needed more time to prepare for the flight, and this was not available.''

The loss of the S-35 plunged the company more deeply into debt than ever before. The plane had not been insured and the situation looked hopeless. The S-35 was widely regarded as a failure, the crash having wiped out in the minds of many the plane's early excellent performances. Sikorsky and the other officers of the company were sure, however, that the S-35 had been one of the finest airplanes of its time. Despite the now empty hangar and a pile of unpaid bills, this certainty gave them the faith to plan again with confidence for the future.

═══════ **9** ═══════

Wings to Link the Americas

From the viewpoint of quality, the first three years of Igor Sikorsky's return to aviation may be rated as a superior accomplishment. His two large milti-engined airplanes, the S-29-A and the S-35, were pacesetters of their day, unique and exciting aircraft which won their share of headlines. His smaller planes, with their all-metal construction and effective G-S wings, performed well above average; one of them, the S-31, took second place in an efficiency contest. The twin-engined S-34 amphibian, a sharp departure from the usual designs of the day, showed Igor's willingness to try radically new ideas. The S-34 was the forerunner of a whole new family of aircraft which made aviation history during the late 1920s and early 1930s and proved to be the most successful airplanes ever to bear the Sikorsky name.

From the standpoint of quantity, Igor's return to aviation was something else again. Only one each of his designs from 1923 through 1926 was built. Each plane was but a prototype of hoped-for production aircraft that never saw the light of day. In the fall of 1926, amid the shambles of the S-35 tragedy, the Sikorsky company could boast plenty of head-lines, but no customers.

This period—perhaps the gloomiest—of Igor's life in avia-tion, turned out to be the "darkest before the dawn." In just thirty-three and a half hours, on May 20–21, 1927, a young airmail pilot named Charles A. Lindbergh changed the whole face of aviation. His epic nonstop flight from New York to Paris gave the world of flight its greatest single lift, launching it on a dizzy climb that has never slackened. Fortunately, the Sikorsky Manufacturing Corporation was ready with a new and unusual airplane to take full advantage of the situation.

First, though, Lindbergh's flight ended a Sikorsky project which was progressing well at the time. Late in 1926 René Fonck, with new financial backing, had returned to try once more for the Orteig prize. Again he chose a Sikorsky plane, this time the twin-engined S-37 which was designed from the start for the transatlantic attempt.

A complete flight test program (such as Igor had wanted for the ill-fated S-35) showed the S-37 to be quite capable of the New York–Paris flight. The new ship's cruising speed of about 120 miles an hour and its range of over 4,000 miles were enough to take the S-37 to Paris with fuel to spare. Aided by the lift of its 100-foot-long upper wing and the power of its two 500-horsepower Jupiter air-cooled engines, the S-37 had the heavy-lift performance required. Take-offs were made with heavier and heavier loads, including the overloaded weight needed for the transatlantic hop.

Late in 1926 Sikorsky Manufacturing Company moved into its third home when it rented space in a factory building at College Point, Long Island, at a point between the present La Guardia Airport and the Bronx-Whitestone Bridge. The company retained its hangar space at Roosevelt Field. about

Built for a second transatlantic attempt by René Fonck, the twin-engined S-37 instead became an airliner in South America.

twenty-five miles east on the Island, but the new plant, close to the waters of Long Island Sound, provided a good site for testing seaplanes and amphibians. Many parts of the S-37 and the S-34 amphibians were built at College Point, using the improved tools and equipment there.

With Fonck's S-37 nearing completion of its flight tests, there suddenly was no longer any reason to attempt the New York–Paris flight. Lindbergh had done it alone and no matter how brilliant a following flight might be it would be an anti-climax. Also, the prize money was gone.

No observer of the time was more impressed, nor probably more relieved, by Lindbergh's single, courageous achievement, than Igor Sikorsky. The historic flight had removed once and for all from Igor the burden and worry of another transatlantic attempt.

"The S-37 was capable of doing the job," he said later. "But after Lindbergh, there was no reason to try. I was more interested in constructive flights. I was glad to get out of these stunt flights where planes were often loaded beyond their capacities and beyond the abilities of their crews. Too many of those early attempts to fly across the oceans ended in tragedy."

Igor's instant respect for Lindbergh the aviator was matched later by his admiration and affection for Lindbergh the friend. The two pioneers, so different in birth and background, found a common bond of interest over the years. Each admired increasingly the other's competence in aviation, as well as the other's beliefs, personality, and worth as a man. Many years later, speaking about aviation in America, Sikorsky said:

"America can be proud that the period which the Wright brothers started was completed by another great American, Charles Lindbergh, and his wonderful flight when he took off from New York and landed, not merely in Paris, but in a definite spot, Le Bourget Field. This flight of one man in a relatively inexpensive airplane, all alone, with no assistance whatever along the route, produced a great impression all over the world, especially in America where the impact of this flight was tremendous."

Asked once why his friend wanted to make the hazardous flight alone, Igor replied: "I had a chance to talk with Charles on that subject and this was his explanation: 'When I go alone I risk my life, not someone else's, and my life, I am the master of it. I can do anything I want. Furthermore, on the way I may find difficulties to solve. If I am alone I am going to solve them. If there is another man I'll want to consult with him. I don't want to risk his life. I *can* risk mine. I want to be in total control of the situation.' My discussion with Charles was over a quarter-century ago, but I remember it very well. Maybe the wording was different, but the meaning is correct. The man wanted complete freedom of decision and action. He took a risk, but he won, and he gave a tremendous push to aviation."

Lindbergh, discussing Igor's comments, added a further thought on the subject. "Possibly a still more important reason for flying alone," he said, "was that the weight of a navigator turned into fuel added hundreds of miles to my range, and extremely accurate navigation was not necessary in order to strike somewhere on the coast of Europe. The additional range would much more than compensate for any possible error in navigation, thereby adding considerably to the safety of the flight, as well as to the probability of success."

An acquaintance of Lindbergh once asked him if Sikorsky, a believer in multi-engined airplanes, had ever mentioned the risk which he had taken with his single-engined *Spirit of St. Louis* over the vast expanses of the ocean.

"No, he didn't," Lindbergh replied. "Igor was designing primarily for another purpose. He was very rational about it. He wanted to build a large transport and for that he had to have power. Even if he had been willing to use a single engine, no engine then in existence had enough power. So he had to use at least two engines. But this did not result in additional safety for the New York–Paris flight. Here is a vital point about the S-35's three engines: actually it was no better off, and probably worse, with three engines. There was a greater chance of engine failure. Loss of an engine on takeoff would have meant a crash, since the ship was too heavily loaded to get off on two engines. Also, an engine failure during much of the flight would have meant a landing in the ocean because the remaining engines wouldn't have power to maintain flight with fuel enough to reach land."

The S-37 was named the *Ville de Paris* (City of Paris). Like the S-35, it was ahead of its time, reflecting Igor's lifelong habit of always thinking in terms of the future. The real need for a large transport airplane in the United States did not arrive until a few years later. The S-37 would have made a good airliner, but there were no airlines. Later, bought by American International Airways, Inc. of Argentina and renamed the *Southern Star*, the S-37 proved its worth. In 1929 it was flown from New York to the Argentine on an historic trip which saw it cross the lofty Andes on the final leg from Santiago, Chile, to Buenos Aires.

From Buenos Aires came a telegram to Sikorsky from the crew of the S-37. "*Southern Star* arrived here today in perfect condition after flight from New York via west coast of South America, crossed Andes from Santiago at 19,000 feet carrying eight people and total useful load of 5,000 pounds. First large transport plane to cross. Congratulations to constructor of such great ship." After that the airline used the S-37 for several years to carry passengers over the Andes between Buenos Aires and Santiago.

With no market for large transports, the Sikorsky company in 1927 struggled to stay in business, selling a few G-S wings and completing the S-36, a twin-engined amphibian. The S-36, two of which were built, supplied important experience in the field of amphibians and led to Igor Sikorsky's first completely successful American-built aircraft.

In the summer of 1927, as Lindbergh crisscrossed the United States in the *Spirit of St. Louis*, the public's interest in aviation soared as never before. New and old aircraft companies alike worked hard to make the most of the new opportunities which seemed just around the corner. Each looked to the future with new confidence, designing everything from the standard three-place open cockpit biplane to closed-cabin monoplanes carrying five or six passengers. Many companies prospered for a while, then fell by the wayside. Others, with better management and stronger financing, grew with aviation and prosper to this day.

Convinced that aviation in America was finally about to "arrive," Igor and his associates decided to make one last effort to build an airplane that would find a market. As they considered what kind of plane to build, they soon saw that one type was absent—an amphibian of good size and with performance equal to the landplanes of the time. This situation, plus their own head start with the S-34 and S-36, gave them their big chance. To make the most of aviation's fast-rising popularity, they decided to build ten amphibians of a new design.

The result was the remarkable S-38, a trail blazer which was easily the best amphibian of its day, proclaimed—and probably rightly so—as "the world's safest airplane." · To appreciate what the S-38 meant to Sikorsky, one needs only to remember that the nine different Sikorsky designs prior to the S-38 had resulted in only ten aircraft. The tenth design, the S-38, produced 114 aircraft.

An odd bird by today's standards, the S-38 bore the stamp of originality. It could be mistaken for no other aircraft and it carried the name Sikorsky throughout the world. Someone's reference to it as "a collection of airplane parts flying in formation" was generally accepted as a fair, though unkind, description of the plane. Watching an S-38 fly overhead, one saw that the main elements—fuselage, wings, engines, and tail surfaces—seemed to be separated, which indeed they were. A closer look showed them to be linked by a collection of struts and braces jutting at various angles. At the top stretched the big 71-foot parasol wing; beneath that were mounted two Pratt & Whitney Wasp engines, and below the engines hung the fuselage-hull from which extended short lower wings carrying two small floats for balance on the water. Two outriggers extended from the upper wing above the engines aft to the fins and rudders.

When the S-38 made its first flight on June 25, 1928, it was an ugly duckling in appearance only. The new ship quickly proved that it could fly as well as the best landplane or seaplane of its size, that it could be controlled perfectly on the water by means of its two engines, that it could be jacked up and lowered by its own landing gear (enabling it to taxi out of the water onto a beach or ramp), and that it could fly on either of its two engines. Equally at home on land or water, the S-38 climbed a thousand feet a minute fully loaded, cruised at about 100 miles an hour and had a top speed of almost 130 miles an hour. Carrying eight passengers and a crew of two, it could cruise about six hours,

S-38 amphibians outside the Sikorsky plant at College Point, New York, in 1928.

giving it a range of approximately 600 miles. A Navy test pilot called it a better ship than any other of its size and power. Igor was proud of the S-38. Here at last, he hoped, was an aircraft that would pay its way and put his company on the map.

In their enthusiasm for amphibian aircraft, Igor and his associates never accepted the official spelling "amphibian," but preferred "amphibion." In their brochures, advertising, and publicity, the Sikorsky people used the latter spelling, declaring it differentiated the airplane from such land and water creatures as frogs, turtles, salamanders, and others. They believed, too, that "amphibion" came closer to the original Greek word. Despite the Sikorsky effort to win acceptance of "amphibion," dictionaries to this day use only one spelling, "amphibian"—for airplanes or frogs. At best, "amphibion" can only be considered as a Sikorsky trade name.

Some people may have smiled as the ungainly S-38 taxied the waters of Long Island Sound off College Point or cruised

An early S-38 Amphibian in the colors of Pan American Airways.

the skies above. But the widest grins probably appeared on the faces of Sikorsky shareholders as orders for the S-38 began arriving. The buyers proved to be many and varied—from the military services to millionaires. The U.S. Navy ordered the first two, followed by Pan American Airways. Other buyers included the U.S. Army and Marines, several individual owners, among them explorer Martin Johnson, and eventually eight more airlines, a charter service, a newspaper, an oil company, and a drugstore chain.

Charles Lindbergh flew an S-38 for Pan American to inaugurate airmail service between the United States and the Panama Canal. The airlines used their S-38s to pioneer air routes in such widely separated areas as the Caribbean Sea, South America, Hawaii, Canada, and several parts of the United States. When the Chilean government bought an S-38, Igor took advantage of the chance to escape a northern winter, flying the amphibian as far south as the Panama Canal. Navigation was easy—he simply followed a south-bound Pan American airliner, also an S-38, the two amphibians zigzagging around the magnificent mountains and volcanoes of Central America. Sikorsky pilot Boris Sergievsky continued the ferry flight south to Santiago, 7,000 miles from New York, the take-off point.

With the first ten S-38s sold and orders still being received, the company found itself badly in need of more factory space. The time had come to expand. The company was reorganized as the Sikorsky Aviation Corporation and enough money was subscribed to permit construction of its own plant. Arnold Dickinson, the company president, and most of the larger shareholders were from New England. When they presented the problem of the new factory's location to Sikorsky, they insisted on one requirement: "Find a place in New England," they said, "preferably in Connecticut, Massachusetts, or Rhode Island."

Martin and Osa Johnson used the S-38 Amphibian on their motion picture safaris in Africa in the mid-1930s. Here, on the Tanganika Plains, Osa Johnson and lions, inspecting one another.

Igor visited the three states. He looked at locations near Springfield, Massachusetts; Hartford, Connecticut; and Providence, Rhode Island. None provided what he really wanted—deep water plus a place for land-based flying. Finally, in the town of Stratford, just east of Bridgeport, Connecticut, he found the ideal site. A stretch of flat farmland at the mouth of the Housatonic River on Long Island Sound lay immediately adjacent to deep water for seaplane operations. And just across the road—Stratford's South Main Street—the city of Bridgeport was building an airport on another expanse of farmland. Landplanes, seaplanes, or amphibians—all could be moved in minutes from the new plant site to their proper operating locations.

At Igor's recommendation, the company bought the land in Stratford in 1928. The following spring a modern aircraft plant appeared where acres of lettuce and cabbage had previously grown. The latest machinery and equipment, ample office and drafting space, and even a wind tunnel supplanted the largely primitive tools of the past. A roadway and ramp reaching an eighth of a mile out into the Housatonic was built for easy launching of seaplanes in the deep water of the river. When completed in the spring of 1929, the new plant was one of the best of its kind in the country. On the wings of the ungainly S-38 the company had finally climbed to success.

Further major changes occurred in 1929. On July 30 the Sikorsky Aviation Corporation became a subsidiary of United Aircraft and Transport Corporation whose interests included the manufacture of airplanes, aircraft engines, and propellers, and the operation of United Air Lines. (In 1934 United gave up its airline holdings, concentrating ever since on engineering and manufacturing.) Under the new arrangement Igor found himself free to work exclusively on engineering advances. Now he could devote all his energies to research and invention, leaving to others the economic problems of a growing company.

The economic problems proved serious. The first two years of the Sikorsky association with United Aircraft and Transport coincided with the start of the great Depression of the 1930s. All over the country business and industry faltered and the ranks of the unemployed reached record figures. Despite its success with the S-38, the Sikorsky Aviation Corporation began to lose money. Assigned to correct this situation was a retired Navy commander and naval aviator, Eugene E. Wilson, who had been serving as president of United's Hamilton Standard Propeller subsidiary in Pittsburgh. Wilson was named president of Sikorsky Aviation in 1929 with orders to cut costs as much as possible without damaging the Sikorsky engineering team. The job proved frustrating but never dull.

In the Sikorsky shop it sometimes seemed that outside interests took priority over building airplanes. When the Grand Duchess Marie visited the plant, former Russian aristocrats left their benches to give full attention as the great lady held court. When Bridgeport's Grand Opera Company—mostly White Russians—performed, the quality of the music was fully as important as an order for more planes. Studying the red ink of Sikorsky ledgers, United's president, the late Frederick B. Rentschler, remarked, "There is a limit to the contribution United Aircraft can make to Russian Relief."

In July of 1929 Eugene Wilson confronted Igor Sikorsky, a man whom he was later to refer to as "one of the great minds, if not the greatest, of the air age." Wilson discussed the problem frankly with Igor and ordered manufacturing costs cut by 20 percent, which meant layoffs. Later he found that the cuts had been made, but that engineering costs had increased by the same amount. And when that budget was cut, labor costs went up once again. Shop foremen, laid off, would show up at drafting boards, and maybe later as lathe hands. Finally, Wilson reminded Igor that the 1929 stock market crash had wiped out many companies and Sikorsky might be next if costs were not brought under control. Igor agreed heartily, but excused his co-workers.

"Mr. Wilson," he said earnestly, "compared with the earthshaking experiences my fellow countrymen have endured in recent years, a stock market crash is but a vibration of a minor order!" At this point, as Wilson later observed, he realized that "the problem of Russian relief was being compounded by a mystical Oriental philosophy of life."

In later years Wilson emphasized his respect for Sikorsky engineering. "However," he added, "its manufacturing suffered dearly from lack of understanding of American mechanical processes. The defect reflected the difference between life in Czarist Russia and in Free America. One followed the 'hit 'em over the head with a shovel' school, while the other relied on the 'varsity or cooperative' approach. Mr. Sikorsky appreciated this, but the organization as a whole had little understanding of the responsibilities that go with authority. It was quite impossible to bring home to these delightful, talented, attractive, and temperamental people the need to fix responsibility for failure as a means of erasing it."

Despite these practical troubles Wilson grew to admire Igor Sikorsky for "his quiet force of personality and truly intuitive engineering genius." He realized that Sikorsky and his technical associates had a talent for using simple, inexpensive methods to come up quickly with the correct answers. Towing scale-model flying boat hulls behind a motor boat with a butcher's scales as a measuring device was an example. (Similar "cut and try" methods later helped bring into being the world's first practical helicopter.) Somehow the company survived the early Depression years until genius and hard work resulted in the huge Flying Clippers which spanned the oceans to bring new and lasting fame to the Sikorsky name.

It was the Flying Clippers which led to the long association and friendship between Igor Sikorsky and Charles Lindbergh. Sikorsky first came to the attention of Lindbergh at the time of the S-35 crash in 1926. Lindbergh was flying the mail on the St. Louis–Chicago run. He had been reading about René Fonck's planned transatlantic flight for the Orteig prize and soon thereafter interested himself in a New York–Paris flight. Lindbergh and Sikorsky first met in 1929 in connection with Lindbergh's pioneering flights with the S-38 and Pan American's plans for a much larger transport. The flier had become a consultant for Pan American that year.

"The S-38 was the most efficient amphibian of its time for Pan American's purposes," Lindbergh recalled many years later. "This ship was essential to Pan American route surveys in the Caribbean. But the company needed a still better airplane, and Igor was well aware of this need."

When Pan American chose Sikorsky to design its new amphibian, Igor realized that he now had the chance to resume building the large planes he had dreamed of as a youngster. Working eagerly at his task, he would visit the Pan American offices in the Chanin Building in midtown Manhattan, bringing his drawings with him from Stratford. Chatting with several of Igor's friends, Lindbergh once recalled those days which proved so vital in ushering in a new era of travel—scheduled air service across the oceans.

"We'd hold conferences," Lindbergh said, "usually in President Juan Trippe's office where there was a long table. Igor would lay his drawings out on the table and we'd gather around—Trippe, Andre Priester who headed Pan American's engineering, Igor, and myself. Mainly we discussed two subjects: first, a plane to replace the S-38, a design that would be larger and have longer range and more power for take-off; and, second, the problem of maintenance of the S-38.

"Operating in a semitropical area, with the added problem of salt water take-offs and landings, the S-38 was a maintenance nightmare. As far as we could tell, those Russian engineers were not much interested in maintenance problems. They would put brass nuts on an aluminum framework and in operation trouble came almost overnight—electrolysis, with white powder forming where the two metals met. Igor used to listen very attentively to these problems, which were a real headache for Priester. Incidentally, they were a remarkable combination—the dynamic and demanding Priester with his Dutch accent and the imperturbable Igor and his Russian accent. Maintenance got better, but the basic problems were never fully solved."

When he first saw the drawings laid out on the table, Lindbergh was disappointed in the S-40 design. He felt that with the cleancut, full-cantilever monoplane types coming along, like the beautiful Lockheed *Vega*, there was need for a cleaner, more efficient plane than the S-40.

"I used to call the S-40 the 'flying forest' because of all its struts," he said. "But Igor sold me on the S-40. He argued that we had to have a larger plane quickly and that time did not permit a radical departure from the previous design. He presented his case tactfully and quietly, yet forcefully, and eventually I came to see that he was right. Priester was even quicker to see that Igor was correct, that this approach would give us a plane of proven design in a short time and that a cleaner, faster plane would have to come later

View of S-40 in the water.

as a second step. The S-40 was not particularly efficient and its range was short. But it was a big improvement over the S-38.''

At first glance the S-40 appeared to be an overgrown S-38, but a second look showed four engines rather than two slung below the big wing. The power plants were Pratt & Whitney Hornets of 575 horsepower each. In contrast to the S-38, a sesquiplane, the S-40 was a monoplane, having no lower wing at all. It was the largest American-built plane of its day, with a gross weight of seventeen tons compared to the S-38's eight tons. It could carry a maximum of forty passengers over a range of 500 miles. With twenty-four passengers, its range was increased to about 950 miles. It was not intended for transatlantic service, but for the 1,300-mile, island-dotted route between North and South America. Test fights showed its top speed to be over 130 miles an hour and its cruising speed about 115 miles an hour. As a flying boat, without its big main landing gear and tail wheel, the S-40's performance showed considerable improvement and its payload increased by 1,800 pounds. Even as an amphibian, it could climb to 6,500 feet on three engines and could hold an altitude of 2,000 feet on only two engines.

Like most Sikorsky aircraft, the S-40 represented a pioneering step forward. Its size exceeded by far the largest amphibian ever before built. The only springs strong enough to support the seventeen-ton ship came from a railroad car. Even the location of the pilots' cockpit raised questions not easily answered at the time. The problem led Igor to call upon Charles Lindbergh for a pilot's opinion. Igor gave him several sketches of various arrangements. These included the pilots' cockpit toward the rear of the ship, as in the Sikorsky S-29 or in the De Havilland DH-4 mailplanes which Lindbergh knew so well. They also included locations in the bow of the boat hull and in the center section of the wing, the highest point in the plane.

"Lindbergh impressed me," Igor recalled in later years. "He looked on in silence so that I could give an uninterrupted report. After all, the design was ultimately my responsibility and I was free to do the design in any way I wanted.

"At the end Lindbergh started to talk in the modest, confident, and firm manner that was characteristic of him. I soon found that he was persuading me of the correctness of his position. The question of where to place the pilots' compartment had been pending for weeks. Yet now it was settled at once by the brilliant ability of Lindbergh to grasp the highlights of the situation, laying aside all that was secondary. His advice was to place the crew compartment forward of the wing, the engines, and the passenger cabin, where the best visibility was possible. This was an example of Lindbergh's outstanding ability (which I observed in a number of cases) to grasp the important points at once. So many people dwell on secondary things, which wastes time. Lindbergh was instrumental and helpful in the construction of the S-40. The cockpit was placed where it should be, about one-third of the way from the wing to the bow."

Lindbergh's attitude about the best cockpit location was changing rapidly about the time the S-40 was being designed. Previously, in flying military aircraft and mailplanes, he had strongly favored a position well aft in the fuselage, since experience had shown that such a location had saved many pilots in crashes.

"In designing a transport plane for passengers," he said while recalling his work with the S-40, "different elements had to be considered. The safety of passengers became of paramount importance. Crashes, which were accepted as an inherent part of flying in the early days, had to be avoided almost entirely if commercial aviation was to be a success. To minimize crashes, it was essential to maximize the pilot's vision. This could be done only by moving the cockpit farther forward. I applied this philosophy to the S-40 in discussions with Sikorsky. I remember clearly the difficulty of taking off in the S-38 caused by spray striking the propellers and being thrown onto the windshield so thickly that you literally couldn't see ahead at all for a number of seconds before the plane got up on the step. I felt it of utmost importance to avoid this condition in future designs and therefore recommended moving the cockpit forward.''

With the opening of the new plant in Stratford, Igor and his family moved into a rented bungalow in the Lordship section of Stratford, on Long Island Sound, a few minutes walk from the beach. The family then included two sons, Sergei, born January 31, 1925, and Nikolai, born August 14, 1926. Also moving to Connecticut were Igor's sister, Helen; her children, Galina and Jimmy Viner; and Igor's daughter, Tania.

More than one hundred of Igor's Russian refugee associates made the move with the company, following the pioneer who had become a kind of father figure for them. Included were such key figures as the Gluhareff brothers, Michael and Serge, of the engineering department; Michael Buivid of the test laboratory; Bob Labensky of the experimental shop; Nicholas Glad, maintenance manager; young Viner, scarcely out of his teens and destined later to become a pioneer helicopter pilot; Baron Nicholas Solovioff, service manager; and Victor Koodroff, tool supervisor.

The little group of transplanted Russians formed a close-knit community, concentrated mostly in Stratford. There, in December, 1929, they founded the St. Nicholas Russian Orthodox Greek Catholic Church. At that time and for the next thirteen years the church consisted only of a chapel in a small frame house at 37 Lake Street about a mile and a half from the Sikorsky plant. After a succession of three priests, the Rev. Stephen J. Antonuk took over the pastorate on August 13, 1930, serving and building the little church for thirty-eight years before he was elected Bishop and transferred to Western Canada.

Father Antonuk's daughter, Olga, choir director for many years, described the church she remembers from her childhood. ''The altar was in the dining room, the congregation in the living room, and the choir in the kitchen,'' she said, ''and we lived upstairs, my father, mother, and I. The vestments were hung in the pantry and the bell was tolled through the kitchen window.''

Today the little house remains as the church rectory, but nearby stands the present church, an imposing brick edifice in the twelfth-century Russian style, topped with gleaming golden ''onion'' domes. The new church was opened November 1, 1942, standing as a monument to the unceasing work of Father Antonuk and the generosity of the Russian community, especially Igor Sikorsky. Father Antonuk's wife, Matushka, an opera star in her native Russia, gave many concerts to help raise money for the church building fund.

''Mr. Sikorsky always gives substantial donations and is very, very kind,'' Olga Antonuk said. ''My mother was seriously injured in an auto accident in 1934. When she got out of the hospital Mr. Sikorsky invited her to recuperate at the Sikorsky home in Trumbull. This was most kind and helpful, for recuperation would have been difficult here in the busy church-rectory.''

Olga was graduated from the New England Conservatory of Music in Boston. Her associations with the Sikorskys, and others of the cultured Russian group, were many. Her concerts and joint recitals with Nicholai Sikorsky, a violinist, provided money for the church. One of her close friends has been Orestes Sergievsky, a ballet instructor in New York, who is the son of Captain Boris Sergievsky, Sikorsky's chief test pilot of the Flying Clipper days.

With Captain Sergievsky as pilot, the S-40 made its first flight in the spring of 1931, rising gracefully from the waters of Long Island Sound while Igor and his associates watched from a motor boat. Other flights followed, confirming the new ship's excellent flying qualities. The big amphibian was then brought back to the factory for painting and interior furnishings as ordered by Pan American. One evening, returning from a flight over New York, the S-40, its engines throttled back, descended toward Stratford in a smooth glide. The fading rays of a setting sun touched the clouds below as Igor left his seat in the pilots' compartment and walked into the cabin toward the smoking lounge at the rear. A crewman switched on the overhead lights. Igor stopped, the scene jolting him with its familiarity. Then he remembered: there were the same walnut walls and passageway, the same doorway to

Cabin of S-40, the walnut paneled passage of Igor's dream at the age of eleven.

the lounge, even the bluish lights and the barely felt vibrations of the motors that he had visualized thirty-one years before. It was his dream as a boy of eleven come true.

On October 12, 1931, the S-40 was flown to Washington where it was christened the *American Clipper* by Mrs. Herbert Hoover, wife of the President. Later that fall Pan American accepted the S-40 and flew it to Miami from where it departed on its first airline flight—to Cristobal in the Canal Zone, by way of Cuba, Jamaica, and Colombia. The historic flight provided an opportunity for two men to plan an even better airplane which would lead to other historic flights of even greater importance. The men: Charles Lindbergh, pilot, and Igor Sikorsky, passenger and observer.

Using the seats in a smoking lounge at the rear of the cabin, the S-40 could carry forty passengers. However, to provide more room for strolling about and to leave the lounge free, the passengers were limited to thirty-two for the S-40's maiden flight. The *American Clipper* flew in the daytime, the passengers and crew staying overnight in hotels along the route. Igor was delighted to take part in the flight, especially, as he put it, "for the privilege of spending much time with Lindbergh, to learn to respect and admire this man tremendously, in every respect." Each evening, with Captain Basil Rowe, a veteran Pan American pilot, and others of the crew, they discussed their ideas for a transoceanic flying boat of the future.

"Lindbergh and I would take the menu," Igor recalls, "turn it upside down and make sketches for a long-range flying boat. We both believed that scheduled transatlantic flying was possible and at that time a flying boat seemed to be the right solution. At those dinners we laid down the basic principles around which to design a transoceanic flying boat. The problem was to combine speed with long range and a payload which would make transoceanic airline routes practical and economical. The fundamental need was to carry enough fuel for a flight of 2,500 miles with a 50 percent reserve to cover a total of 3,750 miles if necessary, at a cruising speed of about 150 miles an hour and a payload far above anything possible at the time. It was taken for granted that we were not ready for nonstop transatlantic operation, but would use a two-stop route—either Bermuda and the Azores, or Newfoundland and Ireland."

Igor handled the controls occasionally during the S-40's maiden flight to Latin America, but he spent most of his time back in the cabin with the Pan American crew. "The more the men knew him the better they liked him," Lindbergh recalled. "He was very open-minded, always listening to discussions and suggestions."

During the long trip several incidents happened which later seemed amusing, but were not so funny at the time. At Barranquilla in Colombia, the S-40 was tied up in a slip for refueling. Lindbergh was standing on the high wing watching the operation when the gasoline suddenly overflowed and ran over the wing and into the water. "When I saw the gasoline hit the water," he recalls, "I noticed that people standing around on the pier were smoking. I yelled 'stop smoking'— and they threw their cigarettes into the gasoline-covered water! Luckily there was no fire, but the trip could have ended right there."

During the stopover in Jamaica, Lindbergh was called upon to make a speech at a dinner for 200 persons. Just before he was to get up from his seat at the head table a waiter carrying a tray of coffee and cream tipped the tray and a whole pitcher of cream spilled down his neck and over his suit. "The audience was about equally divided between English and Americans," Lindbergh remarked. "The English ignored the incident, and the Americans all laughed. It seemed so typical of the two nationalities."

Uncomfortable as it was, the mishap failed to ruffle Lindbergh's characteristic calm. Although he had no chance to prepare a speech beforehand, he stood up and talked for a quarter of an hour, receiving long and warm applause at the conclusion. "An experienced diplomat could have done no better," Igor said later. "He gave his own ideas on the value of air transport for Jamaica because of its location at the crossroads between North and South America. I was surprised to see how quickly he had grasped the situation."

On the final leg of the return trip, the S-40 got off to a late start and it appeared that the Clipper was going to reach Miami a little after dark. Lindbergh had a choice of either landing in one of the island lagoons along the route in daylight, or going through to Miami in the hope that it would not be too dark to land in the bay.

"I was concerned about landing in a lagoon, since we would have no way of caring for our passengers," he said

Huge S-40 flying boat on ramp leading to Housatonic River near the Sikorsky plant in Stratford, Connecticut, in 1931. The forty-passenger ship was used by Pan American Airways to blaze air trails to South America. Smaller aircraft below the S-40's wing is a three-four place S-39 Utility Amphibian.

later. "I finally decided to go through to Miami because it seemed there would be enough light left and the landing area was well protected. However, it was quite dark when we landed, and I could not determine the wind direction. The ship porpoised a bit and swung abruptly to the left. No damage resulted, but one or two passengers who did not have their safety belts fastened were thrown from their seats. That night Igor wanted to take the blame for the porpoising on landing. He said the bottom of the hull had not been designed properly and that landing was not my fault at all."

Igor recalled the incident vividly. "It was very dark when we landed in Miami Bay," Igor said, "and we had no night flying equipment. The ship porpoised a couple of times. Later we had a nice dinner and I said 'Charles, I want to claim part of the credit for that bouncy landing.' And he said, jokingly, 'You can take it all.' I replied, "The fact that the ship jumped so gracefully is because I made an error in the design of the bottom of the hull, and it needs the most delicate landing technique.' The point I want to make is that it was I who made the blunder, not Lindbergh."

When informed, nearly half a century after the incident, that Igor still claimed "credit" for the landing, Lindbergh laughed and said: "That's quite typical of Igor—to take the blame himself and never blame the other fellow. Actually, it was not his fault. At the time he built the S-40, a great deal remained to be learned about hull design. He and Michael Gluhareff used to put a scale model of a hull on the end of a stick and test it at the side of a launch on the river near the plant in Stratford. This method did not of course provide the accuracy obtained later with elaborate instruments and test basins. So it was not surprising that the S-40 and even the S-42 hulls were not ideal. This sort of thing applied not only to seaplanes but to landplanes also—in the design of landing gears, tail skids, and other parts. The knowledge was just not there at that time in aviation. Igor had done a good engineering job and it was the pilot's job to handle the airplane properly. True, the hull could have been better, but the knowledge just wasn't there."

An objective view at this late date might be that the real culprit, quite likely, was the darkness itself and that under the conditions the touchdown in the huge, new amphibian was not bad at all.

The S-40—at the time the largest airplane ever built in America and the world's largest amphibian—fully justified Igor Sikorsky's belief that he should stay with a proven design rather than attempt a more advanced concept. "The increase in size alone brought enough problems," he said later. "We had to hurdle in one jump the gap between an amphibian of eight tons gross weight—the S-38—and one of seventeen tons—the S-40."

Besides the original *American Clipper,* two other S-40's were built—the *Caribbean Clipper* and the *Southern Clipper.* All were flown by Pan American on its routes to Central and South America. The service reached as far south as Buenos Aires, Argentina, and Santiago, Chile, and included stops at such large cities as Rio de Janiero, Brazil; Bogota, Colombia; Cristobal, Panama Canal Zone; Lima, Peru; Kingston, Jamaica; and others, as well as brief stops at more than fifty other points.

After retirement by Pan American Airways, the S-40 Flying Clippers continued in useful service for charter operations. They ran up a remarkable record, never experiencing a crash and logging an estimated total of ten million miles of flight. Although they had become obsolescent by the time of World War II, they were used then by the U. S. Navy to train pilots in the operation of large, four-engined aircraft. and even the student pilots with their dubious skills failed to damage these sturdy ships which were as much at home on the water as in the air.

Even though only three were built, the S-40s contributed far more than their share toward carrying scheduled air service beyond the shores of the United States. Following the S-38 amphibians, conquerors of the Caribbean, the S-40s extended the conquest beyond that island-dotted sea southward throughout the South American continent. They strengthened further the aerial bonds between the Americas, greatly reducing travel time and paving the way for the longer air routes which would soon link the United States with Europe and the Far East.

Small in number but large in accomplishment, the S-40 Flying Clippers earned an enviable place in the annals of aviation, bringing new laurels to their designer, Igor Sikorsky, as he continued his brilliant contributions to the world of flight.

10

Wings over the Oceans

By the time they had returned from the Flying Clipper's historic trip to the Panama Canal Zone, Igor Sikorsky and Charles Lindbergh had made a decision regarding the flying boat design they had sketched on the back of their dinner menus.

Igor felt sure that United, with its growing experience and skills in the three vital areas of engines, propellers, and aircraft, had the all-around ability to achieve the goals outlined for the new flying boat. These goals exceeded the performance capabilities of any aircraft then in existence. He realized the difficulties facing him and his designers. The ideas that now had to be brought to reality had already been discussed over the Sikorsky drawing boards for several years. He knew that the longer range and higher cruising speed specified would require a wing loading almost double that of other planes then in operation—about thirty pounds per square foot of wing area compared to fifteen or twenty. The heavier wing loading meant that the plane would have a higher landing speed. A way had to be found to increase the lift, slowing the plane down for safe touchdowns in the water. Scores of major and thousands of minor engineering problems had to be solved to achieve the over-all goal, a flying boat able not only to span the oceans, but also to earn a profit in scheduled passenger service from continent to continent.

The high wing loading was decided upon after careful

study of the conditions under which the ship would have to operate. The high cruising speeds over long transoceanic routes, with no intermediate landing places, meant that the new flying boat would have to withstand sharply changing weather conditions. A simple areodynamic study showed that the forces imposed by squalls or vertical gusts of air had less effect on high wing loadings. Igor noticed that even nature seemed to agree: large birds that fly over the sea, covering long distances without being able to alight in case of stormy weather, have a much heavier wing loading than birds of similar size that fly over land. (Flight tests later confirmed the soundness of the decision. The new ship flew smoothly and easily in the roughest of weather. It was found, too, that the wing, smaller than that of the S-40, had an advantage in riding out strong winds and squalls while the ship was afloat.)

The new flying boat, the S-42, was designed in 1932 and built in 1933. When it was completed, just before the end of 1933, the S-42 stood as a symbol of the achievements possible through teamwork and the creative spirit of a few individuals. The teamwork was seen in the joint efforts not only of Sikorsky and Pan American, but also of Sikorsky's sister subsidiaries of United Aircraft—Pratt & Whitney Aircraft with its improved Hornet engines and Hamilton Standard with its new controllable pitch propellers. Helpful also, with scientific advice and information, was the Government agency, the National Advisory Committee for Aeronautics (NACA), forerunner of today's National Aeronautics and Space Administration (NASA).

A list, only partial, of the individuals whose talents contributed much to the S-42 would be headed by—in addition to Igor Sikorsky, Andre Priester, and Charles Lindbergh—Sikorsky's Michael Gluhareff, Hamilton's Frank Caldwell, and Pratt & Whitney's George Mead and Andrew Willgoos. Mead and Willgoos headed the small group of engineers whose genius brought into being the Wasp and Hornet engines which set the pace for aircraft power plants for three decades. Caldwell's controllable pitch propeller, the "gearshift of the air," proved eventually to be one of the most revolutionary advances in the history of powered flight. For this achievement, Caldwell received the Collier Trophy, aviation's highest award, in 1934.

Friends for many years, Charles Lindbergh and Igor Sikorsky are shown on the wing of an S-42 flying boat in 1934.

Without the new propellers, the S-42, despite its superb design and four 750-horsepower Hornet engines, would not have met its performance requirements. The blades of earlier propellers, like those on the S-40, could be set at a specific angle while the plane was on the ground, but the angle could not be changed in flight. The setting had to be a compromise between the maximum power (high revolutions per minute) needed for take-off, and the much lower rpm required for the most economic cruising. It was as though an automobile had to remain in second gear both at the start and driving along the open highway. The new controllable pitch blades, on the other hand, could be set at the flat angle needed for full take-off power, and then, when the plane had reached cruising altitude, could be changed to the increased angle that gave the lower fuel consumption needed for long distance flights. The idea was not new; the problem had been to build such a propeller strong enough to withstand the high stresses exerted on the blades. Caldwell's successful design relied on a simple hydraulic mechanism in which oil pressure rotated the blades in their hubs, locking them in either of the two positions. Such propellers installed on Spitfire fighters just prior to the Battle of Britain provided the performance margin that enabled the Royal Air Force to defeat Hitler's *Luftwaffe* in the crucial struggle in the skies over England. Controllable pitch propellers also spelled success for the early passenger transports, notably the Boeing 247 and the Douglas DC-3. Further development of the same basic idea did the same for piston-powered planes from then on, planes, like the Boeing *Flying Fortress* and Consolidated *Liberator* bombers of World War II and the Lockheed *Constellation* and Douglas DC-6 airliners of the late 1940's.

"Our organization," Igor said later, "possessed the experience and skill needed to fulfill the S-42 requirements which were exceptionally high for that time. Among the factors which contributed to the success of this aircraft was the use of the outstandingly efficient GSM wing section developed by Michael Gluhareff who directed the design work and was responsible for this and several other advanced features of the aircraft."

One of the other design features was a new type of wing flap which formed the trailing edge of the wing, except for the outer sections where the ailerons were installed. The specially designed flap offset the two disadvantages of the S-42's heavy wing loading—a long and difficult take-off run, and a fast landing speed. When lowered at a 40-degree angle, the huge flap produced an increase in lift of about 40 per cent and brought the landing speed down to a comfortable 65 miles an hour.

Although the S-42 was completed shortly after Christmas, 1933, solid ice in the Housatonic River prevented a launching and first flight until March 29, 1934. When the big ship was towed slowly along the causeway leading to the ramp, onlookers saw quickly that this was the most beautiful aircraft ever to bear the Sikorsky name. Its very outline spelled simplicity. Gone was the "forest" of external bracings peculiar to the earlier designs. The tail, instead of being supported by outriggers, was attached directly to the hull. The one-piece wing, 114 feet long, with tapering tips, was fastened to the hull by a short, sturdy superstructure. External struts, the largest streamlined Duralumin sections ever produced at the time, ran from the hull to the outer portions of the wing. The four Hornet engines, fitted with the latest rings and cowlings for low air resistance, were faired neatly into the wing. Like most of Igor Sikorsky's designs, the S-42 reached into the future, superior to anything built previously. It was the best flying boat in the world, as it was soon to prove by the truest yardstick of all—the setting of world records.

The new Clipper quickly showed its mettle. Water trials only were scheduled for the first test day. But the S-42, lightly loaded, was skimming along on Long Island Sound, using only about 50 per cent of its 3,000 horsepower, when it suddenly lifted into the air. Pilot Boris Sergievsky quickly throttled the engines and the ship splashed back into the water after only a few seconds of unscheduled flight. Igor, riding in the co-pilot's seat, described the surprise lift-off as a "grand feeling." Pleased with the first tests, he scheduled a real flight for the next day.

The first flight lasted twenty minutes and was fully successful, with an easy take-off and smooth landing. Other short flights followed during the next couple of weeks. In early April, with all studies completed and adjustments made, the flight test program got seriously under way to learn if the new ship's performance would meet its designer's claims. The results proved even better than had been hoped.

Stop watches showed that the new Clipper, flying low over a measured course along the Connecticut shoreline, was hitting 180 miles an hour, well above the top speed guaranteed in the contract with Pan American. The S-42 quickly proved its load lifting abilities also, easily taking off at its full gross weight of nineteen tons, which included a useful load (crew, fuel, and payload) of over nine tons. On April 26 the Clipper set a world record for the greatest payload carried by a seaplane to an altitude of 2,000 meters (6,561 feet). The payload totaled 16,608 pounds (over eight tons) and was carried to an altitude of 16,000 feet, far higher than required for the new record. On May 17, the Clipper set another world record for seaplanes, this time for the highest altitude reached with a payload of 5,000 kilograms (11,023 pounds), the altitude being 6,204 meters, or 20,407 feet.

When it became clear that the new ship's combination of speed, range, and lift exceeded that of any other flying boat

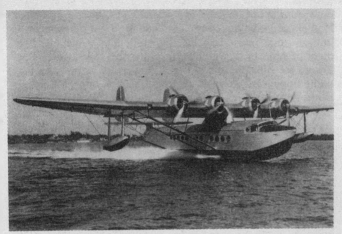

Graceful S-42 Flying Clipper, *far ahead of its time in performance and appearance, skims along on a take-off run. The S-42s pioneered air routes across the Atlantic and Pacific oceans.*

in the world, Igor Sikorsky and his flight crew decided to try for a whole string of world records. At the same time they would use the record flights as part of the S-42's continuing flight test program, checking particularly the cruising speeds and fuel consumption. A course was laid out from Stratford lighthouse, near the Sikorsky plant, to the eastern end of the George Washington Bridge in New Jersey; over Staten Island, New York; eastward over Long Island to Block Island and Point Judith, Rhode Island; and back to Stratford. The course measured 311 miles, just one mile over the 500 kilometers required for world records. An unofficial test run over the course convinced Igor that several world records were within the grasp of the S-42.

August 1 was set as the date when the S-42 would try for eight world records in a single flight. By a rare coincidence, a letter was received that morning at Sikorsky from the National Aeronautic Association urging the company to attempt to set world records. American aviation, still having its difficulties in 1934, was being criticized for having "lagged behind'' European nations in technological progress. France held sixteen world records, not counting light plane records, to the United States' nine. Within an hour after the letter was received, the S-42 was taxiing down the Housatonic River toward the Sound. Aboard was a blue-ribbon crew headed by pilots Edwin Musick, Pan American's chief pilot, Sikorsky's Boris Sergievsky, and Charles Lindbergh (who had driven most of the night to be on hand).

Shortly afterward, at 9:24 A.M., the Clipper passed over the starting point, Stratford lighthouse, at an altitude of 2,000 feet, heading west on course. Ahead lay a four-lap flight of more than 1,200 miles—almost eight hours of flying. If all went according to schedule, the United States, late that afternoon, would be in first place with seventeen records to France's sixteen.

That is exactly what happened as the Clipper, cruising at a speed of just over 157 miles an hour, completed its flight at 5:18 P.M., exactly on time. Four of the records were for speed (157.7 miles an hour) with various payloads over the 1,000 kilometer distance (two laps). Four more were for speed (157.5 miles an hour) over the 2,000 kilometer distance (four laps), again with various payloads. The Clipper carried a payload of 4,400 pounds (2,000 kilograms) and the records were set for zero payload, 500, 1000 and 2,000 kilograms. That evening, Frederick Nielsen, then president of Sikorsky Aircraft, sent a letter to the president of the NAA, with the good news that a single day's flight by the S-42 had vaulted the United States into first place as a holder of world aviation records.

What is the significance of world records? Are they just publicity stunts or do they have real meaning? A quote from the NAA magazine of July, 1934, provides a good answer: "With all the complexity of size and type, the F.A.I. (Federation Aeronautique Internationale) record categories, developed over a quarter-century of aircraft performance, give a thorough and effective yardstick for determination of just whose planes deserve the title of the world's best."

The record flight was one of thirty-two test flights averaging over two hours each during the five-months test program. At the conclusion of the program, pilots Musick and Sergievsky turned in a detailed report on the S-42's performance.

During the S-42 test flight program, Igor Sikorsky talks with Captain Edwin Musick, chief pilot for Pan American Airways.

Among the highlights: at its full gross weight of 38,000 pounds the S-42 had a top speed of 188 miles an hour, a cruising speed of 160, take-off time of 25 to 30 seconds, a range of 1,200 miles with a payload of 7,000 pounds, a range of 3,000 miles with a 1,500-pound payload, a climb of 1,000 feet a minute with four engines, and 400 feet a minute with three engines. These, and a great many other statistics all added up to one vitual fact: the S-42 was entirely ready to establish transoceanic air routes.

The S-42s were designed to carry thirty-two passengers across the Atlantic Ocean by way of the so-called "Steppingstones" route—from New York to Bermuda to the Azores to Portugal. This route was to have been opened in 1935 and was to be followed later by the longer pioneering routes across the Pacific. But things worked out just in reverse: the big Clipper blazed commercial air trails across the

Pacific in 1935 and across the Atlantic two years later.

International politics caused the change in plans. So well was the S-42 designed that the British refused to grant Pan American landing rights at Bermuda because they had no flying boat with which to match the service. So Pan American turned westward to introduce its sleek new flying boats in over-ocean service. The change meant that the airline had to tackle first the long 2,400-mile hop from California to Hawaii rather than the 1,900-mile water jump from Bermuda to the Azores. But the long months of testing had already shown that the S-42 had the performance to handle the more difficult job.

In the fall of 1934 the same S-42 that had set the world records opened service from Miami to the Argentine, cutting the total travel time from eight to five days. Dinner Key, once a little island used by boaters as a stop for midday meals, served as Pan American's Miami base, and became known as the "Gateway to the Americas." Spectators far outnumbered passengers. No visit to Miami was complete without an afternoon at Dinner Key to watch the big Clippers use Biscayne Bay as a runway thirty miles long and seven miles wide.

During World War I the Navy had built a base at Dinner Key, filling in the shallow water to form a "key" or island. In 1930 Pan American bought the island as a base for its new S-38 service to Cuba, using a houseboat as a terminal. A permanent terminal building was completed in 1934, along with hangars for overhaul and maintenance. By 1938 the parking lots at Dinner Key often held 10,000 cars as people jammed an observation deck of the terminal building or lined a sea wall to watch the Clippers land. This colorful era came to an end August 9, 1945, when the last Clipper, a Sikorsky S-42, flew in from Puerto Rico and Jamaica. In later years the city of Miami bought the old Clipper terminal for use as its City Hall and the hangars became a huge convention hall. The Dinner Key Marina appeared where the Clippers once docked, and the romantic era of the Flying Clippers lived only in memory.

In April, 1935, an S-42, fitted with larger fuel tanks than on the earlier S-42s, which gave it a cruising range of 3,200 miles, pioneered commercial air service between the United

States and Hawaii. The first flight, commanded by Captain Musick, started at Alameda, near San Francisco. The Clippers soon extended the transpacific routes all the way to the Philippines and China, as well as southwest to New Zealand and Australia. The steppingstones west from Hawaii were the islands of Midway, Wake, and Guam where Pan American had built bases. The southwest route to New Zealand found the Clippers touching down at bases on Howland Island in the Fiji Islands. By midsummer, 1937, Pan American had completed a million miles of scheduled flying to the Far East, most of it with Igor Sikorsky's S-42s which had pioneered the service.

Despite the political differences which had temporarily prevented an opening of transatlantic air service, the rivalry between American and British aircraft designers had already proven friendly and cooperative. In November, 1934, Igor Sikorsky was invited to speak before the Royal Aeronautical Society in London on "The Development and Characteristics of a Long-range Flying Boat (the S-42)." The British, moved by Igor's modesty and charm, were surprised, and possibly shocked, by the S-42's superiority over the best British flying boat, the four-engined Short *Empire*.

During a discussion following Igor's talk, one British designer ruefully summed up the situation. "In spite of the fact that the S-42 has rather less horsepower in proportion to its weight," he said, "its cruising speed is fifty-two miles an hour faster than that of the English boat; the speed of the S-42 with one of its engines stopped is twenty miles an hour faster than that of the English boat with all engines operating at full power. The S-42 carries nearly 1,000 pounds more payload in addition to fuel for 550 miles increased range. The climb of the S-42 is also better, the landing speed is only about five miles an hour higher, and the time to leave the water is about the same. This improvement in performance can only be described as colossal. The new Atlantic liner *Queen Mary* possesses hardly so great an advantage over the so-called Atlantic greyhounds of the last century as the S-42 possesses over the English flying boat."

A second British designer added that the British would have to take a lesson from Igor's speech and recast their ideas, especially as to wing loading. "It would appear," he said, "that practically all of the improvement in this boat over its predecessors is due to the increased wing loading and aerodynamic cleanliness. In England we have been very loath to work to such high wing loadings because of their effect on landing speed."

The audience showed much interest in the S-42's wing flap which had opened the way toward the long-desired combination of high flight speeds and low landing speeds. Another designer commented: "Flying boats have always been regarded as inefficient in comparison to landplanes . . . It appears, however, that the S-42 is not only ahead of all other flying boats, but that from a profit-earning point of view, it is better than any commercial landplane in this country. At every turn we hear the argument that speed is obtained only by greater horsepower; Mr. Sikorsky has shown, however, that increased speed can be obtained by other means. We have known that in theory, but he has shown it in practice. The great lesson to be learned from his paper is that more courage and forethought is needed."

The president of the Royal Aeronautical Society, J. T. C. Moore-Brabazon, ended the meeting with these warm remarks: "Mr. Sikorsky is indeed a very remarkable man and it is regrettable that he is not an Englishman. The applause which followed the reading of his paper and the discussion was very much above average—and that is a significant fact because the Royal Aeronautical Society is a scientific body, not swayed by sentiment, but one which judges a paper purely on its merits. One hopes that Mr. Sikorsky will visit this country again even before he builds the machine to operate across the Atlantic."

Many years later the question of the flying boat versus the landplane for transoceanic flying was put to a pioneer in both types of flying—Charles Lindbergh. In light of the virtual disappearance of the flying boat, Lindbergh was asked to account for Igor Sikorsky's often-stated opinion that landplanes should not be used over the ocean.

"As of a few years ago, at least (before the jets), Sikorsky still felt it had been a mistake to go to the landplane," Lindbergh said. "I am not sure how he now feels about this. His reasoning was interesting: he believed that passengers would have more room and comfort in a large flying boat. And he argued that the air resistance penalty of a flying boat in relation to a landplane decreased with size. He also cited the high cost of airport construction for large landplanes.

"I favored flying boats at first, but landplanes later, for several reasons. A flying boat has to operate in three elements—land, air, water—and this adds greatly to operating complications. So you gain efficiency with the landplane. Handling a flying boat in water is relatively difficult. There are currents, winds, and tides. Policing a water area is difficult: logs drift in or small boats may appear. You can't fence things out as you can at an airport. Flying is restricted by winter icing conditions, both surface ice and freezing spray. Pan American had to change its operating bases in the winter; there is lots of ice along the U.S.–Europe route in winter, at New York and Newfoundland, for example.

"Another objection I had was that there are a limited number of places where flying boats can get close to cities. I remember, in brainstorming sessions with Michael Gluhareff and others, that Igor once suggested excavating long strips near inland cities and filling them with water, and possibly using an antifreeze mixture to prevent ice in the winter."

Lindbergh said he still believed there might have been a place for big jet flying boats for strategic bombing, pointing out that the Navy had prototypes which were never placed in production. "It's probably too late now for a comeback of the flying boat for such military use," he observed, "but it's interesting to speculate on what might have been. Igor's beliefs about the usefulness of large flying boats cannot be dismissed as entirely wrong. And if he was wrong once in a while, well, that only makes him all the more a likeable human being in my view. He is an extraordinary man in many ways, and certainly one of the greatest figures in the history of aviation."

By the summer of 1937 the political problems with Great Britain had been solved. Imperial Airways Limited was ready with its four-engined *Empire* flying boat, and Pan American had negotiated landing rights in Newfoundland, Ireland, and England, as well as in Bermuda. The first commercial crossing of the Atlantic took place in July and followed the northern route. Harold Gray, veteran Clipper pilot, commanded the S-42 as it lifted from the surface of Long Island at Port

Washington, New York, paused briefly at Botwood, New-foundland, and then rose into the dusk for the long hop to Ireland, Meanwhile, the British flying boat, named the *Cale-donia,* had taken off two hours earlier from Foynes, Ireland, the head start being granted because of the adverse winds faced on the east-west crossing. The two planes passed within sixty miles of each other in mid-Atlantic, exchanging greet-ings by radio.

The S-42 touched down on the Shannon River at Foynes twelve and a half hours after take-off. The British ship landed at Botwood sixteen minutes later, after a crossing of fifteen hours and twenty-eight minutes against head winds. The two flights closed the last gap in round-the-world air transporta-tion, as the transpacific routes had already been linked with connecting flights across Asia and Europe.

Ten S-42s were built, all for Pan American. Two other outstanding Sikorsky designs went into production from 1935 to 1940, the twin-engined S-43 amphibian, also used as a flying boat, and the four-engined S-44 flying boat, the last fixed-wing airplane built by Sikorsky.

The sleek S-43, which made its first flight on June 1, 1935, carried fifteen passengers and a crew of three, cruised at 160 miles an hour, and had a top speed of 182 miles an hour. The S-43 set four world altitude records for amphibians in April, 1936; one record, an altitude of 24,950 feet with zero payload, remains unsurpassed to this day. Fifty-three S-43s were built, all but three being used as amphibians. The U.S. Navy with seventeen, and Pan American with fourteen, were the principal users. Four each were flown by Inter Island Airways of Hawaii and by a French airline, Chargeurs Reuni, from Dakar southward along the west coast of Africa.

On August 7, 1938, a Pan American S-43 began route survey flights between Seattle, Washington, and Juneau, Alaska. This led to completion of the last link in an 11,000-mile air route stretching from Buenos Aires, Argentina, to Nome, Alaska. The new service brought Alaska to within six hours of Seattle and twenty-four hours of New York and any other large city in the United States. At Juneau, passengers could connect with smaller air routes which already were putting the dog team out of business in Alaska by cutting trips of three or four weeks down to three or four hours.

The S-44 came into being as the XPBS-1, a Navy experimental patrol bomber known as the *Flying Dreadnaught*. In the mid-1930s, the Navy's Bureau of Aeronautics, concentrating chiefly on landplanes operating from aircraft carriers, had almost given up on large seaplanes. However, Rear Admiral Joseph M. Reeves, Commander in Chief of the U. S. Fleet, was deeply concerned about the vast reaches of the Pacific and how best to scout them. He raised the question with Eugene E. Wilson, then senior vice-president of United Aircraft, asking if a big flying boat could do the job. Wilson had only recently completed a study of the use of large flying boats to patrol the Pacific, using available harbors as bases. The study, he told the Admiral, showed that flying boats were fully capable of the task. The Navy invited bids from the aircraft industry and Sikorsky won the award with its design for the XPBS-1, which made its first flight on August 13, 1937.

As the Sikorsky design progressed, the Navy developed more interest and approved the building of a second experimental ship, this one to be built by Consolidated Aircraft of San Diego, California. Later, in the competition for a production order, Sikorsky lost to Consolidated which quoted a lower price. The winner, the PB2Y, was the Navy version of the famous B-24 *Liberator* bomber of World War II.

The major effort which Sikorsky had put into the big *Flying Dreadnaught* was not wasted. From the design of the huge Navy plane came the VS-44A, perhaps the most successful flying boat ever used as a commercial airliner. The "VS" stood for Vought-Sikorsky. To make room for expansion of its Pratt & Whitney Aircraft engine plant in East Hartford, Connecticut, United had moved its Chance Vought Aircraft Division to Stratford, combining it with Sikorsky as the Vought-Sikorsky Aircraft Division. The combination lasted from April 1, 1939, to December 31, 1942, the Vought people producing Navy fighters and observation scouts while the Sikorsky group worked on its final flying boat, along with a new contraption cloaked in much mystery, the helicopter.

The VS-44A, an all-metal monoplane with a wingspan of 124 feet and a total of 4,800 horsepower for take-off, cruised at about 210 miles an hour over distances ranging from 3,500 to almost 5,000 miles, depending on the load of fuel carried.

This meant that the new ship could fly nonstop from New York to Rome (over 4,600 miles) carrying a full load of passengers and 1,600 pounds of mail, an unprecedented performance for the time. Aboard, air travelers found new comfort, and even luxury. Seats for the thirty-two passengers were arranged in eight compartments along either side of a central aisle, somewhat in the manner of a first-class train of that era. For overnight flights the ships carried sixteen passengers, with ample sleeping accommodations for all. American Export Airlines, operator of the three VS-44As to be produced, called them its *Flying Aces*. In its advertising the airline praised the new ships' "minimum vibration," "maximum soundproofing," "individual sofas," "full-length beds," "roomy dressing rooms," "full galley for serving hot meals," "snack bar service," "attractive lounge and smoking room," "proper heating and ventilation," and "more square-foot-area per passenger."

The three big flying boats were named *Excalibur, Excambia,* and *Exeter*. Distinguished guests from New York and Washington joined several thousand Vought-Sikorsky employees January 17, 1942, on a concrete ramp outside the plant for a colorful christening of the *Excalibur*. Mrs. Henry A. Wallace, wife of the Vice-President of the United States, swung a bottle of champagne against the plane's bow. The bottle merely bounced back from the ship's Duralumin nose. She tried again, and again, with the same result. The ship's nose, it appeared, would crack before the bottle. Jack Hospers, Vought-Sikorsky's service manager, whose job (and hobby) was solving such problems, came to the rescue of the embarrassed Mrs. Wallace. He taped a length of angle iron to the bow. Mrs. Wallace swung again, the champagne flowed and the *Excalibur* was "launched." The next day the new ship made its first flight.

In operation between the United States and Europe throughout World War I, the *Flying Aces* proved to be the longest-range airliners in the world. They were the only aircraft flying commercial non-stop flights across the North and South Atlantic with full payloads on flights of over 3,100 miles. They set record after record, including the fastest flight from the United States to Europe, 14 hours 17 minutes (3,329 miles, from New York to Foynes, Ireland), and the fastest west-bound flight, 16 hours 57 minutes (Foynes to New York). The *Flying Aces* made the first nonstop flights along such wartime supply routes as Bermuda–North Africa, Africa–Trinidad and Africa–Puerto Rico.

During World War II many high-ranking government officials shivered in the bucket seats of military transport landplanes on the long Atlantic crossing. They had to land at Newfoundland, Iceland, or the Azores for fuel, often in bad weather. Others, luckier, went nonstop in the *Flying Aces*, enjoying the comparative luxury of cushioned seats, sound-proofing, and sleeping berths. Igor Sikorsky's huge flying boats not only outperformed the landplanes of the time, but also showed that the long flight over the ocean could be a pleasant experience rather than a physical ordeal.

Of the three VS-44As built, the second one—*Excambia*—is still flying, the only four-engined flying boat operating commercially today. The *Excalibur* had a brief career, being lost in a bad landing at Gander, Newfoundland, during flight tests. The *Exeter* cracked up after the war in a bad night landing while on a charter flight to South America.

A group of Baltimore, Maryland, businessmen rebuilt the *Excambia* in 1950, fitting it out as a flying trading post for use in the Amazon River, but the plan did not work out. In 1957, W. R. Probert, a former Navy flying boat pilot and president of Avalon Air Transport, of California, found the ship stranded in a harbor near Lima, Peru. Probert ferried the big ship to California in a hair-raising trip that included a couple of forced landings and an eighteen-hour flight from Lima to Acapulco, Mexico, with a wing float, broken on take-off, penetrating the right wing.

Operated by Avalon, the former *Flying Ace* shuttled thousands of tourists between Long Beach, California, and nearby Catalina Island. Ironically, the VS-44A, designed for nonstop service of 3,000 miles or more, was then flying a forty-five mile route which it covered in twelve minutes. Since early 1968, the one-time *Excambia* has been operated by Antilles Airways to ferry passengers among the Virgin Islands in the Caribbean. To Antilles' president and pilot, Charles F. Blaire Jr., the VS-44A is far more than just another airplane. Blair

Huge XPBS-1 Flying Dreadnaught, *built in 1937, was the forerunner of the VS-44A* Flying Aces, *last of the Sikorsky flying boats.*

Sikorsky VS-44A Flying Aces *were the first aircraft to provide non-stop transatlantic service.*

commanded the *Flying Ace* which in 1944 flew the fastest Atlantic crossing. Earlier, in 1937, he had flown the original *Flying Dreadnaught* as a Sikorsky test pilot.

Despite their remarkable contributions to international air travel, the end of the road was in sight for the big flying boats. Sikorsky had made no profit on its ten S-42 Flying Clippers and had lost money on the three VS-44A *Flying Aces* produced. Pan American had turned to the Martin and Boeing companies for future Clippers, but these flying boats, too, were doomed to be replaced by much faster landplanes within a few years.

In 1938 it became the unhappy duty of Eugene Wilson, as senior vice-president of United Aircraft, to break some bad news to his old friend Igor Sikorsky: United had decided, with regret, to close down the Sikorsky division. But Wilson was unaware that Igor had an ace up his sleeve, that he was ready, almost by intuition, to offer a counterproposal. Since as early as 1929 Igor had been working informally with one or two of his closest associates on the idea that had first stirred his interest as a youth in Russia. This was the ugly duckling of the air world, the "impossible," "impractical," ungainly helicopter.

Had the time finally come to make a final try to add a new dimension, the vertical, to flying? Igor, with an eye to the future as usual, thought it had.

11

An Old Dream Revived

One summer day in 1967 Igor Sikorsky sat in his office at Stratford, Connecticut, leaning forward, his hands resting lightly on the table before him. He appeared, as usual, alert yet relaxed. From a corner of the room a motion picture camera zeroed in on him. In another corner a sound technician twirled the dials of his console. From overhead, floodlamps bathed the scene in a hot and brilliant light.

Igor was undergoing the ordeal of a filmed interview, speaking without notes as he recalled for posterity the highlights of his career. The lights bothered his eyes, but he endured the irritation with characteristic patience. As the long interview continued, his answers seemed, almost incredibly, to gain in vigor and enthusiasm.

"Mr. Sikorksy," asked Alvin Sizer, news editor of the New Haven *Register,* who was conducting the interview, "when you were working on your transoceanic flying boats did you ever think of your first love, helicopters? How did you get back into the helicopter game?"

"I was certainly thinking about the first love virtually all the time," replied Igor. "It was back in 1926 and later, in 1930, when I made sketches of an aircraft which was very similar to the VS-300 which eventually was constructed. While we were working on the problem of building an airplane capable of introducing transoceanic flying it was not wise to start something as new as the helicopter. The helicopter was a thing which called for attention, I would say love, I would say all energy, knowledge, and support that a man could put in. And of course it was my ambition to live my life again, to again design an aircraft without knowing how it should be done because no one really knew properly how it could be done.''

Igor looked closely at his interviewer, warming to his subject, forgetting the lights and the intruding eye of the camera. He raised his hands in a gentle gesture and an almost mischievous smile brightened his face as he continued. ''The helicopter was at that time one of the impossibilities,'' he said. ''Many people considered that no helicopter with real control characteristics could ever be constructed. Other pessimists said that even if you did build a helicopter, no one would need it. A good friend of mine, a very prominent designer, a scientist in aviation, asked me when would a helicopter go faster than an airplane? I said, 'The answer is never.' When would the helicopter be more efficient than the airplane? he demanded. I said again, 'Never.' But I told him the helicopter would do a number of jobs no airplane will do, and which, in fact, nothing else will do except the helicopter.''

Igor continued to express his thoughts on the helicopter, pronouncing, as always, the ''ed'' on the end of words as ''approved,'' or ''established.'' It was as though he were reciting the ''Blessed's'' in the Beatitudes. In fact, the trait of accenting the last syllables of words ending in ''ed'' probably derived from his having learned his English from the Bible. It gave his diction an individual quality that has been almost a ''trademark'' of his life in America and added much to the natural charm and effectiveness with which he speaks. As he continued his recollections, Igor emphasized a point that was to bring him much satisfaction in later years—the helicopter's value for saving lives.

''That was one of my dreams, to build this lifesaving machine,'' he said. ''I wanted to do that as long as I'm alive, even if it's the last big job which I did in my life, which perhaps it will be. It had to me a sort of romantic or philosophical appeal. The appeal is this: what kind of machine can give you unlimited freedom of transportation? When you walk you need a trail or something. A pack animal needs even a better trail. A horse wagon needs a road. The automo-

Helicopters first attracted worldwide attention for their performances in saving lives during the Korean conflict. One of the most widely used was the Sikorsky S-51 shown here.

bile needs a still better road. The railroad needs a track. Steamships need a waterway. Airplanes need big airports. If a man is in need of rescue, an airplane can come in and throw flowers on him and that's just about all. But a direct lift aircraft could come in and save his life. Even if a helicopter cannot land (and these were the ideas I had fully before I started it) the helicopter can use a hoist or a cable to contact any place on the ground—on a roof, on water, in a treetop— absolutely any place.''

Early in the interview Igor had discovered that a reel of film lasted just over ten minutes and he had been timing his remarks to end as nearly as possible when the film ran out. Now he concluded his comments on the helicopter: ''Those were the ideas and dreams of why I wanted to start the helicopter, and why I succeeded finally to sell the management of United Aircraft the idea to authorize its construction. Once

I received the okay I promptly started to work. I was not only the designer but the pilot of this aircraft during its first flight when it flew to the altitude of this table, which happened in September of 1939.''

The camera stopped, the lights blinked out, and Sikorsky smiled at the camera crew's exclamations that his timing had been perfect, his concluding words having been spoken just as the film ran out.

When Igor mentioned selling United Aircraft on the helicopter, his mind may well have flashed back to a gloomy day in 1938 when he was called to the office of United's senior vice-president in East Hartford. Igor entered Gene Wilson's office that day, brought his heels together and bowed from the waist in his customary Continental manner. Although he suspected why the meeting had been called, he awaited Wilson's first words. They were quick in coming and were based on a decision that had been reached by United with great reluctance: the Sikorsky division would have to be closed; it had become, in Wilson's words, ''a factory full of wonderful people, but no orders.'' A colleague had told Wilson, ''There's a pearl somewhere in that Russian oyster. If you can find it, save it.'' Wilson had his work cut out for him, and he proceeded with dispatch, speaking kindly, for he admired and respected Igor Sikorsky, but firmly, for business was business with precious little room for sentiment. Only the power of Igor Sikorsky's personality had prevented this action months earlier.

''After long and careful consideration,'' Wilson told Igor, ''it has been decided finally—but with deep reluctance—to discontinue production and engineering development at the Stratford plant. However, because of your personal contribution to aviation we are prepared to consider any individual research program you may propose, providing it is within our means.''

Igor certainly had a research program in mind. However, before outlining it he moved quickly to obtain an important concession upon which all else would depend. After expressing his appreciation for United's consideration in the past and his regrets for the Sikorsky division's failure to live up to expectations, he said:

U.S. Navy/Sikorsky Helicopter picking up an Apollo astronaut crew following a "splash down" in the Pacific. Almost all the astronauts have been picked up by helicopter following their return from space.

"I am sure you realize that whatever contribution I may have been able to make to aeronautics has been the product of diverse intellects working together in freedom and harmony. I am but the coordinator of an engineering team. Therefore, before accepting further responsibility it would be necessary for me to know whether or not my little group shall remain intact."

Sikorsky's appeal, presented earnestly and humbly, made a strong impression on Wilson who quickly appreciated its logic. Of course, the group would remain intact, he told Igor. With this load lifted from his shoulders, Igor relaxed and launched into a detailed explanation of his proposal—the "impossible" helicopter. He outlined the historical attempts to build a vertical lift aircraft and how most had proved to be failures in one way or another. He summarized the entire history of aviation as a record of repeated accomplishment of the "impossible." He outlined all the helicopter's advantages over other vehicles, pointing out that the helicopter would fill the gap between the high-speed, long-range airplane and the low-speed, short trips of various surface vehicles. He said that if the Sikorsky company did not solve the problems of the helicopter, some other company would. He said the helicopter would require little money but plenty of intuitive engineering. He estimated that to build a full-scale, man-carrying helicopter to test his theories would cost no more than $30,000. He advanced a final argument: the helicopter would be ideally suited to saving lives, not to destroying them.

Sikorsky's arguments won Wilson's approval; the company would provide the money needed to build a research helicopter. Although it was far too early to be sure, Wilson felt intuitively that he had "saved the pearl," as advised. How did it happen that Igor had been able to present so many strong arguments for the helicopter at such an early date? Perhaps it was luck; Igor once said that he had been "lucky in timing," that he always seemed to be in the right place at the right time. More probably, however, it was simply his reward for being prepared, for having provided the creative spark that advanced the cause of the helicopter years before there existed any real interest in, or demand for, such a vehicle.

On December 18, 1930, when most of his pioneering work with large amphibians and flying boats still lay ahead of him. Igor Sikorsky wrote a confidential memorandum to United Aircraft entitled "The Helicopter Problem." Prophetic, as usual, he wrote: "a flying machine capable of normally taking off and landing from an area of, say, 120 feet across will offer far greater advantages for everyday use than the present airplane which requires, roughly speaking, at least one hundred times greater area. Such a small place as the size mentioned could very easily be built on tops of buildings, in parks, aboard large steamships, and with very little or no expense could be made available anywhere out of town.

"A flying machine offering reasonable speed and which could be controllable and safe to the extent comparable to the present airplane, also combining take-off and landing ability in such a small area, would be of great value and would be, unquestionably, in considerable demand. The possibility to fly at low speed and to make a slow landing would eliminate most of the dangers now encountered by airplanes in fog. The writer believes that the progress which has been made during the past few years in all branches of aviation industry permits and encourages the building of a practical helicopter which will satisfy all the requirements outlined above."

The memo reviewed past helicopter attempts noting that "many helicopters" were built from 1920 to 1930 and that several proved capable of taking off and hovering briefly over one spot. It noted also that the Cierva autogiro, while not a helicopter, did prove a very important point—that it was entirely possible for a helicopter to make a safe landing in case of engine failure. The helicopter, the memo estimated, was in about the same stage in 1930 as the airplane was some twenty years before.

Igor saw two courses open to United Aircraft: either forget the problem and wait for some other company to develop a helicopter and then enter the field, or, to develop "in a reasonable and economical way our own type of helicopter." Igor favored the second course as best suiting the interests of United and Sikorsky.

The memo concluded by disclosing that Igor had done some helicopter development work in 1928, had added to this work in 1930, and that he now believed these efforts "may result in the development of a practical flying helicopter."

A great many development and production programs of higher priority, including engines, propellers and, of course, the big flying boats, kept the helicopter pigeonholed until the late 1930s. However, Igor and his closest associates pursued the problem whenever they could find a spare moment. One of these men was Igor's cousin, Igor Alexis Sikorsky, who had moved from Russia to France in 1922. Like his older relative, he had become interested in aviation at an early age, influenced by the writings of Jules Verne, Blériot's flight across the English Channel in 1909, and the achievement of his famous cousin in building the world's first four-engined airplane in 1913. In France, Igor Alexis attended the University of Nancy, the Sorbonne, and an aeronautical technical school, then worked as a draftsman in French factories for three years, He came to the United States in 1930 and joined Sikorsky Aircraft the same year.

A popular figure with a pleasant, outgoing personality, Igor Alexis was known as "Professor Sikorsky" or, to his fellow engineers, as just plan "Prof." Despite the nickname, he never did any formal teaching. "Jimmy Viner gave me that name," he said, "when I was teaching him to be a draftsman in 1930." The name stuck and somehow seemed natural for Igor Alexis with his scholarly manner and appearance.

Prof, "a walking encyclopedia" of aeronautical lore, contributed much to aviation with writings and lectures. A handbook he prepared with the late Alexander Klemin on the aerodynamics of rotary-winged aircraft was published in 1954 by the U.S. Department of Commerce. His technical history of Sikorsky Aircraft, from 1909, is a standard reference, one of the most complete of its kind. A bachelor, he liked to keep track of relatives; there were fifty-three in the United States as of his last count. In 1965 he was able to get in touch with a younger brother, still in Russia, after a lapse of twenty-five years. One of his many hobbies was cooking, self-taught, which began as a necessity when he lived in a small apartment near the Eiffel Tower in Paris.

Igor Alexis, who retired in 1967, had been working at Sikorsky only four months when his cousin came to him and began talking about helicopters. "After that I worked on helicopter designs with Robert Kemp, our patent engineer," he said. "This was quite difficult as I spoke very little English and he spoke no French. We used to do a lot of communicating by sign language, mostly just waving our hands and arms about like fighter pilots describing a dogfight."

Vital in Sikorsky's "unofficial" helicopter work of the early 1930s were Bob Labensky, head of the experimental

"Prof" Sikorsky as a young man in Paris.

laboratory; his assistant, Michael Buivid; and a young engineer, J. Russell Clark. But they worked on the helicopter only once in a while since the company's main effort was focused on the Flying Clippers.

"Mr. Sikorsky served as the crēative spirit behind this work on the helicopter," Prof said. "He would have the ideas and it was my job, as a draftsman, to translate the ideas to paper. Then Bob Labensky, who did just about everything, would take the drawings and convert them into hardware; from nothing he would build something. He was a gifted mechanical engineer and without him nothing would have been built. Michael Gluhareff, as chief engineer, would come up with beautiful drawings of a helicopter which might not be correct in every detail. Labensky would take these drawings, making corrections from time to time, and fashion parts for testing. Michael Buivid, who was second in command in the lab, would then handle the more detailed work, such as gears, and bring the job closer to something really workable. Labensky and Buivid were inseparable, a wonderful team. They were good mechanics and dedicated men who worked fourteen hours a day. Michael Gluhareff, by the way, was very skeptical about the helicopter at first, but changed later and became one of its strongest supporters.''

In the very early days of planning a Sikorsky helicopter design argument arose as to which rotor system was the better, the single main lifting rotor, or a multi-rotor system. Many favored the multi-rotor, but not Igor Sikorsky. One of the most influential authorities supporting Igor's viewpoint was Leonard (Luke) Hobbs, an outstanding research engineer who became engineering manager of United's Pratt & Whitney Aircraft division in 1935. Hobbs reasoned that one rotor system was complex enough, so why add more complications by increasing the number of rotors? The single rotor won out and became both the hallmark of Sikorsky helicopters and the standard for the helicopter industry. Today, more than 90 per cent of the world's helicopters employ the single main rotor system.

''The Old Man, as we called Mr. Sikorsky, attacked problems with great persistence,'' Prof once observed, ''and in the end things had to be done his way.'' That does not mean, as others have pointed out, that he ever ordered or demanded or ''pushed anybody around.'' He simply won people to his way of thinking by logic and persuasion sprinkled with equal parts of charm and determination. In a meeting, if his point of view became overlooked or sidetracked for a while, he always brought it back into the discussion quietly, yet firmly, often with his listeners not quite sure how it had happened. Often, because of Igor's kind and courteous manner, an associate would feel that, after all, Igor's opinions had not really differed from his own all along. ''If you don't mind,'' Igor would say, or, ''If this suggestion does not conflict with your own engineering principles . . .'' In the end his associates gave their consent and support to his views not grudgingly, but with loyalty and enthusiasm.

Igor Sikorsky's VS-300 helicopter, designed in the spring of 1939 and built during the summer, was ready for flight tests that fall. The spindly craft, a collection of steel tubing,

In a corner of the Stratford plant, Igor Sikorsky "flies" a helicopter flight simulator. Looking on (left to right): Michael Buivid, Bob Labensky and Michael Gluhareff.

drive belts, and gears, presented an almost ludicrous contrast to the sleek Navy scouts and bombers then moving from the assembly lines of the Vought-Sikorsky plant. The VS-300 closely resembled a helicopter design for which Igor had applied for a patent June 27, 1931, and on which a patent had been granted on March 19, 1935. It had a single main, or lifting, rotor of three blades and a two-bladed tail rotor. The latter served two purposes: it overcame the torque, or twisting effect, of the main rotor, and provided directional, or rudder, control.

As the novel ship took shape in a walled-off corner of the big plant its builders faced a variety of difficulties, the easiest of which was lift. Far more troublesome were the problems of control arrangements, reduction of vibration, and selection of materials which would give the helicopter's moving parts the longest possible life.

Since they would have to learn as they went along, Igor and his associates built their first helicopter as simply as possible. The uncovered welded steel frame could be changed in shape and size overnight. Heavy duty truck gears were used for the transmission and a set of belts permitted almost instant changes in the transmission ratio. Design changes which in most aircraft might take as long as two months were made in a couple of days in the VS-300. Several times the ship was flown in quite a different form than it had had only two days earlier. Eventually some eighteen different control arrangements were tried and the VS-300 took to the air in four completely different configurations before its final design was decided upon. That final design, ironically, was the same as the first one flown and the same as the one for which the patent had been requested eight years before. This was the single main and tail rotor which seemed to provide the best combination of design simplicity and good flight performance.

Igor told an interviewer several years later: "The main problem was control and the difficulty was threefold. First, we had little knowledge of helicopters in general; second, we were building the first helicopter in the world with a single main rotor; and third, we knew practically nothing about how to pilot a helicopter. When trouble came, as it did, we had to decide who was to blame, the designer or the pilot, even when both were the same person. During the early years of the helicopter's development I filled both these positions. So I must take the blame for our occasional flight trouble if I am to accept any of the credit for the helicopter's successes later."

On September 14, 1939, the VS-300 was taken to the factory's backyard for its first flight test. As Igor strapped himself into the open pilot's seat his mind may well have flashed back to 1910 and his first attempt to fly an airplane. The VS-300 looked just as primitive as the S-1 and learning to pilot it would probably prove fully as hazardous and frustrating. The crude copter had four swiveling landing wheels—two at each side, one under the nose, and one toward the tail—to provide the greatest possible stability on the ground.

Historic moment: With Igor Sikorsky at the controls, the VS-300 helicopter lifts inches off the ground in its first flight. The date was September 14, 1939.

On each side ropes ran from the helicopter to stakes on the ground, to restrain the new bird if it tried to leap too high into the air on its first flight.

When Igor started the little 75-horsepower engine the VS-300 vibrated and the controls shook in his hands. He increased the power and the shaking became worse. But he could feel that the craft had power enough to rise, so he pulled up on the pitch control, increasing the bite of the rotor blades. One wheel inched clear of the ground, then another. He added more power and suddenly all four wheels hung clear of the ground. Igor quickly reduced power and pitch and the ship rested again on its wheels. He conferred with Labensky, Buivid, and the Gluhareff brothers, and then made a few more brief flights, just getting the wheels off the ground each time. That was it for the day, a total of about ten seconds in the air. The shaking had been violent, and control difficult, but the VS-300 *had* gotten off the ground and back again undamaged.

Now came the long and painstaking process of developing the helicopter, of unceasing changes and tests. In its first form, or configuration, the VS-300's main control was centered in its single main rotor through an arrangement called *cyclic pitch*. This enabled the pitch of each blade to be changed during its cycle of rotation. By increasing or decreasing the pitch of the blades the helicopter could be tilted, and thus moved, in any direction—forward, backward, or sideward. In its early form the cyclic pitch system gave inadequate control. On December 9, 1939, with Serge Gluhareff as pilot, the VS-300 was moved sideways by a minor gust of wind. The ship touched the ground and in a split second flipped on its side, the rotor blades destroying themselves on the concrete pavement near the factory building. Gluhareff was uninjured, but the copter was badly damaged.

Rebuilding the VS-300 led to its second configuration. Cyclic pitch was abandoned and the ship, in a major re-design, carried three auxiliary rotors at the tail. Two were mounted horizontally at the tips of outriggers while the third was the usual anti-torque rotor. Each small rotor had one blade with a counterweight. An increase in the pitch of the two horizontal rotors raised the tail, while a decrease lowered it. Increasing one rotor's pitch while decreasing that of the other rolled, or banked, the ship. The main lifting rotor, without cyclic pitch, moved the ship only straight up or down. The new arrangement, though complicated, provided more positive control. Restraining cables and weights, previously used, were eased off as the ship began to fly higher and under better control. The flights attracted growing public attention in the vicinity of the plant.

It was in its second configuration that the VS-300 first aroused widespread interest and made its most historic flight. The craft began tethered hops March 6, 1940, first flew free on May 13, and was shown to the public on May 20. The invited guests looked on in amazement as Igor flew the VS-300 backward, sideways, up and down, and even turned on a spot. After the flight one of the guests, Charles L. (Les) Morris, Connecticut Commissioner of Aeronautics, stepped forward to hand the pilot an envelope. "Mr. Sikorsky," he

Changing a wheel in flight was one of the many demonstrations that proved the helicopter's control and versatility. Igor Sikorsky flies the VS-300 while Al Krapish makes the tire change.

said, "I am happy to present you with Connecticut Helicopter License No. 1."

Caught up in the enthusiasm of seeing a helicopter for the first time, the spectators missed an important point: the VS-300 had not flown forward. Queried on this later by Eugene Wilson, Igor replied, "That is one of the minor engineering problems we have not yet solved!" When the ship moved forward the horizontal tail rotors were buffeted by the turbulent air from the big main rotor. An uncertain, unsteady, flight resulted. Despite this, the ship made short "cross-country" flights of up to 250 yards, hovered under good control to pick up objects handed to the pilot by a man on the ground, and made helicopter converts almost every time it flew.

One of the more enthusiastic visitors, and certainly the most influential, was a lean and tanned young Army Air Corps flier, Captain H. Franklin Gregory. A visionary with the toughness to make his ideas come true, Gregory came to the Sikorsky plant in July in his capacity as a leader in the

Army's rotary wing development program. Until then, the program had been chiefly concerned with autogiros—machines which look like helicopters but can neither hover nor rise straight up. Gregory's purpose at Sikorsky was to study and fly the VS-300. He first flew the ship on July 24, making two flights of about five minutes each. After that there was no holding the young flier, who quickly envisioned the military promise of the helicopter. He became the driving force that eventually brought the helicopter into military use.

The flights continued and gradually the little band of pioneers learned the dos and don'ts of helicopter design and flying. Control was lost at a height of fifteen feet one day and a hard landing resulted. The cause: oil dampers installed to prevent vibrations had been left empty to see if they really were needed. They were. Later, Igor was flying forward at thirty miles an hour about twenty feet in the air when one of the tail outriggers folded upward, loosening the drive belts to one of the horizontal rotors. The rotor slowed down and the ship rolled over in the air and crashed to earth on its side. Igor climbed from the wreckage unscratched, looked at the debris for a minute or so, and then quietly said: "I think we will get her home now." The cause of the accident: a crack in the outrigger, the result of the earlier hard landing.

Records and "firsts" came in quick succession during the spring of 1941. Still in its second, or "outrigger" configuration, the VS-300 set an American helicopter endurance record of 1 hour, 5 minutes, 14.5 seconds on April 15. This was fifteen minutes short of the world record of 1 hour, 20 minutes, 39 seconds set by the German Focke-Wulf helicopter in 1937. Two days later the VS-300 became the world's first seaplane-amphibian: supported by two sausage-like rubber floats and balanced fore and aft by a basketball under the nose and a smaller sausage beneath the tail, the ship, its rotors spinning, was pushed out into the Housatonic River. Igor quickly found that he could maneuver as well as any boat—and perhaps better—and took off. After making several landings on the water he flew over the shoreline and landed gently in the grass beyond. The helicopter had proved another point: with floats it could land on any surface where there was room enough to swing its rotors—water, mud, snow, ice, and even on ice too thin to hold the copter. Frank Greg-

Equipped with inflated floats, the VS-300, with Igor Sikorsky at the controls, became a seaplane-amphibian in April, 1941.

ory, looking on, made further mental notes concerning this new bird's value to the military services.

On May 6 the VS-300 was rolled into a field back of the plant for a try at the world endurance record. Reporters, cameramen, and newsreelmen were on hand as Igor felt sure a new record would be set. An oversized gasoline tank had been installed and if the ship could get off the ground with the added weight of fuel (about twenty-nine pounds extra) all would be well. Before the attempt, Igor told the press that this would be a scientific proof of an entirely new principle of flying, namely controlled and sustained flight without the need to move through the air at high speeds. "You will witness the most unspectacular event you have ever covered," he said. "I plan only to hang stationary over one spot for about an hour and a half, and nothing more."

With the engine running at full power the ship hung only a foot or two off the ground and it was touch and go for a while. As the fuel was burned off, however, the copter climbed a bit and finally hovered about thirty feet in the air. As time passed, Igor broke the monotony by turning the ship in different directions at signals from the cameramen below. The company had sent out two cafeteria wagons and spectators enjoyed sandwiches and coffee. For a while the helicopter ground crew played soccer with the basketball that had been used for the seaplane flights. At the edge of the field Igor's wife, Elizabeth, stood by the family car, quietly surveying the scene. A woman who characteristically preferred to stay in the background, this was one of the rare occasions when she left her household duties to share in her husband's aviation activities. The four Sikorsky sons, meanwhile, romped about the field, enjoying what, for them, had become a picnic as well as an afternoon off from school.

When the 1 hour, 20 minute mark was passed, Robert MacKellar, a Sikorsky mechanic, stood in front of the helicopter holding up a sign he had painted for the cameramen: "World's Record Broken. 1 hour 20 min." After that Bob Labensky used a set of binoculars to keep a close watch on the fuel gauge. Just before 2:49 P.M. the VS-300 touched its wheels to the ground to establish a new world record of 1 hour, 32 minutes, 26.1 seconds. The tank still contained two and a half gallons of gasoline, but the engine, running at full throttle, had started to sound rough. With the record in hand Igor saw no point in pressing his luck any further.

When Les Morris left his job as state Commissioner of Aeronautics to become a Sikorsky helicopter test pilot in March, 1941, his chief credentials were a boundless enthusiasm and faith in the new machine. He had yet to fly a helicopter. He learned quickly, however, making his first wobbly flight on May 12 and becoming a vital member of the team which pioneered the helicopter.

In May, Igor decided to return, by easy stages, to the control system that had been used at the very beginning—cyclic pitch in the main rotor. Despite the successes with the three-tail-rotor, outrigger system, it had become clear that reasonably fast forward flight would never be achieved with that method. Lateral, or rolling, control was returned to the

Igor Sikorsky waves a greeting from the VS-300 as he breaks the world helicopter endurance record on May 6, 1941.

main rotor, but fore and aft, or pitching, control was retained at the tail by mounting a single horizontal rotor atop a turret. Directional control remained, as usual, in the single vertical tail rotor.

The VS-300 first flew in its third configuration on June 12. With the cumbersome outriggers gone, the ship had a less complex appearance and showed improved control and smoother forward flight. Soon Morris was flying the ship in graceful curves over the fields and adjacent airport. Though still ugly in its bare-boned look, the VS-300 flew beautifully, responding quickly to the controls and reaching speeds up to seventy miles an hour. For the first time the pioneers knew they had a really successful helicopter. They even covered the forward part of the ship with fabric so that the pilot now sat in a conventional-looking cockpit.

While the VS-300 was moving through its period of growing pains, the Vought-Sikorsky company received an Army contract to build a two-seat helicopter for use as an observation trainer, the XR-4. Frank Gregory, who retired from the Air Force as a brigadier-general in the early 1950s and now lives in Tulsa, Oklahoma, recalled in 1968 his pioneering work with the helicopter.

"Igor and I sat in his car one day at Stratford and discussed in detail what the Army Air Corps needed in the way of a helicopter," he said. "We really designed the XR-4 then and there. We agreed that it must have a closed cabin and be able to carry a pilot and one passenger. I insisted that all the controls be placed in the main rotor—both cyclic and collective pitch—that we must get rid of the two horizontal tail rotors that provided lateral control in the VS-300."

The decision to build the Army ship with a single main rotor and single tail rotor led to the final change in the form of the much-modified VS-300. Since the XR-4 was to be larger and more powerful, it was agreed that the test pilots who were to fly it (Morris and Gregory) should have plenty of experience in a helicopter with similar controls. So, in November, the VS-300 underwent its final major change. On December 8, 1941, the day after Pearl Harbor, the ship was flown for the first time in its final configuration. The flights that day and for the next few days proved shaky and uncertain. Oddly, the VS-300 now did better in forward flight than while hovering. Finally, Igor came up with the answer: the old blade dampeners, which had been left off to improve forward flight, were reinstalled in such a way that they served well both in forward flight and hovering. On the last day of the year the VS-300, as Les Morris said later, was flown "forward, backward, and sideways, and no wobble was discovered at any time."

The Vought-Sikorsky division was split into its original Chance Vought and Sikorsky divisions at the end of 1942.

Vought remained in the rapidly expanding Stratford plant to handle the huge job of mass-producing Corsair fighters for the Marines and the Navy. Vought's employment total topped 13,000. The Sikorsky division, with only a few hundred employees, took over a renovated factory close to Long Island Sound in Bridgeport.

As the VS-300 continued its test flights throughout 1942 and into 1943 it attracted a continual flow of visitors to Stratford and later to Bridgeport. Several veteran airplane pilots tried their hand at flying the helicopter, often with nerve-wracking results. They were startled when movements of the copter's control stick brought results not at all like those they were accustomed to in fixed-wing planes. As an airplane settles to a landing, the pilot pulls back on the stick. In the helicopter a backward pull on the stick starts the ship moving backward. Charles Lindbergh spent a whole afternoon trying to master the helicopter. He analyzed the problems that night and returned the next day to fly the VS-300 without any trouble.

"There was no dual instruction," Lindbergh recalled in 1968, "since the ship had only one cockpit. Les Morris stood out in front and Igor at the side of the ship while I lifted it a few feet off the ground. I've never felt so completely out of my profession. I'd push the stick forward and nothing would happen. I'd push it forward more and, whoosh, the ship would surge ahead much faster than I wanted it to. Then I would ease back on the stick without any effect on the speed forward. I would pull back harder and, whoosh, movement reversed so fast I thought the tail would dig into the ground."

One of the American men of achievement whom Igor Sikorsky admired was Henry Ford. One day he mentioned to Lindbergh that he would like to have the VS-300 placed permanently in the Ford Museum at Dearborn, Michigan. Lindbergh was happy to make the initial arrangements. He discussed Igor's wish with Henry Ford who was delighted to give his approval. So it happened that on October 7, 1943, the VS-300 at the advanced age of four years, reposed on the lawn of Ford's Edison Institute Museum, awaiting its last flight.

With a crowd of several thousand looking on, Les Morris took off and put the little ship through its paces for the last

Charles Lindbergh (right) with Igor Sikorsky in 1943 at Sikorsky Plant, Stratford, CT. V-S-300 in background.

time. He set a landing wheel on the center of a handkerchief placed on the ground, picked up with the nose of the craft a twelve-inch metal ring set on the top of a pole, and did other stunts developed over the years to show the helicopter's precise control and maneuverability.

Igor Sikorsky (right) with Henry Ford after the VS-300's final flight.

Igor Sikorsky pilots the VS-300 helicopter on its last flight, October 7, 1943, when the historic ship was delivered to Ford's Edison Institute Museum at Dearborn, Michigan.

Famed VS-300 found its final home in Ford's Edison Institute Museum.

Pioneers all (left to right): Igor Sikorsky, Orville Wright, and Colonel Frank Gregory, upon delivery of the first helicopter to the military services, an R-4 received by the Army Air Corps at Wright Field, Dayton, Ohio, in 1943.

All hands were saved when the big auto ferry, Skagerak, *sank under mountainous waves off Denmark in 1967. Of the 144 passengers saved, more than half were picked up by Sikorsky helicopters of the Royal Danish Air Force.*

Then Igor Sikorsky climbed into the cockpit, made a short flight and landed gently in front of the grandstand. He and Morris posed for pictures with Ford and Lindbergh. Finally he patted the silver-colored fabric of the VS-300's fuselage. "She was a good ship, a sweet little ship," he said.

The end of the VS-300's historic career marked the start of the helicopter saga. The XR-4 became the R-4, the "world's first production helicopter" and the only helicopter to serve in World War II. From these beginnings sprang the helicopter industry. More helicopter companies were started, turning out hundreds and then thousands of rotary wing craft. The helicopter won first world-wide attention in the Korean conflict and later, in far greater numbers, in Vietnam.

Of all helicopter achievements since the days of the VS-300, none gave Igor Sikorsky more satisfaction than the thousands of lives that have been saved with the new aircraft. The best estimates now put the total at well over 100,000 lives saved by American-built helicopters alone. All of these lives have been spared because of the helicopter's special ability to hover, with most of the rescues taking place under conditions where no other vehicle could have done the job. These lifesaving missions range all the way from a wounded soldier rushed to medical aid or a lost child found wandering in a swamp to mass airlifts of hundreds and even thousands of people in peril during natural disasters such as floods or earthquakes.

The first recorded mercy mission by helicopter occurred January 3, 1944, when a Coast Guard R-4 flown by a pioneer helicopter pilot, Commander Frank Erickson, braved a snowstorm to rush blood plasma to 100 crewmen burned in an explosion aboard a U.S. destroyer a few miles outside New York Harbor. The helicopter rescue hoist, originally developed by the Coast Guard, was first used to save a life November 29, 1945, when two men were lifted from a barge that was breaking up on a reef during a storm.

Individual rescues were many: men hoisted from the roof of a flaming building, sick or injured persons sped to hospitals from ships at sea or from the scene of a highway accident, a badly injured boy plucked from a rocky cliffside, a mountain climber snatched from the snows of an avalanche. When the big auto ferry, the *Skagerak*, was being pounded by mountainous waves in the straits between Norway and Denmark in the fall of 1967, 144 men, women, and children were pulled from the sea, half of them by helicopters of the Royal Danish Air Force, the last ones just before the ship sank. Said the ferry's captain: "The rescue could not have been done had it not been for the helicopters."

The devastating floods of 1955 probably head the list of mass rescues: almost 10,000 airlifted to safety in Tampico, Mexico, 2,500 by rescue hoists; about 1,100 saved in Connecticut and 1,000 in northern California. In the 1960s more thousands were saved following floods in Japan, Germany, and the Netherlands. Over the years helicopters have airlifted food and medicine to hundreds snowbound in trains, buses, and autos, and to many other isolated and starving because of the cruelties of war.

No single organization has used helicopters for rescue more widely than the U.S. Coast Guard in its job of patrolling some 88,000 miles of coastline. A single Coast Guard station gets hundreds of calls for help each year. Most of them come when boaters, hunters, fishermen, and swimmers get themselves into trouble from which only a hovering, direct lift machine can save them. The U.S. Air Force's Aerospace Rescue and Recovery Service depends increasingly upon helicopters as it ranges the world to save lives. The crews of this service's Sikorsky "Jolly Green Giant" helicopters wrote new chapters in selfless heroism in Southeast Asia by snatching hundreds of downed airmen from jungles, valleys, and mountaintops, defying capture and death themselves on almost every flight. The crews of rescue helicopters both in Korea and in Vietnam became the most decorated men of their time. One of them, Captain Gerald O. Young, a "Jolly Green Giant" pilot in Vietnam, won the nation's highest award, the Congressional Medal of Honor.

During his helicopter career Igor Sikorsky rarely passed up an opportunity to stress the helicopter's usefulness for saving lives, or to praise the men whose skill and courage made the rescues possible. He concluded one major address with these words:

"We all read in youth the beautiful stories about the wooden ships manned by iron men. Now the clipper ships, the beautiful ships of the oceans, have almost disappeared. But fortunately for us the iron men are still right here. The iron men of today are behind the controls, no longer of wooden but mostly Duralumin ships of the air, and it is the iron men, the airmen of our armed forces and private organizations, to whom I would like to express now my deepest gratitude for their work, for their skill, abilities, and courage. We, the designers and builders of airplanes, would be building something useless and worthless if it were not for the skill and courage of our airmen whose exploits could fill not merely a volume, but could fill libraries, and would be just as fascinating to read as any brilliant human exploits. The story of air rescues by airplanes, and lately by helicopters, is particularly dear to me, and to my mind, forms one of the most glorious pages of human flight."

Igor Sikorsky foresaw almost limitless uses for helicopters. In 1940 he said, "I foresee the creation of vast new detachments of air cavalry capable of landing large groups of men behind

At Cape Kennedy, huge U.S. Marine Corps/Sikorsky Sea Stallion helicopters were the prime rescue vehicles standing by in case of emergencies during blast-offs of Apollo spacecraft.

the fighting lines." Prophetic words! Time has proved him right in almost all cases. Helicopters have given the Army new mobility, carrying soldiers over barriers that have halted armies since time began. The Navy uses helicopters for antisubmarine warfare, minesweeping, rescue, and supplying ships at sea, as well as to pluck astronauts from the water after splashdown. The Marines have developed a whole new tactic, "vertical envelopment," to hurdle over an enemy's ground defenses. Air Force helicopters, in addition to their world-wide rescue mission, transport personnel and cargo, linking the units of huge missile bases and supplying remote radar outposts.

In civilian life the list of jobs done by helicopters is long and still growing. Heavy industries such as petroleum, construction, and electrical transmission, agriculture, exploration, photography, police and fire departments, airlines, and others, all benefit from helicopters. Presidents, since the days of Eisenhower, have used helicopters to avoid crowds and traffic jams.

Today the companies which produce helicopters in the United States employ some 40,000 workers. Many thousands more work for companies, large and small, which supply the copter builders with everything from rivets to big turbine engines. The helicopter operators—both military and civilian—all over the world raise the helicopter industry total to many thousands more. In the United States alone an estimated 25,000 helicopters have been built since the days of the VS-300. Russia probably ranks second only to the United States in total helicopter production. England and France have substantial copter production, while West Germany and Italy show gains in this area.

With congestion increasing daily on the ground and in the air around our major airports, transportation planners look more and more to vertical lift aircraft, either helicopters or other types, as a partial answer to the problem. The long road to full use of such aircraft, which had its beginning with Igor Sikorsky's frail little VS-300, still stretches far ahead. Nobody believes that more strongly than does Igor Sikorsky.

Many of the more than eighty official honors and awards bestowed on Igor Sikorsky throughout his long career concern his work with the helicopter. He, more than any other person, can rightly claim the title of "Mr. Helicopter," the man who did the most to make the helicopter a practical and useful vehicle. The nickname was first applied to Igor by Secretary of the Air Force Thomas K. Finletter in 1952 as he presented him the National Defense Transportation Award.

"For the creation and reduction to successful practice of a helicopter of superior controllability," said the Sylvanus Albert Reed Award which he received in 1943 from the Institute of Aeronautical Sciences. "A pioneer aeronautical engineer who has created a helicopter of revolutionary implications and given man new freedom of movement in the air," stated the Copernican Citation presented by the Kosciuszko Foundation, also in 1943.

"Your latest achievement, the helicopter, is a vertiable magic carpet which, though now serving the purposes of war, already gives promise in the postwar years of opening new horizons for peace-loving men," declared Rhode Island State College in making Igor Sikorsky an honorary Doctor of Science, again in 1943. Igor Sikorsky's development of the helicopter was "1943's most significant aviation achievement," reads the scroll Igor received as the first annual Fawcett Aviation Award in 1944.

Igor Sikorsky represented the helicopter industry and the armed forces in accepting the coveted Collier Trophy from President Truman at the White House in 1951.

"In honor of his development of the first practical helicopter," said the U.S. Coast Guard in making Igor an honorary Coast Guard helicopter pilot in 1945. "In recognition of his development of the helicopter," is the inscription on the Frank M. Hawks Memorial Trophy presented in 1947. "For design and mass production of rotary wing aircraft," says a Presidential Certificate of Merit signed by Harry S. Truman and presented by the Air Force in 1948.

That Igor Sikorsky was the creative spark which brought the helicopter into being is proved again and again in these formal awards. He was the first American ever to win the Silver Medal of England's Royal Aeronautical Society, receiving this top award in 1949 "for his achievements in the helicopter field." On December 17, 1951, Igor represented the helicopter industry in accepting the 1950 Collier Trophy, the nation's top aviation honor, which was presented at the White House by President Truman.

Igor Sikorsky's return to the helicopter typified his whole life—a dogged refusal to give up on anything until he had seen it through to completion. Whether it was a conference, with his challenge of opposing personalities, or the larger challenge of bringing something brand-new onto the aviation scene, he moved with a force both quiet and irresistible. When he retired as engineering manager of Sikorsky Aircraft in July of 1957, at the age of sixty-eight, he could look back on a career that had been devoted to achieving the impossible: a four-engined airplane at a time when small, single-engined planes brought trouble enough; ocean-spanning flying boats when cross-country flights over the relative safety of the land included ample dangers; and, finally, a machine that could lift itself up by its bootstraps—the "impossible" helicopter.

In developing the helicopter, why had Igor Sikorsky succeeded where scores before him had failed? Paul Cornu and Louis Breguet in France, Juan de la Cierva (with his autogiro) in Spain, Henry Berliner and Georges de Bothezat in the United States, and Dr. Heinrich Focke in Germany, as well as others, all made valuable contributions to the science of rotary wing flight. Yet it was the VS-300 alone which transformed the helicopter from a dream into a reality and led directly to the founding of a whole new industry. The previous designs had languished and led nowhere.

In the view of his friend, Charles Lindbergh, Igor's success with the helicopter has a deeper cause. "His return to the helicopter was an example of Igor Sikorsky's intuition at work," says Lindbergh. "He had not the slightest doubt as to the helicopter's tremendous future. He had this faith right from the early days of the helicopter."

Les Morris, from his vantage point of pioneer helicopter pilot, voiced similar thoughts. "Back of our efforts stood the unswerving faith of Mr. Sikorsky," he once said. "I believe that his success can be charged to his calm, forceful, sometimes dogged confidence coupled with sound engineering and *intuitive* judgment."

Certainly with the helicopter, Igor Sikorsky had revived his youthful dream, had "relived his life," and in so doing had given the world a new kind of flying.

12

Igor and Family

Of Igor Sikorsky's five children, Tania most closely resembles her father in facial features and, one suspects, in temperament and talent, too. In the eyes, which occasionally take on a faraway look, can be noted something of the father's mysticism, a quality of inward contemplation enabling Tania, like her father, to retire within a personal fortress that the world and its commonplace cares cannot enter.

Music and travel are Tania's chief hobbies. She has played the piano since childhood and enjoys her collection of classical records. She travels whenever she can. Like her father, who is known for his rumpled suits and unshorn locks, Tania is not much concerned with external appearances. Housekeeping sometimes gets neglected in the interests of such higher pursuits as reading, writing, and teaching.

Tania was born March 1, 1918, in Kiev. Though still a small child at the time, she remembers the shootings, the bitterness, and the destruction of the horrible civil war that followed the Revolution. When Igor's sisters, Olga and Helen, fled Russia in 1923 with Tania and Helen's two children, Dmitry and Galina Viner, they had a visa for a six months' stay in the United States. However, they had no intention of ever returning to Russia. Soviet officials became suspicious and at the last minute revoked the visa. But Olga and Helen, fearing this, had already gathered the children and left Kiev on the midnight train to Moscow. From there they fled east by rail to Latvia, the revocation of the visa following but never catching up with them. The storm-tossed crossing of the North Atlantic was the last leg of their flight to freedom.

After arrival in the United States, Tania attended a Roman Catholic parochial school on Long Island and, from 1929, the public schools of Stratford, Connecticut, graduating from Stratford high school in 1935. She attended the University of Connecticut for one semester, but left in 1936 to marry George von York, a former Russian naval officer then working as a mechanic in the Sikorsky plant. Olga, with whom Tania lived, had taken in Russian refugees from time to time as boarders and young von York was one of these.

A son, Boris, was born to the von Yorks December 14, 1937, and later Tania decided to complete her interrupted

Left: *Tania as a teenager at the beach in Stratford. Right: George von York, Tania's husband, working on engine of the S-38.*

education. This she did in a remarkable display of energy and intelligence covering the next ten years. She graduated from the Junior College of Connecticut in 1943 with an associate in arts degree and from Barnard College, New York, in 1945 with a bachelor of arts degree in history. She enrolled in Yale University where she was awarded a master's degree in history in 1946 and a doctor of philosophy degree in sociology in 1951.

Three more children were born to the von Yorks—Elizabeth Anne in 1947, George in 1955, and Peter in 1956. Tania's husband died in 1962. She has been a teacher since 1957, first at the University School in Bridgeport where she taught history, English, and French and, since 1964, at Sacred Heart University, Bridgeport, where she is an associate professor of sociology. She has had a number of articles published and is working on a book dealing with the sociological problems of religion in modern society.

For her doctorate, Tania wrote a study of the Russian refugee community called "The White Russians of Bridgeport." The thesis so impressed her professor that he suggested it be published as a book. Tania, who had become increasingly interested in Russian history, converted her thesis into a book on the history of the Russian Revolution under the title *Russia's Road to Revolution* which was published in 1963 by the Christopher Press of Boston. The book examines the underlying causes which brought on the Revolution, and describes the event itself, including its impact on the world. A searching and colorful work, it has become a standard textbook and reference.

The eldest of Igor Sikorsky's four sons, Sergei, was born in New York City on January 31, 1925. He attended grammar school in Nichols and Long Hill, Connecticut, and in 1943 was graduated from the University School, a private school in Bridgeport, after taking a college preparatory course. In his senior year he attended classes at night so that he could work at the Vought-Sikorsky plant during the day. Under the direction of Eugene Gluhareff, son of Michael Gluhareff, he helped lay out the original design of a new two-seat helicopter. Ten years later the very successful Sikorsky S-52 showed a remarkable similarity to the early design. A development

Tania teaching a sociology class at Sacred Heart University in Bridgeport, Connecticut.

of the S-52, the turbine-powered S-59, set a world helicopter speed record of 156.005 mph in 1954.

After high school Sergei enlisted in the Coast Guard. He was assigned to an experimental helicopter unit at Floyd Bennett Field, Brooklyn, New York, under Coast Guard Commander Frank Ericson, one of the pioneer helicopter pilots. One of Sergei's duties was to demonstrate the use of a helicopter rescue hoist fitted to a Sikorsky R-4. This was part of Commander Erickson's work in developing the hoist and "selling" it to government and military officials. The helicopter was so new at the time that its rescue potential was almost unknown. As Erickson barnstormed from base to base, Sergei served as the "guinea pig," riding the rescue hoist. "During those years, 1943 and 1944, I guess I spent more time on a rescue hoist than anyone else in military service," he said later.

Upon leaving the Coast Guard, in 1946, Sergei worked a while as a staff writer for the *American Helicopter Magazine,* a monthly publication edited by Russian Prince Alexis Droutzkoy. Then, using the G.I. Bill of Rights, he enrolled in the art school of the University of Florence, in Italy, graduated in 1951 with a B.E. degree in Fine Arts. He began in those years to develop his talent for languages. Today, besides English, he speaks fluent Russian, Italian, German, French, and Spanish, as well as some Japanese.

When he graduated from art school, Sergei accepted a job offer from Joseph Barr, then president of United Aircraft Export Corporation. His work ever since has largely been with United's overseas sales effort, especially that of Sikorsky Aircraft. Except for ten months in Japan and a year with Sikorsky at Stratford, he was based in Germany, traveling extensively throughout Europe.

As director of Sikorsky products—Europe, Sergei Sikorsky often finds himself helped by the magic of his father's name. Beyond that, his own outgoing personality and superb knowledge of his field have won him many friends throughout Europe. With his correct Continental manner, he seems today more European than American. His ability with languages puts him in constant demand as an interpreter. For several years he was especially helpful to a small group of American aerospace editors at the Paris Air Show who were astute enough to enlist his services. He took them through the Russian helicopter and airplane displays, enabling them to talk with Russian engineers, pilots, and technicians, including the famous designer Mihail Mil.

Of the four Sikorsky sons, Sergei, of medium height and with thinning hair, most closely resembles his father. A few years ago when he affected a mustache, the resemblance to a young Igor Sikorsky (as seen in an oil painting done some twenty-five years ago) was startling. Sergei is the only one of the four sons to choose aviation as his career. A man of buoyant good humor, he is a non-stop storyteller, given to detailed and articulate phrases. The events he observes or the people he meets are, to Sergei, not merely interesting or unusual, but "incredible." He moves quickly, abruptly, and seems happiest when "on the go," or in the give-and-take of a conference or social gathering. Like his father, he is a careful listener, but is ever eager to expound his own views, which he does clearly and with confidence. Like most people, he seems least comfortable at his desk, faced by a pile of paper work.

Despite his active professional life, Sergei finds time to pursue several hobbies. He holds American, German, and Swiss private pilot's licenses and has logged about 800 hours in various light planes. This sometimes helps him cover his beat in Europe. He favors high-performance autos, too, and has owned a series of rugged sports cars. These, also, have helped him move quickly about Europe. He continues his art, doing drawings, cartoons, and often illustrating his helicopter briefings with blackboard sketches. His interests extend to astronomy, archeology, and handguns. (He is an above-average marksman.) His reading in archeology has led him to a new interest—underwater mining and agriculture, which he believes hold much promise for man's future. To prepare for more serious work in this field he began scuba diving in October, 1967. He enjoys music of all kinds, but favors the classical.

Igor's second son, Nikolai, was born August 14, 1926, in New York City. His early schooling was the same as that of Sergei—grade school in Nichols and Long Hill, Connecticut, and then to the University School, Bridgeport. At an early age Nikolai showed a strong musical talent and has devoted his life to music. He was an accomplished violinist early in life and has excelled at that instrument ever since. After high school he did a tour of duty in the Army, being stationed in Berlin as an interpreter attached to the staff of General Lucius Clay. Out of the Army, he resumed his musical career, studying with leading teachers in New York. He later studied music for three years at the University of Mexico in Mexico City where he became fluent in the Spanish language. His later studies at the Julius Hartt School of Music of the University of Hartford in Connecticut were aimed at obtaining a master's degree with the ultimate hope of teaching music.

Nikolai, a ruggedly handsome man, is a husky six-footer with dark hair and the strong features of his mother. Friendly, gregarious, and with a ready smile, he has been his father's companion and good right hand in recent years, accompanying Igor on various social engagements. Occasionally, as

Igor Sikorsky (left) and his eldest son, Sergei. The latter is the only one of the four Sikorsky sons to choose aviation as a career.

at the big Reading, Pennsylvania, Air Show in 1968, he ably represented his father, accepting a plaque in Igor's behalf. Of the four brothers, Nikolai remained closest to the family fold, long a cheerful aid to his parents. Married in 1968, he now lives near Hartford while he pursues his musical career.

Born in Bridgeport, July 20, 1929, a third son, Igor I. Sikorsky, Jr., attended grammar school in Nichols and Long

Hill, Connecticut, and is a graduate of Choate School, Wallingford, Connecticut. His tour of duty in Air Force intelligence found him stationed in Austria where the proximity of the Soviet occupied zone made him especially useful.

Igor, Jr., is a graduate of Yale Law School, 1956. Much interested in politics of the Hartford, Connecticut, area, he started his law career with the firm of Alcorn, Bakewell and Smith at a time when Meade Alcorn was National Chairman of the Republican Party. He left the firm after about seven years to open his own law offices in Hartford.

He retains an active interest in local government, having served as chairman of the Simsbury, Connecticut, Zoning Commission. He is active in the Civil Rights movement, being a commissioner of the Connecticut State Commission on Human Rights and Opportunities. He likes to write and has completed two novels (both unpublished), several magazine articles, and a study of the 1964 Republican Convention.

George Sikorsky, youngest of the Sikorsky sons, was born December 18, 1931, in Bridgeport, Connecticut. He is the individualist of the family, and probably the one least concerned with material possessions. In the words of one friend, "George has carried on an unspoken rebellion against the Establishment, being somewhat cynical and skeptical of a number of things the rest of the family considered worthwhile, which might be summed up as the external attributes of success. He is the brain of the family, very analytical, with an almost dispassionately, mathematical mind."

A graduate of the University of Florida, specializing in mathematics, George worked for several years in computer programming at Poughkeepsie, New York. He finally decided that this work did not suit him either personally or financially, and made a major change in his career. From friends in the construction industry he found that electrical installers were earning more than he was with all his mathematical skills. So he left his job and became a duly paid-up union electrician. Later, he returned to his original field and now works for a computer company near Poughkeepsie.

As youngsters, the Sikorsky children watched the great and the near great of aviation come and go in their home. Lindbergh, Andre Priester, and others from Pan American were occasional guests. Roscoe Turner visited a few times. A guest for lunch one day was Captain Eddie Rickenbacker, just back from his ordeal on a life raft in the Pacific, emaciated and still walking with a heavy cane. The youngsters watched with awe the entourage of reporters which followed Lindbergh around. "One or two cars filled with the press would pull up behind Lindbergh's car and just wait," Sergei Sikorsky said. "The reporters would just sit around and wait and watch until Lindbergh finished his lunch and the business that had brought him to our place. Seeing this, I first began to realize why Dad had tried so seriously to keep us out of the limelight."

One hot Sunday afternoon in the mid-1930s is known in both the Sikorsky and Lindbergh families as "the day of the water fight." On that day, Sergei Sikorsky recalls, his parents informed the children that the Lindberghs and their children were coming for a visit. "We were told to put on our best clothes," Sergei said, "and we kids expected a serious and boring afternoon. But suddenly we found that Lindbergh was not only a legendary figure, but an incredibly charming and warm person, and very human. Anne Lindbergh, too, we found just as charming and human. Ten minutes later, while Dad and Mom and the Lindberghs had coffee in the living room, we were outside with the Lindbergh children. I believe there were three at the time—Jon, Land, and Scott.

"It was a hot and muggy afternoon. How it all started I don't know. All of a sudden the barriers were down and we were all tumbling together in the backyard when the water fight began. I believe it was George and I and a Lindbergh against the others. Anyway, the teams were mixed. One side had a hose and defended a fortress, while the other attacked with five or six buckets of water from a nearby faucet. After ten or fifteen seconds someone turned the hose on full force and the battle raged at full fury. I guess the hose changed hands a half dozen times and the buckets too. After about twenty minutes of this the noise proved too much and our parents came out. We were all sopping wet—and in our Sunday best.

"I remember Dad apologizing to the Lindberghs. I recall the water spurting from Jon's sneakers as he climbed into the car for the trip home, and Lindbergh calmly turning at the sound and saying, very quietly: 'I think you had better take your sneakers off and put them in the trunk of the car.' The Sikorskys offered the Lindbergh children some dry clothes, but I don't remember if they accepted the offer or not. We visited back and forth later and there were no hard feelings.''

During the 1930's and 1940's the Sikorskys lived in several houses in the Bridgeport area. They left the bungalow near the beach in the Lordship section of Stratford in 1930 to move seven or eight miles inland to a rented Colonial house in Nichols, just north of Stratford. Their final child, George, was born while they lived there. They bought the house in Nichols, but sold it two years later to move again, this time to a larger Colonial in Long Hill, a section of Trumbull, just north of Bridgeport. In 1950 they moved into the present family home, a big farmhouse on a hilltop in Easton, a few miles farther north.

Igor described his home in Easton as ''a typical farmer's house in which the former owner had added two rooms and to which we added a dining room (by transforming a porch), and a pleasant living room with a picture window giving an excellent view of the surrounding countryside, mostly fields and woods.''

The house is set on a tract of several acres. Despite his advancing years, Igor himself has kept the ground neat and the grass cut, mainly through mechanization in the form of two tractors—a Ford and a smaller International Cadet. He found he had to cut the grass once a day, for about an hour, to keep up with the job. ''I cut it section by section,'' he said, ''and when I'm through with the last one the first is usually ready for cutting again.'' Most of the time he uses a rotary mower attached to the back of the Ford.

Igor built a small observatory in the backyard of the home in Long Hill. ''Nicky and I would look through the telescope,'' Sergei recalled, ''and Dad would tell us that the day would come when men would land on the moon, saying he was 'absolutely confident' that we would see that day, but not so sure he would.''

Peering at the moon through their father's telescope, the boys looked at the lunar surface as though it were only 6,000 miles away, rather than the actual 240,000 miles. ''The moon suddenly became to us a very definite piece of real estate, not at all remote,'' Sergei said. ''And hearing these predic-

*Mrs. Elizabeth Sikorsky with the Sikorsky sons in the mid-1930s.
Left to right: Igor, Jr., George, Nikolai, Sergei.*

Elizabeth Semion Sikorsky in the late 1920s.

tions from Dad was quite an experience, for this was at a time—about 1932—when anyone who talked rockets or space travel was either a nut or at best a science-fiction writer.''

In later years Sikorsky often discussed future technology with his son, Sergei. Since Sergei was the only one of the boys to follow aviation as a career, he and his father seemed able to communicate very well with each other in technical areas.

''One of the most important truths that my father taught me in recent discussions,'' Sergei said, ''is that it is terribly important not to become so locked into one field of technology that you are unaware of other events. Scientific predictions, for example, have to be tempered with a broad knowledge of what is going on in other fields such as biology and astronomy. It is fascinating how clearly my father proved to me that one must be constantly alert and open-minded in order not to become entrapped by developments in other fields that suddenly impact into your field of technology. Only with this broad outlook, my father told me, can you evaluate current and future trends with any hope of guessing right for the next ten to twenty years.''

Social evenings at the Sikorsky home were by no means solemn. Anne Lindbergh, an accomplished author and poet in her own right, found Igor a fascinating conversationalist. ''The evenings there,'' she recalled, ''were gay, lively, and full of discussions, many of them about politics and world conditions or plans for world improvement. . . . Sometimes the discussions turned to war, which always distressed Mrs. Sikorsky. Igor was always very gentle and lovely to his wife. When she would protest if there was too much talk about war, he would answer her with a gentle 'Yes, that's right, Elizabeth, but—' I picture him as always listening to everyone with extreme reverence for anyone—always listening. He was not one to talk a great deal, but when he spoke everyone listened.''

Igor's achievements in the world of aviation have shown him to be ''his own man,'' an independent thinker, a genuine original. These qualities are also seen in his appearance, his hobbies, and his other interests.

Although he is a man of medium height, soft-spoken and retiring in manner, Igor's inner strengths command attention wherever he appears, whether with small groups of before large audiences. Had he chosen a political career he would have been a cartoonist's delight with his gleaming, semi-bald dome and the fringe of gray hair all around it; the strands which seemed always to hang just over his collar at the back of his neck; his broad "ski-jump" nose, the sparse gray mustache and the rather long, somber face dominated by the quizzical, yet kindly eyes. The strength of the face was matched by a sturdiness in the body which was marked by the sloping shoulders of an athlete, a compact build, and large, strong hands.

Igor's clothes, too, rarely went unnoticed, chiefly because throughout the years he gave them little thought. Baggy tweed suits, neckties that clashed with his suit or shirt, and thick-soled suede shoes worn for comfort and not appearance were long his sartorial trademarks. In the days of the VS-300 he was known for the Homburg hat clamped squarely on his head as he put the open-frame ship through its paces. In later years he often sported a baseball cap while driving his Volkswagen between home and office.

At the conclusion of an annual United Aircraft stockholders' meeting in a hangar at East Hartford, Connecticut, a few years ago, the several hundred persons attending retrieved their topcoats from racks. The last man to leave took the last coat left. "Someone took my new coat," he exclaimed, "and look what they left me. The cuffs and collar are frayed. What a swap!" The mistake was corrected the next day and the coats exchanged. The stockholder was slightly embarrassed to learn that the coat he had been complaining about so loudly was Igor Sikorsky's.

Until recent years Igor took full advantage of his love of travel, using planes, trains, or his own car, depending on the circumstances. He drove his car throughout the United States and several times into Mexico. When distances required that he use the airlines, he would rent a car upon arrival and explore new areas. In a few places where the scenery was especially beautiful, as in the Canadian Rockies, or between Colorado and California, he went by train.

One hobby which kept him on the move was his love of volcanoes. "I don't pretend to be a scientist," he once said, "but I am still interested in volcanoes as a mighty and magnificent natural phenomenon. So I traveled to see them and I read what I could about them." He enjoyed his visits to Mount Vesuvius in Italy and to the volcano Izzalco in San Salvador which he first saw while on an air trip through South America. When he read that Izzalco was starting a violent eruption he flew there from Connecticut and organized an exploration party of Indians to obtain the closest possible view.

Igor's favorite volcano is Parícutin in Mexico, near the city of Uruapan, about 200 miles west of Mexico City. He visited it four times, once by helicopter when he looked down into its glowing crater and took pictures. Parícutin was born February 20, 1943, in a cornfield when a cloud of smoke began coming out of a small opening in the ground. In the weeks that followed, explosions hurled rocks high into the air and ashes shot upwards thousands of feet. Within a year the volcano was 1,500 feet high, ashes and lava still poured from it, and the nearby village of Parícutin was almost buried. Clouds above the volcano glowed red from the hot rock below.

The U.S. Army Air Corps sent a new Sikorsky helicopter to Parícutin in the summer of 1945. The area lies about 7,200 feet above sea level and the purpose of the expedition was to determine the helicopter's performance at the high altitude. A second purpose was to help the National Research Council gain more knowledge of volcanoes. Igor Sikorsky accompanied the expedition, along with a group of scientists and educators. More than 100 helicopter flights were made over the volcano to observe it and take pictures.

Mountain climbing was for many years another of Igor's interests. "I loved it dearly when I could do it, which has been all my life until recently," he said in 1968. "I have been to the Rockies many times, and to the Green Mountains of Vermont and the White Mountains of New Hampshire dozens of times, and to the Canadian Rockies. I usually drove a car to the point where I had to start walking. I walked alone; I do my best thinking during walks along mountain trails or in woodlands."

Igor's love of solitude is familiar to all who have known him. One summer Saturday a dozen years ago a United Aircraft employee visited an amusement park with his wife and young son. They saw an elderly man seated on a bench watching the merry-go-round. He wore a sweat shirt and old pair of slacks and looked vaguely familiar. Suddenly they realized the stranger was Igor Sikorsky. They introduced themselves and Igor greeted them warmly. He explained why he was sitting in the park some fifty miles from his home. "I just like to watch the children enjoying themselves," he said. "And the merry-go-round reminds me of a carousel I once rode in Russia."

For one who has spent a lifetime peering into the future, Igor Sikorsky shows a very human nostalgia that sometimes takes him far back into the past. The humble hotel in which he lived while seeking an engine for his first helicopter still

Igor Sikorsky (right) with a Mexican geologist near the Parícutin volcano.

stands in a back street of Paris. In 1947, when the Paris Air Show was resumed following a lapse during World War II, he said to a few friends one night, "Let's find that hotel where I stayed in 1909."

In high good humor he led them to the building, pointing out the window of his room. He showed them the little sidewalk cafe in front of the hotel where he used to stop for an *aperitif* and to write out his notes and make sketches at the end of the day. In 1909, even as today, he allowed himself one glass of Dubonnet wine before ordering supper.

"It's the same cafe, the same tablecloths," he told his friends, and then added with a twinkle in his eye, "and the same girls sitting about."

In 1958 he flew from Paris directly to the Brussels World's Fair in a Sabena Airlines Sikorsky S-58 helicopter. Once again, before leaving Paris, he wandered the streets of the city, noting that everything was almost exactly the same as a half-century before. He enjoyed especially his visit to the Paris Heliport, which was on the site of the old Issy de Moulineaux Aerodrome where, in 1909, he had first seen an airplane fly. When the girl at the Sabena ticket counter had trouble spelling Igor's last name she finally asked him if it were the same as the line's helicopters. Igor answered "yes" and modestly let the matter end there.

Sometimes when he pursued his hobby of astronomy, Igor's thoughts would go back to 1905 and 1906 when his father took him to the Austrian Alps on vacation. Father and son used to stay at a little mountain hotel in Berchtesgaden, later the infamous retreat of Adolf Hitler, but then a sleepy little village. Walking down from the mountains at night they had a clear view of the stars, a view impossible from cities with their smoke, dust, and lights. The little hotel still lies nestled among the towering peaks and Igor took great pains to make sure his own children visited there.

"Three generations of Sikorskys have stayed at that hotel," Sergei Sikorsky said recently. "And Dad would like a fourth, his grandchildren, to go there too."

With advancing years, Igor grew more conscious of his origins and his family, more aware, as Tania once expressed it, "of his kin and kind." He showed a desire for all his

For the first time in many years the Sikorskys had a family reunion at the testimonial luncheon in New York for Mr. Sikorsky's eightieth birthday. Left to right: Igor I. Sikorsky, Jr. and his wife; Mrs. George Sikorsky; Nikolai Sikorsky and his wife; Igor I. Sikorsky and Mrs. Sikorsky; Mrs. Sergei Sikorsky; George Sikorsky; Mrs. Tania von York; and Sergei Sikorsky.

children to get along well with each other and displayed much personal interest in them.

In rearing his children he proved himself a very good father, chiefly through the example of his own life. The demands of his career, as well as his soft-spoken and mild manner, made it necessary for much of the strong discipline to be applied by Elizabeth.

Tania once summed up her father's impact for good on his children. "He has a lot of personal warmth," she said. "He has a tremendous sense of decency, of what is right and wrong, of what is appropriate. He communicated much of this to his children. He is a man of strong convictions and faith and is much concerned that this should get across to his children and his grandchildren."

Igor Sikorsky's retirement years, which began in 1957, gave him a wonderful opportunity to think, to write, and to add further to his contributions to aviation and to his fellow man. He made such effective use of this opportunity that few ever thought of him as retired.

13

Retirement Years

"Rare is the man of vision whose dreams become reality. Rarer still is one whose vision brings a better life to others while fulfilling his own. Such a man is Igor I. Sikorsky—no less a pioneer, dreamer, and inventor today than a half-century ago when he flew his first airplane from a pasture in southwestern Russia to launch a career unmatched in aviation annals."

These were the opening words of a gold-edged scroll presented to Igor Sikorsky by his friends and associates when he retired as engineering manager of Sikorsky Aircraft, May 25, 1957. On that day, at the age of sixty-eight, Igor Sikorsky's impact on aviation appeared to have been completed. Three aeronautical careers, each studded with success, lay behind him. What more remained? Was it not time now to rest on his laurels, to accept an occasional invitation to speak, and to devote himself to one of his favorite pastimes, travel?

In contrast, the next decade found Igor Sikorsky as active as ever. Retained by the company as an engineering consultant, he became, as one writer put it, a sort of "resident genius." He reported daily to his memento-filled office at the plant in Bridgeport, putting in a full day's work. In the summer of 1957 when a new engineering building was opened adjacent to the then two-year-old main plant in Stratford, Igor went along, moving into a sunny office with drapes in which was woven a rotary wing pattern. The office provided shelves for display of the most prized of his souvenirs and trophies. On the walls appear signed photographs of national figures, including President Eisenhower.

When visitors came to his office, which was often, he showed them one item which he prized most—a framed display containing two small photographs. One shows Igor and pilot Les Morris with Henry Ford, Charles Lindbergh, and Henry Ford II when the VS-300 was turned over to the Ford Museum in 1943. In the second picture Igor is greeting then Lieutenant-Colonel Frank Gregory, with Orville Wright looking on, as the XR-4 was delivered to the Army Air Corps at Wright Field, Dayton, Ohio, in 1942. Within the same frame appears a place card for a testimonial dinner in honor of the Wright brothers April 16, 1938, in Dearborn, Michigan. On the card are the autographs of Orville Wright and Henry Ford.

"I am not a collector of autographs," Igor often told his guests as he showed them this souvenir, "but this is so special. I believe this is the only place where the signatures of both these great men appear."

Sometimes Igor led a visitor to a spot at the rear of the office. There, back of a sofa, reposed the gnarled limb of a cherry tree, mounted and black with age. It was the branch that the S-29-A struck during the hazardous night landing on Long Island in 1924. "I kept this," he would say, "as a souvenir of a narrow escape."

In 1968 Igor's advancing years, especially his failing eyesight, forced him to reduce the length of his work day. Yet he continued to appear at his office each day, keeping up with his correspondence and handling the few interviews and special chores which he deemed most necessary. Often he joked about his age, especially when called upon to speak at the annual dinners of the Sikorsky Quarter Century Club. In October, 1968, speaking to a group of newly hired young engineers, he showed slides of his career. As the first picture was flashed on the screen, he said:

"I do this not because I attach any particular importance to these things, but because I want to speak to you about something which, perhaps, I am one of the very few who can still speak. The only indisputable qualification which I

* MR. I. I. SIKORSKY

Orville Wright

IN HONOR OF *Henry Ford*

WILBUR AND ORVILLE WRIGHT

The Dearborn Inn • April Sixteenth, Nineteen Hundred Thirty-Eight

Obviously enjoying each other's company are aviation pioneers (left to right): "Casey" Jones, Roscoe Turner, Igor Sikorsky, "Eddie" Rickenbacker, Grover Loening and Frank Gregory.

can claim for the honor of addressing you is that I am still alive; and most other ones are not!''

Despite his retirement status, Igor Sikorsky's mail and the demands on his time continued to be heavy. Requests for signed photographs and copies of his autobiography arrived from throughout the United States and Europe, along with occasional honors, awards, and invitations to lecture. Sometimes a Russian-American friend would send him a holiday greeting card which showed that the sender was still struggling with his adopted language. A New Year's greeting one year was a beautiful card entitled ''In Sympathy.'' No matter how they are addressed, the letters manage to reach his office. He has been called Count Sikorsky, Rev. Sikorsky, Honorable Igor Sikorsky, S. Korsky, and Si Korsky. Occasionally a correspondent will editorialize, as ''Mr. Igor Sikorsky, America's Greatest Airplane Designer,'' and ''Mr. Igor Sikorsky (famed aero engineer).''

Age and health forced Igor to all but eliminate trips too far from home. Visitors, mostly young people, continued to show up at his office just to shake his hand. After his talk to a group of graduate engineers late in 1968, young men would arrive from time to time to meet him. Igor would offer a chair and chat with each for a few minutes. One and all received the same greeting or attention from Igor Sikorsky. He had but one code of conduct—kindness to a person and respect for individual dignity.

In 1964 Connecticut Governor John Dempsey and other officials visited the Sikorsky plant to commemorate the twenty-fifth anniversary of the first flight of the VS-300 helicopter. Igor, surrounded by VIPs, spotted a secretary who had been with the company since the early 1930s but whom he had not seen in recent months. He tried to get through the crowd to greet her, but could not. Finally he managed to reach her side to extend his hand with the greeting, "How are you, Miss Catlin? You're looking very well."

When Miss United States, Diana Lynne Batts, was ushered into Igor's office a few years ago, her manager said proudly that she was going to Washington the following week to meet the President. "No," said Igor, noting the statuesque beauty of his guest, "the President is going to meet her." Then he added with a smile, "The rest of us have to work so hard to gain recognition, but you, you just have to stand there and be yourself."

David Rynne, guard in the Sikorsky main lobby, observed Igor's kindness almost every time that the company founder left his office in the engineering wing to visit the main administration building. One rainy day Rynne saw the familiar Volkswagen move slowly by the lobby entrance. The car passed up vacant parking places near the entrance, rolling all the way to the distant end of the line of parked cars. Igor emerged, walked back about a hundred yards, and entered the lobby dripping wet.

"Mr. Sikorsky," Rynne said, "you can use the places right out in front."

"No, thank you," replied Igor, "those are for visitors and salesmen. They work hard."

One day Rynne, while busy talking to a visitor, noticed that Igor was standing near the desk looking into the distance.

Candid shots reveal Igor Sikorsky's genial personality.

After a while he sensed that Igor wanted to say something to him, but that he did not want to interrupt. Finally Rynne turned and asked, "Mr. Sikorsky, is there something I can do for you?"

"No," Igor replied. "I just wanted to wish you and your family a Merry Christmas." To express that kind of thought he had waited patiently for minutes.

Few persons know Igor Sikorsky better or hold him in higher esteem than Catherine Simokat, his secretary since 1948. "I think his secret for success is that he dispenses with all things that should not be worried about," says Mrs. Simokat. "He thinks only of the big things. If he cannot change something he does not worry about it. Sometimes I used to get upset if I thought he was being overlooked or not treated right since his retirement. But he always calmed me down and I've come to see that he was right."

His secretary knows Igor Sikorsky as one who never shows anger, has never raised his voice, and always keeps his emotions under control. "Working for him has been a delight, as well as a rare privilege," she says. "He's so considerate and kind. He prefaces every order with something like 'when you find time,' or 'if you don't mind,' or 'would you be so kind as to do the following.' He has always paid little attention to his clothes," she says. "His suits may be either old or new. But somehow what he wears neither adds or detracts from him as a person. The same is true of the furniture in his office. He could use an orange crate as a chair and still be Mr. Sikorsky."

Have his advancing years dimmed Igor Sikorsky's enthusiasm for the new or the unusual in the world of aviation? Hardly, if his visit to the 1967 Paris Air Show is any indication. There, on the morning of June 1, Igor joined thousands of other spectators at famed Le Bourget Field awaiting the arrival of two U.S. Air Force helicopters which, almost incredibly, were nearing completion of the first nonstop helicopter crossing of the Atlantic Ocean. All morning there had been conflicting reports as to the expected time of arrival of the two copters, Sikorsky S-61 "Jolly Green Giants" of the Aerospace Rescue and Recovery Service. The ships were flying from New York to Paris along a 4,270-mile route somewhat north of the 3,610-mile course flown by Charles

At LeBourget Field, Paris, in 1967, the Sikorskys, father and son, greet the crew of a helicopter which had just flown nonstop from New York to Paris.

Lindbergh forty years before. To make the long flight, the copters, each carrying a crew of five, were refueled in the air from two Lockheed HC-130 Hercules tanker planes.

When the two copters landed, clad in their coats of green and tan camouflage, Igor looked on proudly. Doffing a jaunty cap, he greeted the tired flight crews and posed with them for pictures. It was difficult to say who was the happier—Igor at the success of the flight, or the crews, who were surprised and delighted to find the helicopter pioneer among the first to shake their hands. "This is one of the happiest days of my life," Igor told Majors Herbert Zehnder and Donald Maurras, commanders of the helicopters. "I express my deep admiration for this brilliant flight which takes us another step forward in the history of aviation." On display at Le Bourget for the next few days, the two helicopters were then packed into a transport plane and flown to Vietnam where they began the dangerous job of recovering downed air combat crews from enemy territory.

The Paris Air Show, as usual, provided Igor and his son, Sergei, the opportunity for a most welcome reunion. After the excitement of the transatlantic flight had subsided, father and son sat huddled over coffee at a table in the United Aircraft chalet. They sat alone, at a table in a far corner of the room; no one interrupted them, for it was clear the Sikorskys wanted it that way.

Igor has always enjoyed life and brightened the days of those around him. A visiting reporter, discussing VTOL aircraft which rise vertically by the sheer power of jet thrust engines, asked him: "What happens, Mr. Sikorsky, if an engine fails on take-off?" With hardly a hesitation, Igor answered, "We then have what we call the 2P situation—parachute or prayer—in which we do not pray for our safety, but for our ultimate destination!"

Once, sitting on a patio during a social gathering of friends and associates, Igor suddenly exclaimed, "Look, the satellite!" It was during the days of the first Russian Sputnik, and several persons dashed from the house asking, "Where, where?" Igor pointed up, and there it was—the moon!

When television cameras were set up at Sikorsky Aircraft for an interview of the Navy helicopter crew which picked up the Apollo 7 astronauts, Igor begged off because of the discomfort which the lights would inflict on his eyes. Then he added with a quick grin, "It's really not because of any humility."

The number of honors and awards received by Igor Sikorsky during his long career totaled more than eighty by 1969—approximately one for each year of his life. Throughout his retirement the honors and invitations continued to arrive, unsought, but always accepted with grace and modesty. When it was possible to attend a dinner or ceremony in his honor, he was present. When not, he would be represented by his sons, either Sergei or Nicholai, or by a Sikorsky Aircraft official.

In 1967, in a single month, he received the John Fritz Medal, awarded since 1902 "for scientific or industrial achievement in any field of pure or applied science," and the Wright Brothers Memorial Trophy, awarded since 1948 "for significant public service or enduring value to aviation."

Igor was justly proud of the Fritz Medal. In receiving it he joined an illustrious roster on which appear such names as Alexander Graham Bell, Thomas Edison, George Westinghouse, Guglielmo Marconi, Herbert Hoover, and Vannevar Bush. Except for Sikorsky, the name of only one other man of aviation appears on the long and distinguished list—Orville Wright.

In 1964, the twenty-fifth anniversary of the first flight of the VS-300 brought a surge of new recognition to Igor Sikorsky. The American Helicopter Society presented him with an inscribed silver bowl and John Buehler, then the society's president, described him as "one of the truly great inventors of all time." Buehler thanked him in behalf of the hundreds of thousands of people whose livelihood and careers have evolved from the design, manufacture, and operation of helicopters the world over. "I particularly thank him on behalf of the many people who are alive today because their lives have been saved by helicopters," Buehler said. "I am sure that the multitudes of the future, who will reap the benefits as vertical lift aircraft grow to their full potential, will regard him as one of mankind's great creative geniuses."

A plaque presented to Igor by the Sikorsky Quarter Century Club also stressed the helicopter's role as a saver of lives. The plaque said: "The preservation of lives, when all other means would have failed, may truly be traced to the hand and mind that gave us the helicopter and guided the VS-300 aloft on its first flights a quarter century ago."

At a luncheon in New York to mark the VS-300's twenty-fifth anniversary, Lee S. Johnson, then president of Sikorsky

Igor Sikorsky receives National Medal of Science from President Johnson in White House presentation in 1967.

Aircraft, told the 100 aviation leaders present: "If ever there was an authentic pioneer in any area of man's endeavors on this planet, it is the man whom we salute today."

The anniversary year left permanent marks at the Sikorsky plant and at the Bridgeport Municipal Airport. An oil portrait of Igor, done by his fellow Russian, Chaliapin, of *Time* cover fame, looks down upon all who enter the Sikorsky main lobby. At the airport a large bronze plaque on a wall of the terminal building states: "On September 14, 1939, the first flight of the Sikorsky VS-300 helicopter took place a half-mile east of this spot. This historic flight, with Igor Sikorsky, the inventor-designer at the controls, led directly to the founding of today's helicopter industry and the establishment of vertical aircraft as an integral part of world aviation, both military and commercial."

Bathed in a spotlight, Igor Sikorsky delivers an eloquent acceptance speech upon receiving the Wright Brothers Memorial Trophy in Washington, D.C. in 1967.

June 6, 1968, was "Igor Sikorsky Day" at the annual Reading, Pennsylvania, Air Show, largest of its kind in the country. Igor did not attend, but his son, Nikolai, went to Reading to accept an award for his father. There he heard Paul Holt, a Sikorsky vice-president and then president of the American Helicopter Society, say: "Look at any great company and you will find that what is today a great institution began as the product of a single man's drive and brains. Mr. Sikorsky is just such a man and the result has been an entirely new industry and the concept of vertical flight which is only at the beginning of its usefulness despite the strides that have already been made. . . . His life and work illustrate the spark which moves mankind ahead."

Among the most recent honors that have come to Igor Sikorsky was his enshrinement on December 17, 1968, in the Aviation Hall of Fame at Dayton, Ohio. Age and health prevented Igor's attendance, and he was again represented by his son, Nikolai. On hand to describe Igor's many contributions to aviation was Lieutenant General James H. (Jimmy) Doolittle who was disappointed that his good friend could not also be present. The dinner audience attending the enshrinement ceremonies heard a message which Igor had taped in his Stratford office a few days before.

"Dayton holds a number of important memories for me personally, besides being the place where the Wright brothers were born," the message said in part. "Almost fifty years ago my first work for the government of the United States took place here in Dayton on what was then called McCook Field. The next important item connected with Dayton was the delivery by air of our first military helicopter and I was co-pilot of this aircraft in 1942. I would, furthermore, be very happy to be here, to meet friends, to meet the organization which bestowed on me this great honor, and in particular to see General Doolittle for whom I have immense respect and admiration."

Also admitted to the Aviation Hall of Fame the same night were Amelia Earhart and Rear Admiral Richard E. Byrd, posthumously, and Colonel John A. Macready, pilot of the first "dawn-to-dusk" flight across the United States, who was present in Dayton.

If Igor Sikorsky had any objections to these and other honors given him, it was that they took time and effort from other pursuits which, to him, had far more importance. First, of course, came his job as an engineering consultant. As always, his mind leaped ahead, thinking of new designs and new ways of improving present designs. In 1963, in a six-page memorandum to management, he wrote, "We must remain on the alert to eliminate any defects in our ships even though neither the customer nor the FAA may require such modifications."

He emphasized the necessity to lengthen the production life of current helicopters by a constant program of design improvement. He stated (and many of his co-workers agreed) that one older type of Sikorsky helicopter, if it had been modernized some years before with turbine engines, would have been far better than a competitive type still in wide use

Igor Sikorsky with his famous friend, General Jimmy Doolittle, upon receiving Distinguished Citizen Award in 1958.

with the military. He suggested, some three years before it could actually be carried out, a detailed program to prove the industrial usefulness of the flying crane helicopter. He outlined in detail many new ideas for research in helicopters and vertical lift aircraft—types in which rotors could be stopped or retracted in flight, or winged ships with direct jet lift—so that speeds even greater than the speed of sound could be attained while still retaining the ability to take-off and land vertically.

The memorandum outlining his views ended with typical expressions of modesty, warmth, and optimism. "The foregoing suggestions," he wrote, "obviously represent a few personal ideas. The most important work is well attended to by the experienced personnel of this organization to whom, on this occasion, I wish to convey my friendship and respect. . . . We have every reason to enter the coming decade with bright hopes and expectations."

Whenever he is asked about the future of the helicopter, Igor knows that the questioner is really saying: "Won't it be replaced by more exotic and faster types of vertical lift machines?" Of the proposed aircraft that can take off and land like a helicopter, but fly at airplane speeds, he told one reporter:

"I believe that the airplane requiring very long runways is here to stay for an indefinite future because you cannot build these wonderful characteristics of high speed, endurance, and tremendous range and lifting capacity without giving the airplane a chance to take off at high speed. That is one end. On the other hand, I believe the helicopter is also here to stay because the helicopter has the efficiency and the ability to approach the ground without doing damage to the ground or endangering the people on the ground. Now between the two there is undoubtedly room for an aircraft usually known as the VTOL aircraft. . . . It is quite probable that there will be missions which call for this very aircraft and which will justify its existence. However, it is my firm belief that this type of aircraft will never replace the pure helicopter or the pure airplane in their legitimate, respective fields of application."

Igor is justly proud of his contribution to the flying crane helicopter, or Skycrane. "The crane is probably the most important thing that I have done in retirement," he said in 1967 in reply to a question. "I am happy to have suggested it and I know that it is a success and that it will develop a very important and very valuable line of aircraft."

The flying crane represents another in the long line of "impossibles" which have dotted Igor Sikorsky's career. It is a new kind of helicopter that has proven and continues to prove its usefulness both in war and peace.

Igor argued in support of the new aircraft with the same zeal that had given the world its first practical helicopter nineteen years before, and the Skycrane is largely his creation. Long before the first flying crane appeared, Igor talked of the idea with anyone who would listen. His son, Sergei, drew sketches of what the new ship would look like, depicting some of the many new tasks it might perform. The sketches appeared in January, 1958, in United Aircraft's quarterly magazine, *The Bee-Hive,* to illustrate the first article ever published on the new concept. The drawings proved stunningly prophetic: ten years later they were republished along with photographs of the Sikorsky S-64 Skycrane performing precisely the same jobs that Igor Sikorsky's fertile mind had foreseen.

In Sergei's drawings, the Skycrane looked (as indeed it does today) like a giant praying mantis. Instead of the conventional passenger or cargo cabin, the crane helicopter's fuselage was a long, slender boom extending from the top of the pilot's cabin rearward to the tail rotor. Below the boom there was space for carrying all kinds of external cargoes, especially loads too long or bulky to fit within a cabin.

"The crane helicopter," Igor Sikorsky told his listeners in 1957, will have one unique characteristic that will place it far above the abilities of any other vehicle: there will be no limitations as to the place where it may pick up or discharge cargo. It will have no limit, either, as to the size or bulk of the object to be carried, providing the weight does not exceed the aircraft's capabilities. Thus it does not matter what the bulk of the cargo or how inaccessible the spot of departure or arrival."

The skeptics asked Igor what jobs the crane helicopter could do. He replied that it would be the key to the creation of new industries and enterprises. It could be used, he pointed out, to carry small, prefabricated houses, small sections of bridges, sections of power transmission towers or radar towers. It would be especially useful in the many places where cargoes cannot be carried because there are no roads or railways. Bulldozers and other construction equipment, he said, could be carried to strategic spots. In power line construction, for instance, the crane could airlift the bulldozers to clear areas for later erection of the towers, followed finally by stringing the wires from tower to tower, all done by the Skycrane. The new aircraft, Igor said, could reduce the time and cost of such jobs as laying oil pipelines across many miles of difficult terrain.

Prospecting for oil and minerals, he said, often involves much hauling and relocating of equipment and living quarters. With the new kind of helicopter, he predicted, such loads could be airlifted from place to place in a small fraction of the time required with dog teams, mule trains, and canoes.

Igor reminded people that enormous areas of the earth's surface are without roads, rails, waterways, or airports, and can be reached only by helicopter.

As Igor Sikorsky recommended, the Skycranes were built and almost all of his predictions for the new aircraft came true. The S-60, a research aircraft with a six-ton payload and powered by two conventional piston engines, proved the concept sound, carrying, over a two-year period, all kinds of objects.

Igor Sikorsky showed that the years had not lessened his daring spirit. To study the vibration levels of a pod, or van, that could be picked up and carried about by the Skycrane, he asked that a pod floor be built and attached to the aircraft. Four bucket-type seats were bolted to the floor and seat belts installed. With some urging, three engineers consented to accompany Igor on a flight aboard the open platform.

Donning crash helmets and flight suits, the four strapped themselves into the seats. Soon they were cruising along at the dizzy altitude of 1,500 feet, suspended just below the fuselage. They found the ride amazingly smooth, the rotor vibrations hardly being transmitted to the suspended flooring. One engineer placed a dime on the floor, carefully standing it on edge. The dime remained standing, proof of the lack of vibration.

Igor became curious about the ride at the back of the floor. To the dismay of his companions, he unbuckled his seat belt, stood up and strolled calmly along the narrow platform. His curiosity satisfied, he returned to his seat and strapped himself safely in again. Had he thought, as he walked, of his stroll atop the fuselage of the *Grand* almost a half-century before? After the breath-taking episode, nobody thought to ask him. A photograph of the Skycrane with the four helmeted figures huddled on the open platform brought gasps from many readers of the magazine, *Aviation Week,* when the picture appeared on the cover a short time after the flight.

Successful test flights of the S-60 led to development of the S-64 which had two gas turbine engines and could lift loads as heavy as ten tons. Shortly after the Army's first S-64 flying cranes reached Vietnam in 1965, they began performing precisely the kinds of jobs that Igor had forecast for them eight years earlier.

Hazardous flight on an open platform slung beneath the S-60 Skycrane showed that Igor Sikorsky had lost none of his youthful daring. The helicopter is at an altitude of about 1,500 feet.

Many of the peacetime predictions for the Skycrane also began to become realities. The big helicopters helped oilmen shuttle heavy equipment to offshore drill rigs, and to reach remote, inland areas previously inaccessible for exploration. In Colombia, in South America, a Skycrane carried 2,000 tons of supplies and equipment needed to set up a drilling rig deep in the jungle. To slash a road through the tropical wilderness from a beachside base camp to the drill site would have taken many months of punishing labor. The Skycrane did the job in 125 flying hours. Similarly, Skycranes are helping in the search for the vast new reserves believed to lie beneath Alaska's north slope.

"Our helicopter can now carry a load of ten tons," Igor said in 1967. "I predict that in the near future the load can easily be doubled. And in the foreseeable future we could build a ship carrying forty, fifty, and eventually a 100-ton cargo. Now who needs such enormous cargo? Wouldn't it be better, for instance, in the cabin-type helicopter to have five aircraft carrying 100 men rather than one carrying 500 men? That probably is true. But with the flying crane this is not necessarily true. In many cases, military as well as commercial, it is important to carry an object without first chopping it to pieces. The object may be a missile, a big cannon, a huge heavy tank or, in the commercial field, it may be oil-drilling equipment or any kind of machinery. In such cases it would be incomparably more convenient to carry these objects in one piece and then to store them where they are needed rather than chop them into little pieces and carry them away."

With the newer, heavier-lift Skycranes envisioned by Igor Sikorsky, it appears that men, for the first time, may be able to explore the world at will. If so, mankind will once again be indebted to one man and his ''impossible'' dreams.

Soaring with the Mystics

Of all of Igor Sikorsky's interests outside of his career, by far the most meaningful is his philosophy. The endless hours that he has spent reading in the late night hours in his study, or deep in thought as he strolled alone along a mountain trail, have found expression in his books on religion and philosophy. And nowhere do we come closer to the real man than when we read his thoughts on mankind, the world, and the universe.

Readers have found Igor Sikorsky's writings searching and provocative and expressed with clarity and firm faith in God. The marvelous order found in the universe, the great forces and natural laws that span billions of light years of space to hold it all together, have, for Igor, but one cause—a Supreme Intelligence. These beliefs he has expressed in two books, *The Message of the Lord's Prayer* (published in 1942 and reprinted in 1963) and *The Invisible Encounter* (1947), and in such more recent pamphlets as *The Evolution of the Soul* and *In Search of Higher Realities*. The latter appeared in the American Bible Society's publication, *World-wide Bible Reading*, in 1965 and provided the title for his latest book, completed but yet unpublished.

Reading these works inspires a new appreciation of the intellect behind them. Persons who have worked with Igor Sikorsky for years find themselves struck with the sudden realization that there really are two Igor Sikorskys. The first is the man they have known, the practical inventor of material devices, whose humility and kindness inspire a loyal following. The second emerges as a lonely man, immersed in a ceaseless search for higher truths, reaching out for something far beyond the grasp of human intelligence. As he projects his mind into the vastness of the universe, this other Igor Sikorsky appears alone, as a man is alone on a mountaintop at night, with only the distant stars as companions.

The realization that there are two Igor Sikorskys, the practical doer and the mystic, gives new meaning to a view once voiced by Anne Lindbergh. "The thing that's remarkable about Igor," she said, "is the great precision in his thought and speech, combined with an extraordinary soaring beyond facts. He can soar out with the mystics and come right back to the practical, to daily life and people. He never excludes people. Sometimes the religious-minded exclude people or force their beliefs on others. Igor never does."

Charles Lindbergh expressed it another way. "I think part of Igor's greatness," he said, "lies in his extraordinary combination of intuition with science and engineering. I know of no one else who has such a combination. Bellanca may have come close. I think it was this intuitive gift that kept Sikorsky interested in the helicopter and brought him success in that field too. There was always religious depth in back of Igor, a mystical contact. He would often go off alone. I recall one time he went to Colorado, to a beautiful and quiet area, simply to contemplate and to give rein to his intuition. He mixed mysticism in with science and aircraft design. If you selected the outstanding figures in aviation Igor would be a strong contender for top place. Also, as a man, not just an aviation pioneer, he's one of the greats of his time."

Igor Sikorsky's thoughts about the universe and what lies behind it led him to realize the tremendous importance of the Lord's Prayer. His book, *The Message of the Lord's Prayer*, a slim little volume of eighty-seven pages, has had an impact far beyond its modest size. "A beautifully written, warm and reverent analysis of the greatest of all prayers," said one review. "One of the outstanding books of the year," said another.

During the centuries since the time of Christ, familiarity and repetition have caused many persons to overlook the ex-

Igor Sikorsky visiting an ancient Egyptian temple during the fall of 1938.

traordinary message of the Lord's Prayer. It remained, ironically, for a man of science to analyze the prayer phrase by phrase to reveal its full meaning. In this unusual book, which he dedicated to his wife, Elizabeth, Igor Sikorsky expresses his beliefs in a final destiny for man and a higher order of existence.

The Lord's Prayer, as Igor describes it, was so written that it can be understood by a child, but can also guide the wisest and most educated person. So carefully were the words of the prayer selected that there can be no doubt of their meaning, no matter when they appear or into what language they are translated.

The prayer, as Igor analyzed it, is really two prayers. The first includes the lines, "Our Father which art in heaven, hallowed be thy name. Thy kingdom come. Thy will be done, on earth as it is heaven." These lines deal mainly, Igor says, with man's final eternal destinies in relation to God and the universe. The second prayer, "Give us this day our daily bread. And forgive us our debts, as we forgive our debtors. And lead us not into temptation, but deliver us from evil," deals mainly, in Igor's view, with man's present-day material and spiritual needs. "It is a plain request," he wrote, "to man to forgive his personal enemies, to cancel all ill thoughts against them before starting to pray for his own forgiveness."

As Igor wandered through the deserts of the Holy Land before World War II, the idea for another book came to him. It took form during the 1940's and appeared in 1947 as *The Invisible Encounter*. The book was a plea for spiritual rather than material power as the great need for modern civilization. It opened with a highly original study of Christ in the wilderness where he was tempted three times by the Devil, and tells how he resisted the temptation. The book then describes how man, from earliest times, has again and again submitted to temptation by choosing material gains over spiritual rightness and how these choices have led the world into "one of the darkest periods of human history." Modern man, Igor wrote, either rejects Christ or ignores him, while accepting more and more the principles which He condemned.

What does the future hold for a world that relies on the material rather than the spiritual? The book quoted several philosophers and prophets whose answers are far from encouraging. Heinrich Heine foresaw 120 years ago the world wars which have already occurred. V. Soloviev, a philosopher of the nineteenth century, foresaw a totalitarian world state headed by a dictator. H. G. Wells, writing before World War II, predicted the "concealed aims and secret preparations and the fears and suspicions" which have followed that war.

Wells's last book, *Mind at the End of Its Tether*, written shortly before his death, declared that ". . . the end of everything we call life is close at hand and cannot be evaded. . . . The writer is convinced that there is no way out or around or through the impasse. It is the end."

Igor Sikorsky believed that Wells had discovered "the total, final, and hopeless bankruptcy of radical materialism. . . . As a nonbeliever, he had no recourse to the light of Divine guidance. . . . And as long as he considered the force of human intellect alone, he came to a definitely correct conclusion. . . . It is the end."

In probably the strongest words he ever wrote, Igor then

Igor Sikorsky visiting a prehistoric Inca burial ground in the highlands of Peru in the early 1930s.

described in terrifying detail "the probable shape of events . . . under the power of a totalitarian, radical, materialistic dictatorship." Finally, he wrote, when "rage among the deceived, regimented and enslaved human masses could no longer be restrained . . . an all-crushing outburst of desperate violence would destroy world tyranny by exterminating the bitterly-hated new ruling class at the cost of destruction of a large part of mankind and of final ruin of Western civilization. The rest of the human race might be driven to degeneration and extinction as a result of unrestricted use of atomic, biological and other new weapons during the final outburst of the suicidal, worldwide civil strife."

How can mankind avert a violent end? Only, Sikorsky says

in his book, "by a sufficiently powerful and vast religious and moral revival." Abraham Lincoln's statement, "with malice toward none, with charity for all, with firmness in the right, as God gives us to see the right," provides, in Igor's view, a guiding light which should be followed as closely as possible. "This wise and noble sentence," Igor said, "represents an ideal which cannot materialize in full in this world, but the principles which it expressed so clearly and forcefully were never so thoroughly disregarded as they were in our time in the totalitarian mass murders and concentration camps . . . and in a number of other acts which determined the course of events and consequently carried mankind to the edge of a precipice."

Despite the world disaster foreseen in *The Invisible Encounter,* Igor ends on a characteristic note of faith: "Whatever evil may come to us in this life is trivial when measured against the greatness, power, and splendor of the material and spiritual universe. Our concerns sink into insignificance when compared with the eternal value of human personality— a potential child of God which is destined to triumph over life, pain, and death. No one can take this sublime meaning of life away from us, and this is the one thing that matters."

In a lecture on "The Evolution of the Soul," Igor declared that man's moral personality, or soul, must advance in keeping with his rapid scientific progress. He noted that "no organized society can exist unless there is a certain amount of genuine high and noble impulses among its leaders and members."

What led Igor Sikorsky to put such deep thought and effort into religious and philosophic books? First, many Russians of his time were mystics given to analyzing life and death. In Igor's case he was conditioned by his father's background which included a deeply religious family headed by a priest. Also, Igor Sikorsky and his friends had gone through the shattering experience of watching their Russia come to a violent end. They wondered about the terrible forces which caused the everyday struggles they saw all about them.

In the second place, Igor's long interest in ancient history and archaeology, as seen in his many visits to Egypt and the Holy Land, played a part. His analytical mind, when he thought of politics and religion, forced him to try to figure out the basic reasons and causes for what he saw happening all around him. Then, too, Igor had achieved fame at an early age, being a kind of elder statesman at thirty-five, admired and respected in his field. He did not have to prove his ability either to himself or to his contemporaries. His associates, loyal and skillful in their own right, picked up much of the burden of daily work and details, leaving Igor more time than most people have to do abstract thinking— to ponder on the world, the universe, and higher realities. Despite the early struggles, set-backs, and disappointments, things generally worked out quite well for him. Said his son, Sergei, "My father once said he had been lucky in timing, that he always seemed to be in the right place at the right time."

Throughout Igor's retirement years many writers and reporters visited his office for interviews. All received the same gracious reception and thoughtful answers, regardless of whether their readers could be numbered in thousands or millions. One interviewer mentioned the Sikorsky autobiography, *The Story of the Winged-S*. "That book paints quite a picture of a young scientist who had to work where individuality played a big role. Do you think this same opportunity is present today for the young scientist to get ahead and achieve something, or are science and research largely matters of a team getting together today?"

"Well, certainly teamwork enters more than ever before," Igor replied, "in science and perhaps in every other branch or technique. Nevertheless, I am convinced that the work of the individual still remains a very important factor, still remains the spark that moves mankind ahead even more than teamwork. Teamwork comes into existence after the spark, the intuitive spark of a living man, starts something. Then later comes the teamwork to give a bigger body to the little soul which he created."

He touched on the same theme later at the Wright brothers dinner in Washington, D.C., drawing sustained applause when he said: "There is still a wide field left for the initiative of an individual man. Therefore, it is my firm conviction, approaching the end of my life and having seen something and having worked myself, that still nothing can replace the free work of free men; that's where the real progress is started.''

Once a reporter asked Igor about the grim picture of the twentieth century painted in his book, *The Invisible Encounter,* written twenty years before. ''You say that the world seems to be on a path of moral decadence which may prove disastrous. Have your views changed any in the past two decades?''

''My views,'' Igor answered, ''are essentially the same, although perhaps I would like to correct them as follows: Danger is there; there is no doubt of that. However, hope also increases somewhat as time goes on because a large number of people begin to recognize the nature of the danger and the need to defend certain things which for a time seem to be thrown out. Now religion was apparently thrown out. Of course, in religion it is necessary to get rid of such things which represent pure superstition. But religion has made a powerful return and it will survive as human idealism will survive. This higher nature is what mankind has to revive; otherwise it will certainly face a great danger.''

Igor moved quickly to the role of science in the dangers facing mankind. ''Science is neutral,'' he said. ''That is the trouble with science. It is strictly neutral to good and evil. The same radio will transmit an excellent and elevating appeal, or the most dastardly lies, promoting hate. . . . Science is something of which mankind must be careful. A kid on a bicycle represents less danger to himself and others than the same kid placed in a high-powered car, or in a jet plane. Nevertheless, this is the order of destiny and history that we have been given by science. That's that. So, I have to hope.''

As an intuitive engineer, Igor has never underestimated the revolutions that man's technology can bring about over the long run. He remembers that people once told him that trans-oceanic flying and supersonic flight were impossible. Today, although he does not foresee migrations to other planets, he does believe that we will one day be able to travel to the planets as easily as we now fly to Europe. He remains, somehow, always optimistic that the engineering barriers of today will become meaningless tomorrow. He even feels, mostly by intuition, that it is not entirely impossible that man will develop some means of traveling beyond the speed of light, thereby breaking another "impossible" barrier.

"All the purely engineering predictions," he once remarked, "invariably tend to be optimistic over the short range, but almost childishly pessimistic over the long range. Most of these technicians who have taken a chance with their predictions have been far more successful (or correct) than those who have restricted their predictions strictly on the state of today's technology."

During the filmed interview in 1967, the reporter, Alvin Sizer, questioned Igor about his views on future relations between the United States and the Soviet Union. "Do you think these two great countries, great by their culture and traditions, and yet now on the opposite sides of the political poles, may ever become friends again?" Sizer asked.

Igor prefaced his reply by touching briefly on the historical friendship between the two countries. He noted that during the American Civil War the Russian emperor sent his fleet as a gesture of help to the North. He noted also that Russia's sale of Alaska to the United States was "more in the nature of a gift."

"The main point," Igor said, "is that seldom in the history of mankind has there been a situation where a nation has been so sharply divided between government and the people as in Russia. The same is true in East Germany; there is no difference between the East Germans and the West Germans, but in one case they happen to be under Communist rule. Russia happened to be the first, so to say, victim of Communism, but not necessarily the promoter. Communism is not a Russian creation and Marx was not a Russian. So we must remember that it is the Russian government which is our adversary and which wants to destroy free life everywhere in the world.

"As for the people, there is no reason for enmity; even now the people of Russia are friendly. When we speak of Russia we must remember, besides the government, that there is a great people whose history is over a thousand years old and that Russia is a cultured nation that has produced many great men. We could talk endlessly about the great scientists of Russia. And in respect to art, when the names of Tchaikovsky and Rachmaninoff are mentioned there is no need even to identify them. Behind all this we must visualize the great, wise, and good Russian people who are the parent of it all. I would say that the present radical socialism will disappear, while Russia and the Russian people will remain. And Russia and Russian people are inherently, normally, and naturally friends of America.''

"Then you are not completely pessimistic about the future of the world in spite of the many dangers?'' the reporter asked.

"I think we are in danger,'' Igor replied, "but I think that the danger may go too. From all that we hear it seems there is a tremendous moral and religious revival going on even in Russia. It's underground, but it's a living movement.''

In a new book, *In Search of Higher Realities,* in manuscript form in 1969, Igor Sikorsky seeks the meaning and objective of the life of man. "What relation, if any,'' he asks, "can there be between mankind and the incomprehensibly tremendous universe which appears to be so utterly inaccessible and indifferent to the grade of life that exists on this planet?'' The true meaning of life cannot be found, he concludes, within the limits of earthly existence. In general, despite man's material advances, "True progress in the wisdom and happiness of mankind has remained small or nil.''

In the opening chapter of this newest work he states that "by applying reverently and yet boldly modern knowledge and methods of thought to the question about the meaning of life it will become possible to arrive at conclusions that are closer to the truth and incomparably brighter and more inspiring than the traditional religious ideas of olden times, not to mention the pessimistic and hopelessly empty philosophies of materialism and atheism.''

In the fall of 1968 when his manuscript, *In Search of Higher Realities,* was nearing completion, a reporter asked Igor to sum up the thoughts contained in the 600-page work.

"Yes, I certainly can do that,'' he replied. He lapsed into silence for almost a minute, collecting his thoughts, his eyes taking on the familiar inward look. Then he began, speaking slowly.

He said that the book was an expression of the questions and disappointments raised in his mind by world history and current world events. After nearly eighty years of life, he was voicing his conclusions on the meaning of the message of Christ. Earthly events, because of man's freedom of will, are following a turbulent and often tragic course, he said. Yet despite this lack of direction by Providence, individual man in a mysterious way can receive Divine guidance. Man, he declared, has the chance to freely recognize and select between good and evil, between truth and lies. This led to his views on a life after death.

Because man has free will, he explained, "some individual beings after death will undergo a process of being born again into a life of incomparably greater magnitude, splendor, and happiness. The ones who will not qualify will go into eternal sleep of final disintegration which will be as complete as if they had never existed. This idea is believed to follow exactly the ideas expressed by Socrates and I believe it to be the true meaning of the message of Christ.

"This means that the future eternal life may be only a happy eternal life, as I personally reject completely any ideas of Hell in any form. Hell would mean deliberately inflicting suffering—whether physical or mental—and deliberately maintaining a conscious existence for the only objective of inflicting this suffering."

The reporter looked up from his notes and Igor, sensing further questions, quickly continued.

"The process of being born into eternal life is a complete mystery," he said, "because it begins in a temporary, material, mortal world and leads into a higher immortal, eternal order of realities completely unknown to us. However, it is my belief that every being that would be born would carry all the better qualifications of the intellect and soul into the higher order. The being would also undergo a process of immense growth and an increase of all powers and faculties which it had previously and would acquire a number of faculties completely unknown to us. It would do this in the way in which eyesight is completely unknown to worms, jellyfish, and other living beings which are blind.

"The qualifications and faculties of this new living being would enable it to become a citizen not only of a planet or a solar system, but of the universe with the ability to move from place to place, from star to star, and from galaxy to galaxy. This higher divine order of existence, which religion

Igor Sikorsky with model of helicopter.

calls the Kingdom of God, will be a place of eternal light and truth and happiness. It would be inhabited by living beings for whom the iron rod would be unnecessary and the qualifications for entrance may be explained as being the character of a living being which can live with others and obey God and truth with no need of an iron rod of any kind.''

He paused a moment, then added a concluding thought: ''This general philosophy permits an optimistic outlook to the whole of Creation and to the turbulent earthly process of life which then assumes a meaning.''

It was obvious that Igor Sikorsky, who had long since defeated fear in a lifetime of faith and accomplishment, had come to the nighttime of his life equally unafraid of death.

Late in 1968 Igor confided to a friend that illness had kept him confined to his home for several weeks that summer. "I had scheduled my departure from this world for 1968," he said with the customary twinkle in his eye, "but someone has apparently canceled my passage. Maybe I'll reschedule it for the coming year."

An Era Ends

On October 25, 1972, Igor Sikorsky sent the following letter to Jerome Lederer of the Flight Safety Foundation, Arlington, Virginia:

"Dear Mr. Lederer: Please accept my sincere thanks for your recent letter and for the enclosure describing the São Paulo helicopter rescues. [The courageous and dramatic rescue of 450 persons from the top of a blazing thirty-story office building in São Paulo, Brazil.] I had it read to me (my eyesight has failed to such an extent that I can no longer read) and found it interesting indeed.

"I always believed that the helicopter would be an outstanding vehicle for the greatest variety of life-saving missions and now, *near the close of my life,* I have the satisfaction of knowing that this proved to be true.

"It was good hearing from you and I thank you again for sending me this information. With kindest personal regards, Sincerely, I. I. Sikorsky."

It was a strangely prophetic letter, and the last he ever dictated, for on the following morning Igor Sikorsky died of a heart attack at his home in Easton, Connecticut, in his eighty-fourth year. He had left his office early on the twenty-fifth, saying that he was feeling tired, and that he might take a few days off to rest up a bit.

About a week before his death, Igor Sikorsky said to his secretary, Catherine Simokat, "Katusha, would you get that poem out again and read it to me;" "That poem," his favorite, was the following excerpt from Tennyson's "Locksley Hall":

For I dipt into the future, far as human eye could see,
Saw the Vision of the world, and all the wonder that
    would be;

Saw the heavens fill with commerce, argosies of magic
    sails,
Pilots of the purple twilight, dropping down with costly
    bales;

Heard the heavens fill with shouting, and there rain'd a
    ghastly dew
From the nation's airy navies grappling in the central
    blue;

Far along the world-wide whisper of the south-wind
    rushing warm,
With the standards of the peoples plunging thro' the
    thunder-storm;

Till the war-drum throbb'd no longer, and the battle-
    flags were furl'd
In the Parliament of man, the Federation of the world.

It will come as no surprise to anyone who knew Igor Sikorsky that those were his favorite lines. A pioneer always, he spent a lifetime reaching into the future. And, though deeply concerned at the crises that seem always to confront mankind (as revealed in his writings), he remained to the end essentially optimistic and hopeful.

He was an unusual man whose death can be considered to mark the end of aviation's pioneering era. And all his life Igor Sikorsky combined brilliant achievements and deep intellectual thought with the greatest humility and kindness. In the last few years of his life, though virtually blind with glaucoma, he insisted on walking to the offices of other engineers rather than asking them to come to him. "But they're younger than you; they should come here," his secretary

Pioneers, old and new: Igor Sikorsky meets astronaut Neil Armstrong, October 29, 1970. Armstrong's greeting reads: "To Igor Sikorsky—with admiration and respect of a junior exponent of vertical takeoff and landing."

would protest. "No," he'd reply, "they're busier. Don't disturb them. I'll go to them."

To Mr. Sikorsky, his secretary of twenty-five years was always "Katusha," the Russian equivalent of Kate or Kitty. He never failed, both when arriving at the office and leaving it, to shake her hand. And when he left he'd usually say, "Thank you, Katusha, you have been a great help to me." In the last four or five years of his life she read all his correspondence to him.

At his desk in Sikorsky Aircraft's main lobby, Guard David Rynne long observed the passing parade. His favorite was Igor Sikorsky. "He loved people," said Rynne. "And people, meeting him for the first time, seemed to sense they

In contemplative mood, Igor Sikorsky gazes from window of Presidential helicopter during test flight over Bridgeport in late 1960s.

were in the presence of greatness. Even though they'd spent only thirty seconds or a minute with him, they would often say to me later 'What a wonderful person,' or 'What a great man!'."

One morning many years ago Igor Sikorsky drove up to the main gate at the old Vought-Sikorsky plant in Stratford, stopped and then discovered he had forgotten his badge. "I'm sorry to have bothered you," he said to Guard Herbert Smith, and immediately drove home to get the badge. "He got away before I could suggest that he go to his office and I'd have a temporary badge sent to him," Smith recalled in 1973. "He always called me Mr. Smitty and he'd stop and say 'hello' every morning. But he wouldn't break the rules."

Igor Sikorsky was an unsurpassed listener. During interviews, or with friends, or when just meeting people casually, he gave others the courtesy of listening intently to their views or questions. His reply would be a quiet "Yes, I understand," or "I see what you mean," followed by a pause to compose his thoughts. The ultimate answer would invariably be clear, thoughtful, and complete. For many years the Sikorsky lectures and speeches delighted his audiences. The Russian accent, amusing at first to the uninitiated, quickly captivated his listeners, while the content and humor of his talks made them always lively and never too long.

During the last five or six years of his life Igor Sikorsky bore the burden of failing eyesight with a quiet dignity. "Reading is absolutely impossible for me now," he told an interviewer in May, 1971. "I have someone read to me and I think a great deal. It was Pasternak, I think, who mentioned that there is a time when one must find support and strength within himself."

He refused, as long as possible, to let his failing vision change the normal course of his life, continuing, for example, to drive his Volkswagen between his home in Easton and the Stratford plant. How he managed it was and remains a source of wonder. Finally, however, in about 1970, his wife Elizabeth took over the driving chores. Until the end he walked alone through the plant, although willing hands were always ready to help.

In his home workshop only two days before he died he demonstrated his skills with the power saw for his much-alarmed daughter-in-law, Siegrid, wife of his eldest son, Sergei. "Don't worry," he told her as he held a block of wood to the whirling blade. "I know exactly where to put it."

Siegrid, a former German airline stewardess, was taking flight instruction at nearby Bridgeport Airport and was only a few days from obtaining her private pilot's license. Igor was to have been her first passenger. "I want to fly once again," he had told her some weeks before, "to be in an airplane again, with my hands on the wheel and to feel the

In late summer of 1972, sculptor David Kintzler puts finishing touches on clay portrait of Igor Sikorsky in the aviation pioneer's office.

The lifelike clay bust of Igor Sikorsky is viewed by Mr. Sikorsky and sculptor David Kintzler.

vibration of engine and propeller. Do me a great favor and let me be your first passenger.'' Siegrid had agreed.

Igor Sikorsky has a deep, almost religious love of astronomy and it was here that his failing eyesight struck perhaps its cruelest blow. One cold and brilliant night in 1970 he stepped outside to look at what he called his ''old friends,'' the stars and constellations. ''He came back into the house,'' Sergei recalled later, ''visibly depressed, and said with sadness, 'I can no longer see the stars.' ''

But he never remained sad for long. Siegrid had arrived in a new Pinto, and Igor had to try it out. Then he suggested that she drive him on the coming Sunday (October 29) to Bantam where the Sikorskys had a small summer house. He proposed that they leave at exactly 2:00 P.M.

''He had an obsession with time,'' Siegrid recalled. ''He always had to know exactly the time of day; he had clocks and watches all over the place. If eyedrops had to be applied at 12:20 A.M., then they were applied at 12:20 and not at 12:25. He asked us to find him a watch on which you push a button and the watch later signals when a full hour is up.''

In September 1972 I visited Mr. Sikorsky in his office where a young sculptor, David Kintzler, of Huntington, Connecticut, was putting the final touches on a clay sculpture of the aviation pioneer. I mentioned the company's plans to unveil the sculpture, in bronze, in the main lobby on March 5, 1973, the fiftieth anniversary of the company's founding. ''My last ambition,'' Mr. Sikorsky said, ''is to be here at this desk next March 5.'' A few weeks later, when someone reminded him of the March 5 date, he remarked, ''I don't know if I'll quite make it or not. I'm tiring very easily lately.'' And then he added, thoughtfully, ''But I'll be there—one way or another.''

I spoke with Igor Sikorsky only once after that—in October about a week before his death. Mayor Nicholas Panuzio of Bridgeport had suggested that Bridgeport Municipal Airport (situated in Stratford) be renamed Igor Sikorsky Airport, ''if the helicopter pioneer would permit it.'' I was calling to ask Mr. Sikorsky's permission. ''I will say yes,'' he answered, ''with gratitude and humbleness.'' And then, thinking of the other fellow's problems, he wondered if pilots might have trouble with the word, Sikorsky. "Maybe," he suggested, "in radio calls they could just use the word, Igor."

On the last night of his life, his wife Elizabeth, a dedicated, self-effacing source of immense strength to Igor throughout their marriage, read to him from Dostoevsky, his favorite author. He retired at about 10:30 P.M. The next morning (as events were reconstructed) he arose, put on his bathrobe and went into his adjoining studio where he turned on the light. He returned to the bedroom and was found lying alongside the bed, his face serene, without a trace of pain or shock.

"My father," said Sergei Sikorsky, "died as he said he wanted to—without becoming a burden to anyone—and still at the height of his mental and spiritual powers."

Today Igor Sikorsky sleeps on the crest of a grassy hill in Stratford, a site which he and his wife had chosen, "because it's on a hill." He was laid to rest on October 30, a sunny but wind-chilled day, to the muted voices of a Russian a cappella choir. A flight of five Sikorsky helicopters passed slowly overhead, their engines throttled, as hushed as the mourners below. And far above, by an almost incredible coincidence of timing, two jet contrails formed a great white cross against the bright, blue sky.

The praise, honors, and awards which came to Igor Sikorsky throughout his life (totalling 111 at the final tabulation) continued to come to him after his death. Editorial writers saluted him equally for his human qualities and his contributions to aviation.

John Pinkerman, aviation editor of the Bridgeport *Times-Star* during the 1930s (later editor, Copley News Service, San Diego), knew Sikorsky well. In November 1972, he wrote that "those who scoff at the Great American Dream should have known Igor Ivanovich Sikorsky. . . . I will long remember an interview way back then, when I asked him what he credited most for his success in convincing the skeptics of the value of large, multi-engined aircraft and helicopters. 'It's your country,' he said, 'and it's my country too. [Sikorsky was naturalized an American citizen in 1928.] There is the unlimited opportunity for creativity in the United

Honor guard stood by as body of Igor Sikorsky lay in state at St. Nicholas Russian Orthodox Greek Catholic Church in Stratford, Connecticut, October 30, 1972.

Igor's nephew and four sons were among the pallbearers as casket left the church.

Bishop Joasaph of Edmonton, Alberta, Canada, a long-time friend of the Sikorskys, conducts graveside services at St. John's cemetery in Stratford as family and friends pay final respects.

In a last tribute, five Sikorsky helicopters fly over Mr. Sikorsky's grave during burial ceremony, October 30, 1972.

States—there is no limit to what a man can do if he tries hard enough.'

"Sikorsky predicted someday there would be huge airplanes flying around the world. How big? 'Eighty tons or more,' he said. I talked later with other aircraft people and U.S. military men. Eighty-ton passenger planes? Ridiculous, they said. 'That guy's a dreamer,' one so-called expert scoffed. Who was right? Today there are Boeing 747s flying with ease, and fully loaded they weigh 710,000 pounds—355 tons. The helicopter was Sikorsky's first love, and again those who should have known better laughed at him . . . Despite the skeptics Sikorsky pioneered a whole new global industry.''

Wrote Claude Witze, senior editor, *Air Force* magazine, "The death of Igor Sikorsky in his eighty-fourth year has closed the second chapter in the history of aviation. The first was written by the Wright brothers. This extraordinary man, credited with genius, spirituality, humanity, integrity, self-discipline, courage, and the unlimited practice of hard work, probably accomplished more than any other single person in the history of aviation to date . . . Igor Sikorsky wrote more than a chapter in the history of aviation. He wrote a chapter in the history of free men.''

Jerry Hannifin, TIME magazine aviation editor and long-time admirer of Igor Sikorsky, said in TIME's science section, ''. . . the helicopter did not become a commercial reality until, with persistence and engineering skill, Sikorsky perfected it. . . . He resourcefully used a single rotor with a small vertical propeller at the tail instead of the double, opposing rotors that had troubled his predecessors. Explained Sikorsky: 'Two women in the kitchen get in each other's way.'

"Sikorsky's helicopters began to demonstrate their military agility as early as World War II. In Korea and Vietnam they totally revolutionized airborne tactics. But Sikorsky, who was deeply committed to his Russian Orthodox faith, was far more proud that his helicopters had become an invaluable instrument of peace.''

To the end of his life Igor Sikorsky personally signed all the Sikorsky Winged-S rescue certificates which, with lapel

Jimmy Doolittle unveils bronze bust of Igor Sikorsky at ceremony held at the Sikorsky Aircraft plant in Stratford on March 5, 1973, to mark the fiftieth anniversary of the company.

pins, were sent by the company to pilots and crews of Sikorsky helicopters involved in life-saving missions. By mid-1974 more than 25,500 certificates had been awarded to heroic helicopter crews, both military and civilian.

The ceremony marking Sikorsky Aircraft's Golden Anniversary on March 5, 1973, was a simple, moving affair. As Joseph A. Owens, editor of the Bridgeport *Post and Telegram*, reported, "Everyone involved in the planning and executing of the event was loyal to the characteristics of the man they honored. The people of Sikorsky Aircraft admired him so much, everything had to be done just so. And it was."

The program was held in the jam-packed, and newly renovated, lobby of the Sikorsky plant, and the highlight was the unveiling of the bronze bust of Igor. It was done by Jimmy Doolittle, who once again voiced his views of Igor Sikorsky which form the foreword of this book.

In the life-sized figure, David Kintzler, the sculptor, captured the sober, thoughtful mood, reflecting the mysticism and long career of the intuitive engineer. The sculpture had been started in the summer of 1972—none too early as events turned out. The final sitting took place only a short time before the aviation pioneer's death. Igor peered intently at the likeness, ran his hands over it, and observed, "From what I can see it seems very good."

After the unveiling, Sergei responded for the family, briefly and eloquently: "Speaking for the Sikorsky family, I would like to express our sincere thanks for your presence here today, to record the fiftieth anniversary of this company and honor the memory of the man who founded it.

"During the last years, I was fortunate enough to spend considerable time with my father, preparing for a series of lectures describing his aviation career. The memory of these discussions will remain one of the great treasures of my life. He was, as we all know, a man of vision—who told us boys in 1935–1936 that man would most certainly reach the moon in our lifetime, if not in his. He was a humanist—proud that the helicopter's first military operations were to save lives, and that this prime mission has continued to this day. He lived with aviation, with religion, and with God. He knew all of them well.

"In conclusion, I believe that much of these thoughts might best be summed up in the words of an old Russian proverb: 'Weep not that he has gone; be grateful that he was' . . ."

An anniversary luncheon followed, with further words of praise from Connecticut Senator Abraham A. Ribicoff, Governor Thomas J. Meskill, United Aircraft president Harry J. Gray, and Sikorsky president Wesley A. Kuhrt.

On June 24, 1973, the Bridgeport Municipal Airport, situated in Stratford adjacent to the original Sikorsky Stratford plant, was renamed the Igor I. Sikorsky Memorial Airport in a brief ceremony which opened the annual Barnum Festival air show. Again, a Sikorsky son, this time Nikolai, voiced words of appreciation for the Sikorsky family. "My profound regret," he said, "the one I feel I share with all of you, is that he is not here himself to receive and acknowledge in his own inimitable way the great honor being extended to his name. He was a humble man, perhaps the most humble it has ever been my privilege to know. Yet he had a keen

Jimmy Doolittle and Elizabeth Sikorsky view the bronze bust of Igor after the unveiling ceremony.

Jimmy Viner (left) and Nicholas Glad, both among the original Sikorsky employees when the company was founded in 1923, pose with the bronze sculpture of Igor Sikorsky, March 5, 1973.

Sergei Sikorsky (left) and Elizabeth Sikorsky inspect details of the bronze bust of Igor Sikorsky.

Aviation pioneers Juan Trippe (left) of Pan American World Airways, and Jimmy Doolittle found the Sikorsky Golden Anniversary luncheon a good chance to recall the old days.

awareness of the importance, even the magnificence, of man's capacity to combine wisdom, will, and work into achievement. And he was highly appreciative of its recognition wherever, and to whomever, it was extended.

"The most important single place in the unfolding of his creative achievement was not miles but mere yards from where we stand today. The pioneering amphibians, the mighty transoceanic clippers, the first tentative hops of the little VS-300 which soon grew into a mighty leap ushering in a new epoch in man's domination of the air—all were conceived, created, and sent out into the skies of the world from that group of buildings just across the road to the east of us. So you see that it *is* fitting that we honor him here.

"On behalf of his family I wish to express our deepest gratitude to all of you who have made this occasion possible."

Through the long years countless letters came to the desk of Igor Sikorsky. The correspondents ran the gamut from school children to helicopter pilots to seasoned veterans of aviation's barnstorming days, and almost all expressed a common theme: admiration and respect for the humble Russian immigrant.

One, dated November 22, 1972, arrived, of course, too late. "At age thirty-four and as a helicopter pilot and instructor," it said, "it occurs to me that too seldom do we take the effort to convey our admiration and respect to those who have contributed to our lives (and particularly to aviation). All too often we speak unheard praise or lastly, send flowers where they cannot be enjoyed. No compliment from me can parallel the fame and acclaim that your career has deserved and earned, but I did wish a moment from your busy schedule to tell you how much I've admired you. I hope that good health and every kindness and good fortune will always be yours."

On October 31, 1972, Franklin T. (Hank) Kurt, an aviator and aviation executive of more than four decades' experience, penned a letter from his retirement home in South Brooksville, Maine. The letter, to Harry M. Lounsbury, executive secretary of the American Helicopter Society, termed Igor "one of the most gracious gentlemen of all time" and "one of aviation's very greats."

At renaming of Bridgeport Municipal Airport as the Igor I. Sikorsky Memorial Airport on June 24, 1973, were: (l. to r.) W. A. Kuhrt, then division president, Sikorsky Aircraft; Ferris Howland, Federal Aviation Administration; Nickolai Sikorsky; Elizabeth Sikorsky; the Most Rev. Michael Jelenevsky, St. Nicholas Russian Orthodox Church; and Bridgeport Mayor Nicholas Panuzio.

• • •

From the ancient city of Kiev in the Russian Ukraine to a hilltop in Stratford, Connecticut, for Igor Sikorsky the long voyage of love, wisdom, and personal achievement is over. But for the world there remains the priceless heritage always left by intelligent men of action, integrity, and good will—words and deeds of widespread benefit to mankind. And for others—his family, friends, and associates (and perhaps the thousands who knew him by reputation only)—there remains the growing realization that they had been brushed by greatness and had benefited, each according to his own awareness and capacities.

INDEX

About the Author

FRANK J. DELEAR, an aviation historian, is the author of five books and many features for newspapers and magazines. His books include FAMOUS FIRST FLIGHTS ACROSS THE ATLANTIC; AIRPLANES AND HELICOPTERS OF THE U.S. NAVY; HELICOPTERS AND AIRPLANES OF THE U.S. ARMY; and THE NEW WORLD OF HELICOPTERS. His book IGOR SIKORSKY: HIS THREE CAREERS IN AVIATION won the 1970 Aviation Writers Association Award as "an outstanding biography."

A native of Boston, Delear retired in 1977 as public relations director of Sikorsky Aircraft Division of United Technologies, and resides in Centerville, Massachusetts, on Cape Cod.

A Note About
the Bantam Air &
Space Series

This is the era of flight—the century which has seen man soar, not only into the skies of Earth but beyond the gravity of his home planet and out into the blank void of space. An incredible accomplishment achieved in an incredibly short time.

How did it happen?

The AIR & SPACE series is dedicated to the men and women who brought this fantastic accomplishment about, often at the cost of their lives—a library of books which will tell the grand story of man's indomitable determination to seek the new, to explore the farthest frontier.

The driving theme of the series is the skill of *piloting*, for without this, not even the first step would have been possible. Like the Wright brothers and those who, for some 35 years, followed in their erratic flight path, the early flyers had to be designer, engineer and inventor. Of necessity, they were the pilots of the crazy machines they dreamt up and strung together.

Even when the technology became slightly more sophisticated, and piloting became a separate skill, the quality of a flyer's ability remained rooted in a sound working knowledge of his machine. World War I, with its spurt of development in aircraft, made little change in the role of the flyer who remained, basically, pilot-navigator-engineer.

Various individuals, like Charles Lindbergh, risked their lives and made high drama of the new dimension they were carving in the air. But still, until 1939, flying was a romantic, devil-may-care wonder, confined to a relative handful of hardy individuals. Commercial flight on a large scale was a mere gleam in the eye of men like Howard Hughes.

It took a second major conflict, World War II, from 1939 to 1945, to provide the imperative that required new concepts from the designers—and created the arena where hundreds of young men and women would learn the expertise demanded by high-speed, high-tech aircraft.

From the start of flight, death has taken its toll. Flying has always been a high-risk adventure. Never, since men first launched themselves into the air, has the new element given up its sacrifice of stolen lives, just as men have never given up the driving urge to go farther, higher, faster. Despite only a fifty-fifty chance of any mission succeeding, *still* the dream draws many more men and women to spaceflight than any program can accommodate. And still, in 1969, when Michael Collins, Buzz Aldrin and Neil Armstrong first took man to the Moon, the skill of piloting, sheer flying ability, was what actually landed the "Eagle" on the Moon's surface. And still, despite technological sophistication undreamed of 30 or 40 years earlier, despite demands on any flyer for levels of performance and competence and the new understanding of computer science not necessary in early aircraft, it is piloting, *human* control of the aircraft—sometimes, indeed, inspired control—that remains the major factor in getting there and back safely. From this rugged breed of individualists came the bush pilots and the astronauts of today.

After America first landed men on the Moon, the Russian space program pushed ahead with plans for eventually creating a permanent space station where men could live. And in 1982 they sent up two men—Valentin Lebedev and Anatoly Berezovoy—to live on Solyut-7 for seven months. This extraordinary feat has been recorded in the diaries of pilot Lebedev, DIARY OF A COSMONAUT: 211 DAYS IN SPACE.

The Bantam AIR & SPACE series will include several titles by or about flyers from all over the world—and about the planes they flew, including World War II, the postwar era of barnstorming and into the jet age, plus the personal histories of many of the world's greatest pilots. Man is still the most important element in flying.

The history of man in flight...
THE BANTAM AIR AND SPACE SERIES

The Bantam Air and Space Series is dedicated to the men and women who brought about this, the era of flight—the century in which mankind not only learned to soar the skies, but has journeyed out into the blank void of space.